CONTENTS

PREFACE

The material in this book is designed for **a more in-depth investigation** of the material found in the shorter *Trust and Follow Jesus: Conversations to Fuel Discipleship*. Each chapter contains two parts: the first part is the exact same material that is found in the briefer, first book, and the second part is the in-depth material which backs up the first part. This book is designed for leaders or spiritual seekers who want more depth.

These two books were created because it is important to have a good understanding of Jesus and his gospel. One's understanding of Jesus and the gospel determines the kind of disciple that a person becomes. At Renew.org we champion a fundamental dictum traced back to Dallas Willard: *the Jesus you preach, the gospel you uphold, and the faith you coach will determine the disciple you make.*

Jesus' kingdom is the greatest thing in human history! That reality calls us to invite people into a relational but counter-cultural mindset. We believe there are eight beliefs that, while they may be difficult for many to accept today, are nonetheless core truths:

- God exists and he wants us to seek him, including with our minds.
- Jesus is a historical person, and the Gospels are reliable guides to his teachings.
- The Bible is the reliable guide to God's truth.
- God is loving, but he is also holy and his wrath is real.
- Jesus is the only way God makes us right with himself.
- Repentance and baptism are integral to true conversion.
- Saving faith is a faithful faith; it means living as a disciple of Jesus.
- The local church is essential for discipleship.

We want people to become disciples—or continue growing as disciples—with rock-solid convictions. That is why we will look at the core things that God desires for everyday disciples to learn and re-learn so that we can trust and follow Jesus today. Furthermore, we desire to follow him in joyful submission, rather than cave into the culture around us.

Please note that there are two levels of material in each chapter. There is an introductory, bullet-point section (just like in the shorter handbook), followed by a more comprehensive and thorough discussion of the main points. The first section is drawn directly from the book *Trust and Follow Jesus: Conversations to Fuel Discipleship*. The second section is for leaders who could use more in-depth teaching material, as well as for people who want to review the material year after year. We encourage repetition of study which enables the material to become the DNA of disciples and disciple-makers in a church. Several well-known churches follow this approach very effectively. It creates theological alignment around these teachings for the whole church.

There are three keys to remember as you embark on a plan to go over this material with others:

1. **Life-on-Life** – We cannot state strongly enough that the goal is to cover this material in a life-on-life context, as opposed to a simple educational context. The format is designed for open, honest sharing together. Please set the example each time for others by sharing your personal reflections. We want to follow and be like Jesus, who invited those he was discipling into a relationship.

2. **Meet weekly, keep it small, and preferably gender-based** – We recommend that you meet weekly in a relational place, such as a coffee shop or in a home. We believe that, ideally, you start with two to four other people of the same gender in your meeting. This will help the group with transparency and encourage deeper discussion. Before you jump into these studies, you might first want to complete the spiritual biography exercise described in the *Starting a Discipleship Group* quick start guide (a free download at Renew.org), as well as in *The Disciple Maker's Handbook*. A spiritual biography will help you start with a strong relational tone. Seek to keep the number of meetings on the material in this book to seven or eight meetings only (including the introduction).

3. **Review the questions and/or read the chapter before each meeting** – The study is formatted for people to read the material in *Trust and Follow Jesus: Conversations to Fuel Discipleship* before the meetings so that you can use the meeting time to talk about your answers to the questions. If you decide to read the chapter at the meeting, plan on at least an hour and a half for your meeting time, and consider keeping the group to four people or less (so you can cover all of the material).

I hope and pray that this book will help you to trust and follow Jesus and encourage others to join you on that grand quest.

Dr. Bobby Harrington
Easter 2020

CHAPTER 1

God

Key Theme: Humans intuitively know that God exists and there are good reasons which support this truth, but we must carefully weigh the different things Scripture teaches us about God: some are more important than others.

et's start the conversations with a story from the Bible. The story takes place around 50 Common Era (CE) in Ancient Athens. It's about the Apostle Paul, an early church leader, and it is recorded in the 17th chapter of the book of Acts (verses 16-31):

While Paul was waiting for them in Athens, he was greatly distressed to see that the city was full of idols. So, he reasoned in the synagogue with both Jews and God-fearing Greeks, as well as in the marketplace day by day with those who happened to be there. A group of Epicurean and Stoic philosophers began to debate with him. Some of them asked, "What is this babbler trying to say?" Others remarked, "He seems to be advocating foreign gods." They said this because Paul was preaching the good news about Jesus and the resurrection. Then they took him and brought him to a meeting of the Areopagus, where they said to him, "May we know what this new teaching is that you are presenting? You are bringing some strange ideas to our ears, and we would like to know what they mean." (All the Athenians and the foreigners who lived there spent their time doing nothing but talking about and listening to the latest ideas.)

Paul then stood up in the meeting of the Areopagus and said: "People of Athens! I see that in every way you are very religious. For as I walked around and looked carefully at your objects of worship, I even found an altar with this inscription: to an unknown god. So you are ignorant of the very thing you worship—and this is what I am going to proclaim to you.

"The God who made the world and everything in it is the Lord of heaven and earth and does not live in temples built by human hands. And he is not served by human hands, as if he needed anything. Rather, he himself gives everyone life and breath and everything else. From one man he made all the nations, that they should inhabit the whole earth; and he marked out their appointed times in history and the boundaries of their lands. God did this so that they would seek him and perhaps reach out for him and find him, though he is not far from any one of us. 'For in him we live and move and have our being.' As some of your own poets have said, 'We are his offspring.'

"Therefore, since we are God's offspring, we should not think that the divine being is like gold or silver or stone—an image made by human design and skill. In the past God overlooked such ignorance, but now he commands all people everywhere to repent. For he has set a day when he will judge the world with justice by the man he has appointed. He has given proof of this to everyone by raising him from the dead."

What is your gut reaction to this story?

_____

_____

How does it feel to know that God made you in the hope that you would personally seek him out as described below?

God did this so that they would seek him and perhaps reach out for him and find him, though he is not far from any one of us.

_____

_____

What steps would you need to take to seek God, to reach out for him and find him at a deeper level?

_____

_____

_____

_____

Our Awareness of God

When the Apostle Paul talked to the people in Athens, he assumed a perspective about God. It is something that I have found to be true today—people intuitively and subconsciously know that God exists. I know that may sound naïve and unreasonable to some, especially to proclaimed atheists who claim there is no God. But I have found that, after years of careful investigation and personal experiences, even when studying with atheists in a graduate philosophy department, it is true.

Everyone intuitively senses that God exists.

If this is true, then why are there atheists? One reason could be that people have been trained to think of life as if there is no God. Or people often simply dislike religion and reject "the gods" that they know about or hear about from others. And others, frankly, don't think about God because they want to be their own god.

However, I find that most people will affirm, in the right circumstances, that a higher power is out there. This lines up with what the Bible teaches—that our consciousness of the created world itself somehow tells us God exists. Consider a verse from the book of Romans in the Bible:

> Romans 1:20 - For since the creation of the world God's invisible qualities—his eternal power and divine nature—have been clearly seen, being understood from what has been made, so that people are without excuse.

This verse not only tells us that God exists, but also that everyone _knows_ about God's eternal power and divine nature.

This discussion guide only delves into the arguments for God's existence in a cursory fashion. We hold to the assumption that you, the reader, believe in God, but also that you may need help determining if the God revealed by Jesus is the true God and Creator of the world. Or maybe you just need help trusting and following Jesus.

Our approach, beginning in the next chapter, will be to start with the historical reliability of Jesus. We will see that there is a solid basis to believe that the Gospels give us an accurate portrait of Jesus from history. That perspective then becomes the foundation upon which we can show what Jesus teaches us about God in the Gospels. We will see that there is good reason to believe that the Gospel writings in the Bible accurately record his words. We will also provide a few perspectives on the creation-evolution discussion that many find helpful.

But before we jump into the historicity of Jesus, let's come back to how we think about God, especially the use of reason. Many people think faith and reason are in conflict with each other. That could not be further from the truth.

The Value of Reasoning in Our Discussions

The Bible tells us that Jesus was once asked about how to inherit eternal life. As you read Jesus' answer, ask yourself: How does this apply to me?

> On one occasion an expert in the law stood up to test Jesus. "Teacher," he asked, "what must I do to inherit eternal life?" "What is written in the Law?" he replied. "How do you read it?" He answered, "'Love the Lord your God with all your heart and with all your soul and with all your strength and with all your mind'; and, 'Love your neighbor as yourself.'" "You have answered correctly," Jesus replied. "Do this and you will live" (Luke 10:25-28).

When Jesus tells us that to inherit eternal life we must love God, Jesus describes a love that is holistic. He describes four different ways to love God—with one's heart, soul, strength, and mind. Let's talk about the four aspects Jesus describes.

The hardest one of the four aspects of loving God for me is . . .

_____

_____

The easiest one of the four aspects of loving God for me is . . .

_____

_____

Explain in a sentence how you feel about your two answers.

_____

_____

One of the things many people have a hard time with today is approaching the Bible with an emphasis on loving God with "the mind." Yet, if we seek a balanced approach to God, the mind will be an important part of how we love God holistically. All parts are important, so we don't want to neglect any aspect; we want all of them.

But, as a part of a holistic approach, the Bible tells us that the use of reason and factual thinking are important. They are necessary to properly love God. The Bible has an ancient proverb that helps us on this point.

Proverbs 24:3 describes the use of reason in a short but profound statement:

By wisdom a house is built, and through understanding it is established.

How is it that wisdom and understanding are necessary to build the foundation of a house for a spiritual life?

_____

_____

Once the house framework is established by wisdom, understanding, and reason, then other aspects of the house can be added.

After the mind sets the foundations, which is the next most important aspect to you—heart, soul, or strength—and why?

_____

_____

The Three Elements of the Faith

There is one more thing to establish upfront as you build the foundation of a spiritual house for your life. People who have spent time studying the Bible say that they are constantly surprised by how simple and relevant its message is for our time. They point out that after a person spends the time to understand the teachings of Jesus in their original setting, then they usually find that Jesus is the most important source of meaning, hope, and direction in life.

But we want to help you by *keeping it simple* (without being simplistic).

So we are going to focus on the essential elements of the faith taught in Scripture. People have found it helpful to summarize a specific way of looking at the various elements in the Bible. Think of concentric circles with core elements in the middle, and moving outward, the elements become more personal or relative.

We call it, "The Three Elements of the Faith." For more information about this model, you may want to read the short book I wrote with Jason Henderson called, *Conviction and Civility: Thinking and Communicating Clearly about What the Bible Teaches.*[1]

In this study, we focus on the essential elements (and those teachings which are integrally related to them). In other resources through Renew.org, we offer help with the important elements, as well as the personal elements. Here is what we mean:

a. There are essential elements (or teachings) in the Bible that are *essential to your eternal destiny and standing with God.*
b. There are secondary elements in the Bible that are *important for your ongoing faithfulness to God and for living as God intended.*
c. There are third-level elements that God leaves for us to decide as *personal preferences or truths about which there is a lack of decisive evidence one way or the other.*[2]

This model and its three levels—understood as teachings and our faithfulness to these teachings—helps us make sense of the Bible. It also helps us prioritize certain teachings over others in the early phase of our journey, as we explore biblical truth. Let me explain each level in more depth.

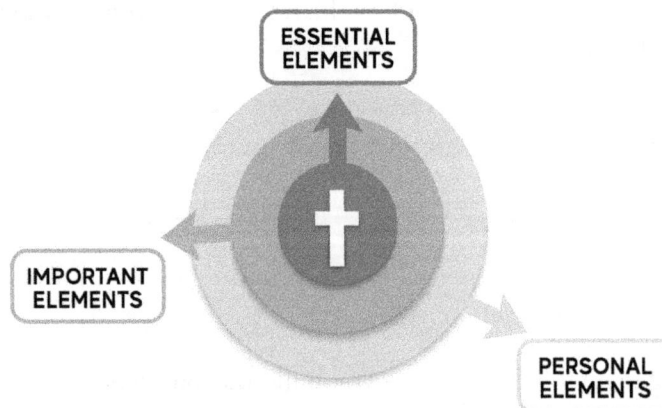

1. Essential Elements

The word "gospel" is not a commonly used word today. As noted above, it is the core essential of the Bible and it simply means "the good news." Jesus Christ himself, especially through his death and resurrection, is the "good news"—the best and most important announcement that anyone could ever hear. Consider these things:

- This gospel is the central message of the holy Scriptures and the key to understanding them.[3]
- This gospel focuses on Jesus Christ, on his person and teaching, his launching of the kingdom of God, his redemptive work on the cross, and his enthronement as Lord and King.
- This gospel proclaims Jesus Christ as the living Savior, King, Teacher, Life, and Hope of all who put their trust in him. It tells us that the eternal destiny of all people depends on whether or not they are in right standing with God through Christ.
- We must respond to Jesus and his gospel by faith. Saving faith is the ongoing decision to trust and follow Jesus—which is to become his disciple. We commit to trust and follow Jesus through repentance, confession, and baptism.
- Saving faith is allegiance, loyalty, and faithfulness. It's a commitment to be a disciple of Jesus. False gospels merely call for mental assent (e.g., believe the fact that Jesus died on the cross) or some sort of emotional warmth toward God (that is, just trusting God to take care of everything without following Jesus' teachings). Faith means that we surrender our lives to be disciples of Jesus. It is a life of trusting and following God through Jesus.

The gospel is so simple that small children can understand it, and it is so profound that studies by the wisest theologians will never exhaust its riches.[4] This is the core of the Bible. It is that which calls us to make the decision to trust and follow Jesus.

2. Important Elements

When we are focused on the gospel and adhere to the path of discipleship, we have a center point for our faith. This is the core teaching of the Bible. Other biblical truths, however, are also important to us because they come from God. These are the important elements. We seek to understand and live our lives in light of *all God's truth*. But we must be clear: our eternal destiny is not dependent on these secondary, yet important truths. People who completely trust in Jesus and have committed themselves to the path of discipleship often disagree on these important biblical teachings.

Important truths are things like how the local church should be structured (e.g., should it have a pastor or multiple elders; should they be male or female). It might also be something like whether or not a church truly practices active discipleship or if they truly teach and help people to love and take care of one another. It could be how the church practices accountability (e.g., how should people be held accountable for the way they live their lives). Or it may be our understanding of predestination and free will.

We know that on many of these matters sincere Christians divide into different churches. Also, as individuals, sometimes our convictions about biblical truth at this level mean that we cannot "do church with other good Christians." We believe, as a general principle, that these issues do not destroy our salvation or make us "lost." Yes, these doctrinal differences are important and we need to strive to be faithful in our understanding and practice of each one; yes, we must strive to believe and follow all of God's truth; yes, these matters have a big impact on the health of the local church and the health of our faith over the long term; and yes, we need to listen to one another and exhort one another to make sure that we are being faithful to God's truth in all things.

But no, we don't have to get everything just right to be saved. The gospel teaches us that we are all imperfect and struggling children who will *never get it all right* and who can only be saved by "grace through faith" (Ephesians 2:8-9). So we must often agree to disagree with our brothers and sisters and practice our faith differently. We are still united through our core faith in Jesus, but we often are not united in the same local church when this happens.

3. Personal Elements

There is a third level of diversity among Christian people that we should also acknowledge. At this third level, we can almost always stay together in a local church. We function together because we agree on the gospel and on the important, but secondary, elements of the faith. But on this third level of personal matters, where issues are less clear, God does not have a set path all of us must follow. Because the issue is relative or not clear, we agree to disagree. Some matters in the Bible are disputable or some are very hard to understand. This compels us to adopt a stance where we respect honest, personal differences, while still being in close fellowship in the same church.

Here is an example of what I mean. While upholding that the Bible is the inspired and reliable word of God, some Christians believe the days in Genesis 1 represent literal twenty-four hour periods of time (that is, God created the world in six of these twenty-four hour periods), and some Christians, with the same high view of Scripture, do not believe this view is accurate. How we understand personal truth is important in terms of our view of the authority of God's Word, but bright, godly, and sincere Christians have different understandings on something like how creation and evolution fit together. One's stance on this doctrine is a personal position; there are many questions, and there is a lot of ambiguity as a person comes to their best understanding. That's okay.

We might take something like having a glass of wine. Some Christians can drink any alcohol, while other Christians cannot. The Bible teaches that it is wrong to get drunk (Ephesians 5:18), but that's the only clear line that can be drawn.

As another example, take the interpretation of many parts in the book of Revelation. Some Christians believe that the book of Revelation must be literal in most aspects, and others do not believe this. In each of these areas, we can witness a unity-in-diversity type of mentality, as godly, Jesus-focused people have different interpretations. Again, each of these matters remains important to us as individuals. While the Bible teaches that, at this level, we will still have to give an accounting of ourselves to God (Romans 14:10-12), none of these matters determines our status as children of God. Therefore, we must be careful not to insist that our belief is the right one *for everyone else*. This is a matter of profound humility. These matters are grey—not black and white. We have great freedom of conscience to believe and practice what we personally think is God's best.

Again, in this book, we are going to focus mostly upon the essential truths. It will involve understanding various important truths, but the essential ones will be central.

We want you to see this paradigm upfront, so that it can help you see the relative weight of various teachings in the Bible. We want to focus on the most central ones.

How would you explain, in your own words, the different elements?

Essential element: _____

Important element: _____

Personal element: _____

This leadership guide was written so that people can revisit the same material year after year. When mentoring others, the group leader often needs to know more background information. In my roles as point leader for Discipleship.org and Renew.org (national collaboratives of disciple-making leaders), I found that several well-known churches follow this approach very effectively.

This leadership guide seeks to establish the key basics or elementary teachings of the faith (Hebrews 6:1-3; Ephesians 4:4-6). There are seven main concepts:

1. **Jesus in History.** Jesus was a real historical person, and most of the key elements of his life have been acknowledged and accepted by historians.
2. **Scripture.** God inspired the Bible and gave it to us for guidance.
3. **God's Holiness.** The Bible reveals that our core problem is sin, which separates us from a holy God. We must own it and repent of it by faith.

4. **God's Love.** Jesus demonstrated God's love when he came to rescue us by his cross and enthronement as Lord and Messiah. We are to respond and place our faith in him.
5. **Lord and King.** True faith in Jesus means that we have a faithful faith that leads us to both trust and follow Jesus as our Lord and King.
6. **Commitment.** We make the commitment to turn to Jesus and place our faith in him through repentance, confession, and baptism.
7. **Discipleship.** We live as disciples (that is, followers of Jesus) by relying on God's Spirit and living out our faith with a local church.

For some people, these concepts are new. For others, they are the basics they have believed for years. Again, those who master this material will be the most effective at reaching other people who do not know Jesus and entering into a relationship where they can help these people to trust and follow him. We commend that as the path for everyone.

Which of the seven teachings described above are you most excited to dig into during the upcoming conversations (and why)?

_____

_____

_____

_____

God

"There are times when I wake up in the middle of the night and ask myself, 'What if I am wrong, what if there is no God?'" This answer of mine surprised Roberta. She did not expect it because she thought that those of us who are in the ministry are so sure of our beliefs that we never doubt. Roberta's husband and I played hockey together. One night a group of hockey players and our wives got together to socialize and have fun.

In the middle of a lively conversation, Roberta lowered her gaze, looked me in the eyes, and asked me the piercing question, "Do you ever have doubts?"

"Yes," I said, and then after my admission, I added, "I think every true believer experiences times of questioning."

Honest questions are good and healthy in the development of one's faith. When I face doubts, I just go back over all the reasons (personally, experientially, and factually) that led me to believe in Jesus Christ and the Bible. Upon reflection and review, I renew my faith and re-commit myself. Such occasions are neither rare nor threatening for me.

The most interesting comment that night, however, came from Roberta. As far back as Roberta could remember, she always considered herself to be non-religious. But after I told her how I handle doubt, Roberta made a confession. "Well," she said, "I often wake up in the night with a question that I can't shake." She became very serious and added, "Sometimes I have grave doubts myself, and I wonder, 'What if I am wrong?'" Her words just hung in the air. Then Roberta topped it off: "I am afraid that I might be wrong and that I might go to hell." Rarely are people so honest. Roberta was awakening to the fact that she had been pushing God out of her life for a long time.

The Bible teaches that we all intuitively and subconsciously know that God exists. As humans, our interaction with the created world somehow tells us that there is a God. Consider the following verse from the book of Romans.

> For since the creation of the world God's invisible qualities—his eternal power and divine nature—have been clearly seen, being understood from what has been made, so that men are without excuse (Romans 1:20).

Like Roberta, most people sense that God is there, and we should turn to him. You might want to go back through the verse and underline the two things that the Bible says everyone knows about God: his eternal power and his divine nature.

Sensing that God exists, however, does not remove all doubt. I have met many people who question God's existence, from friends in philosophy classes at graduate school to concerned Christians who grew up going to church. It is one thing to have questions about God and experience doubt, but atheists go one step further and state that there is no God. Atheism, so I have found, is almost always driven by psychological factors. It is usually *not* a rejection of God, but a rejection of a God or a religion the atheist doesn't like. More often than not, atheism is a rejection of the oppressive religion held by someone close to the atheist, often the atheist's father.

Rarely is there a hard-core atheist who is *not* ultimately rejecting something that he or she relates to God or holds against God. Often, there are good reasons for such a rejection, but the rejection goes too far. Rebellion against one form or another of oppression can be an over-reaction in the opposite direction. This atheist syndrome is described and illustrated from the lives of many famous intellectual people like Sigmund Freud, Charles Darwin, Karl Marx, and others in the book, *The Atheist Syndrome*.[5]

It is easy to see how some do not believe in God because of those who represent God. But most would agree that, in the end, this is not a good basis for rejecting God and saying that he does not exist.

A second reason that causes many to doubt God's existence is the moral expectation factor. Many of us wonder if there is more evidence than the intuitive conviction or deep-seated hunch we get from looking at the world. Many of us want more evidence because the stakes can be pretty high. After all, if we admit in our heart of hearts that there is a God, we know that there are moral implications for our lives. Many of us push God out of our consciousness so we can avoid giving up sin or so that we will not have to admit that what we have done is wrong.

The Bible teaches that many of us subconsciously move away from God in this way. We cling to practices and behaviors that we know are wrong, and our knowledge of God becomes darkened. This is not just true for individuals; it can also be true for an entire culture. The Bible describes the ancient culture of first-century Rome with these words:

> Furthermore, since they did not think it worthwhile to retain the knowledge of
> God, he gave them over to a depraved mind, to do what ought not to be done.
> They have become filled with every kind of wickedness, evil, greed and depravity.
> They are full of envy, murder, strife, deceit and malice (Romans 1:28-29).

The Bible teaches that when some cultures reject God, they easily develop a common mindset that is depraved or inclined toward sinful behavior. This mindset can keep people away from Christians and biblical truth.

The Bible also describes the reason that many reject spiritual truth with these words. The words in these verses are strong, but they can be applied to many people. Some reject the truth about God because they do not want to have their sinful ways exposed.

> Everyone who does evil hates the light and will not come into the light for fear
> that his deeds will be exposed. But whoever lives by the truth comes into the
> light, so that it may be seen plainly that what he has done has been done through
> God (John 3:19-21).

This explains why each of us needs to weigh out the reasons that we believe or do not believe in God. One major struggle, if the Bible is true, may be the one within our own hearts. We want to be honest with our deepest motives.

There is a third reason that people struggle with actively believing in God—science. Many believe that a commitment to good science means that we cannot believe what the Bible teaches. This contention is simply not true. A lot has been written to show how science and the Bible are compatible.[6]

At the same time, many of us need to see objective facts that confirm what we intuitively believe to be true. We believe, but we need help with our doubts. Because God made the universe, the world, and everything in them, his creation should provide us with confirmation of his existence. We will look at the evidence which provides this confirmation.

Who Started the Big Bang?

Many people do not realize that our intuitive conviction that God exists can also be shown to be objectively true. I grew up near the Rocky Mountains of Western Canada. As a teenager, I would often spend weekends in the winter skiing. Sometimes, I would look out over the mountains from a chair on the ski lift. The tall, snow-capped mountains were ruggedly set against the backdrop of the light blue sky and filled with beautiful evergreen trees. The scenes were simply majestic. In such breathtaking moments, I would say to myself, "Wow, God made this." I could not imagine that such a world "just happened" by chance.

Most of us share these sentiments. We look at the world and ask, "Where else could this have come from?" Something made this world. Our natural reaction is to say, "God made it."

Many of us were taught that the universe is infinitely old. Yet science has now demonstrated that the universe also had a beginning. Astronomers and astrophysicists are convinced that the universe—and all time, space, matter, and energy—literally sprang into existence *out of nothing*.[7] The universe began with the "Big Bang." As the brilliant English scientist Stephen Hawking stated, "Almost everyone now believes that the universe, and *time itself*, had a beginning at the Big Bang."[8]

Before the "Big Bang," the universe and everything else did not exist. There was no time, no matter, no energy, and no space. Stop and think about this for a moment. The implications are astounding:

- There was no yesterday, no today, and no tomorrow, no beginning, no end.
- There were no dimensions, no up, no down, no back, no front.
- There was no matter, no atoms, no elements of any kind.
- There was no energy, no power, no motion.

Absolutely nothing existed. Nothing! Then—out of nowhere—everything that exists sprang into existence. There was a "Big Bang," and everything that exists was created in that instant. As apologist William Lane Craig says, "Physical space and time were created in that event, as well as all the matter and energy in the universe."[9]

In every other realm, we know that "something" *cannot* come from "nothing." So where did the universe come from? Think for a moment about the possible options! If all physical elements were created in the moment of the "Big Bang," they could only have been created by something non-physical. There is only one good answer: God. Only a non-material being like God could create the physical universe. Only God is invisible, eternal, and all powerful. As the Bible says, "By faith we understand that the universe was formed at God's command, so that what is seen was not made out of what was visible" (Hebrews 11:3).

Philosophers have developed a very simple summary of the "Big Bang" argument for God's existence:

- Whatever begins to exist had a cause.
- The universe began to exist.
- *Therefore*, the universe had a cause (God).[10]

The person who does not believe in God is in trouble at this point. How can he or she explain the beginning of the universe? An advocate of the Big Bang Theory, if he or she is an atheist, must hold that the universe . . . came from nothing . . . and by nothing.

The Bible makes it clear that the creation of the universe is the work of God. In fact, the first verses of the Bible could not be clearer: "In the beginning God created the heavens and the earth" (Genesis 1:1).

Life Springs into Existence!

The creation of the universe sets the stage for the creation of life on planet earth. Scientists tell us that the simplest forms of life appeared on planet earth soon after it formed.[11] Without God, there are no known explanations for the creation of biological life. Biologists and biochemists have tried to explain the origin of life in different naturalistic ways (without God), but the more we learn about biological life, the more we learn about the miracle that was required for it to have started. Stated differently, if we assume that there is no God, we are at a loss to explain how life started.

Students have been taught that life just happened on early earth. And scientists used to think they could replicate the process in a laboratory. They have given up on such projects—they do not have a clue about how to create life from non-living materials. Harold Morowitz was a mathematical biologist who specialized in this field. In his article, "Biological Self-Replicating Systems," he said that if you take all the possibilities or random combinations from the beginning of time until now, it is impossible to find a mathematical model that will explain the creation of life. [12] Morowitz also said that the random assembly of the most basic building blocks of life, including something as simple as a functional protein is unexplainable.

There are various ways in which scientists try to describe the odds of the simplest blocks of life forming by chance (without God).

- The odds of the building blocks of life "just happening by chance" are the same as a Boeing 747 being created accidentally by a tornado whirling through a junkyard.[13]
- The odds of the building blocks of life "just happening by chance" are the same as a man finding the same grain of sand after being blindfolded and randomly dropped in the Sahara Desert three different times.[14]

- The odds of the building blocks of life "just happening by chance" are the same as believing that monkeys typing on computers could randomly create the entire 30 volume *Encyclopedia Britannica* without error.[15]

The appearance of life on the planet is a miracle that points to God.[16] There is a simple way to sum up this evidence as an argument for God's existence.

- Biological life resulted either from chance or design.
- The odds that life began by chance are so small as to be equal to zero.
- Therefore, life began by design (by God).

There is no known process on earth or in the universe as a whole that can explain the origin of life.[17] The belief that God created life is the most satisfying explanation.[18]

The evidence is very strong that planet earth—as a life-supporting planet—is unique. The evidence is so compelling that scientists now refer to it as "The Anthropic Principle."[19] This principle states that planet earth appears to have been uniquely designed. Planet earth has a "just right design" making it appear to have been uniquely made to support human life.

Here are some of the things that must be "just right" for a planet to support life:

- The galaxy in which the planet exists must have a "just right" age.
- There must be a "just right" distance between galaxies.
- There must be a "just right" galaxy.
- There must be a "just right" location within the galaxy.
- There must be a "just right" distance between stars (sun).
- There must be a "just right" distance from super nova eruptions.
- There must be a "just right" age of our sun.
- There must be a "just right" distance of the planet from the sun.
- There must be a "just right" position of the stars in a planetary system.
- There must be a "just right" axis position on the planet.
- There must be a "just right" rotation period on the planet.
- There must be a "just right" thickness of planet's crust.
- There must be a "just right" ozone level on the planet.
- There must be a "just right" gravitational influence from a moon.

These are just a few of the parameters that must be "just right" for life to exist on earth. Scientist Hugh Ross, in conjunction with various physicists and astrophysicists, has worked out the probabilities that another life-supporting planet or moon exists anywhere else in the universe.[20] He writes, "A calculation of the probability for there existing just one naturally occurring planet anywhere in the observable universe with the capacity to support physical life . . . is less than 1 chance in 10 to the 174 (the number 1 followed by 174 zeros)."[21]

If we put this statistical probability in layman's terms, we could say that the odds of there being a life-supporting planet or moon elsewhere in the universe are the same as *one person* winning the lottery a million times *in a row*. Again, the odds of planet earth just happening by chance are almost indistinguishable from zero.

The Wonder of a Human Being's Design

During my years of ministry, many women have told me that one of the greatest joys they have experienced is that of giving birth. They have intimately experienced conception, the earliest and more advanced movements of the baby, and finally, the birth. Most mothers feel that they have participated in a miracle. More women than I can count have said to me, "There is no way that you could have a baby and not believe in God."

What is it in the experience of pregnancy and childbirth that makes so many women say such things? I am convinced that they say it because they have come into intimate contact with the incredible and unexplainable design of life. In the face of this miracle, they intuitively realize that the processes of human life could not just have evolved by chance. In the face of such experiences, most women cannot help but point to God.

There are two basic ways to explain the development of human life. Either we are the result of chance, or we are the result of design (by God). The dominant way used in Western society to explain the development of human beings still goes back to naturalistic evolution (evolution without God), the theory originally proposed by Charles Darwin.

The theory can be summarized in the following manner:

- The universe and planet earth developed (as a suitable place for life) *by the smallest possible mathematical chance.*
- Then, over billions of years, biological life sprang into existence on earth *by the smallest possible mathematical chance.*
- Then, once life started, it evolved into more complex forms through numerous, successive, and slight modifications *by the smallest possible mathematical chances.*

Consequently, human life and all other advanced forms of biological life are *the result of chance groupings of the smallest possible mathematical chances.*

But the factual probability that life happened this way is very problematical—as Stephen Meyers points out in his book, *Signature in the Cell: DNA and the Evidence for Intelligent Design.*[22] In fact, on probability grounds, the statistical odds of each one is statistically equivalent to zero.[23] Most people are also unaware that the fossil record *does not* support the theory of naturalistic evolution, as most, if not all, species (properly defined) just sprang up in the fossil record with no transitional forms.[24] Those scientists, mathematicians, and thinkers who have looked at the evidence with an open mind, point out that evolutionary theory (when it does not depend on God) should now be put on trial and declared "invalid."[25]

The creation model, which holds that God guided the creation of all life forms, culminating in the special creation of Adam and Eve, is completely compatible with the fossil record and biological evidence.[26] When the statistical odds of life just happening by chance are added to the picture, the view that God made everything is highly sensible and scientific.[27] The facts we are learning about both the physical and biological world are causing more and more scientists and mathematicians to believe in a personal God, a development that runs directly counter to what was predicted sixty years ago.[28] Naturalistic evolution and blind chance simply cannot explain what we observe in the universe and in this world.

At the beginning of this section, I mentioned my friend Roberta's confession about her doubts. That night began a process whereby she confronted her doubts and ended up admitting that she had always sensed that God was there. Roberta needed an environment where she could be honest about her doubts and ask questions. Who would have predicted that a group of hockey players and their wives would provide what she needed? She also needed to see the reasons that cause people to believe in God and become Christians.

Evidence (like that presented above) caused her to open up and started a process which eventually led her to embrace the belief that she had tried to repress all of her life. She is now a devout Christian.

The Bible indicates that, in a way, everybody is like Roberta. We all intuitively or innately know that God exists and that we are morally responsible to him. Evidence and sound reasoning help us to know that our intuitive inclination is based on a solid, objective foundation.

The Storyline of the Bible

To understand the Bible, it is helpful to have an idea of its broad storyline. This storyline can be summarized using seven important and basic teachings. These teachings provide the broader context for you to make the decision to trust and follow Jesus (that is, to be his disciple).

This might be described as the "Grand Story" of the Bible. Carefully read through it below because it will set up everything you will learn in this study guide. Do not worry if you cannot make sense of it all just yet, because the key teachings will be explained in due time.

The major focus in the Bible is that Jesus is the "Christ." The word *Christ* is the same as *Messiah* ("Christ" is from Greek; "Messiah" is from Hebrew). They both mean "the anointed one." Therefore, when we say "Jesus Christ," we are not saying that his first name is "Jesus" and his last name is "Christ." In the time of Jesus, that kind of designation was accomplished by saying "Jesus of Nazareth" or "Jesus, son of Joseph."

Instead, we are describing his identity: "Jesus *the Messiah*" or "Jesus *the Anointed One*."

Jesus the Messiah (Christ) is the main character in the most important story ever told. Human history before his birth leaned forward—waiting and longing for his entrance into the world. And after his short life on earth, history is now leaning forward again, with eager anticipation of his return at the end of history as we know it. You can understand Jesus' identity as the Messiah in light of the Grand Story of the Bible. Here it is in a brief outline form.[29]

1. Creation: The Bible begins with God calling all things into being. Every part of creation is declared *good* by the Creator. God's creative work climaxes in his creation of human beings, uniquely made in his image to display his character and to exercise his rule in the world as his representatives. The first human beings, Adam and Eve, enjoyed warm and close fellowship with God in the Garden of Eden.

2. Curse: God is both holy and loving. We were created to glorify him and to have an intimate relationship with him. Tragically, Adam and Eve were deceived by Satan to question God's faithfulness, and as a result they willfully chose to rebel against God's clear command. By their decision, human beings are now spiritually broken and separated from God. We are incapable of undoing the effects of sin; we desperately need God's saving intervention.

3. Covenant: God reached out to sinful humanity in grace in several ways. He rescued a man named Noah and his family in a time of judgment, making a covenant with him not to destroy the earth in a flood again. Then, he offered a covenant to a man named Abraham, a covenant which became an outline of his redemption plan in history. God promised to create a nation from Abraham and to bless all people of the world through him. Abraham believed God and accepted his covenant, and God eventually made Abraham's descendants into twelve tribes who became slaves in Egypt.

4. Covenant People (Israel): The Grand Story of the Bible continues with the descendants of Abraham. We see how God, using Abraham's descendant Moses, liberated the twelve tribes from bondage in Egypt. God showed his love for the Israelites by giving them special gifts. Three gifts are notable: the Ten Commandments and the Law, sacrifices for sin, and a special Promised Land (known today as Israel) for their twelve tribes. Then, God found in one of their kings, whose name was David, a faith so pleasing that God made another promise to fulfill his commitment to bless all people. He said that one of David's descendants would become the messianic King. His kingdom would never end and would be a paradise for God's people. This Messiah would also judge those outside his kingdom.

5. Christ (Messiah): Jesus came as this Messiah, our King, and in him, the kingdom of God broke into this sin-permeated world. Jesus came to reveal the true nature of God and to restore and redeem God's original intent for humanity. Jesus' mission led him to the cross, where he suffered and died to save all people, both the Jews and the Gentiles (that is, those not physically descended from Abraham). After three days, Jesus rose from the dead, freeing us from Satan, and then he ascended into heaven. He is coming back again to fully restore God's kingdom. By repentance and faith in Jesus and his finished work on the cross, we can enter into his kingdom reign. He takes our sin away, he gives us the gift of the Holy Spirit, and we are adopted into his Father's family. Our old identity is dead, and we become a new creation through the grace of God, by faith in Jesus and what Jesus has done for us. We now live a new life, trusting and following him as his disciples. This teaching is called "the gospel," which means "the good news." Really, it is the best news anyone can ever hear!

6. Church: Before Jesus returned to the Father in heaven, he gave his apostles and followers a commission to carry on his teachings and make disciples. After ascending to heaven and sitting enthroned, he sent the Holy Spirit and established a global community for those who placed their faith in him. Jesus is the head of this body, and he calls those in his church to use the gifts and the message he has given them to be disciples who make disciples. Disciples are people who love God, love others, and live out God's kingdom reign in word and deed by reaching out to those who do not know the gospel and by showing compassion toward the poor and the oppressed. The life and teachings of Jesus form the blueprint for the mission and identity of the church, and the Holy Spirit unites disciples from different cultures, places, and times into one body—the body of Christ.

7. Consummation: Jesus promised his followers that he will return one day to fully remove the effects of the curse and usher in the age to come where sin, death, pain, and sadness are gone forever. This is the blessed hope for all disciples of Jesus. Until that time, Jesus offers humans a standing invitation into his "already-but-not-yet" kingdom. He offers salvation to us by grace through faith. Grace is God's unearned favor through which he offers us forgiveness and life in his kingdom, and we respond to this offer by faith, which is expressed as trusting and following Jesus. When Jesus comes back, he will judge those living as well as those who have died. Those who did not respond in this life to God's gracious invitation to be redeemed will be punished for their sins in hell. Those who trusted and followed Jesus will experience everlasting joy with God forever in the new heaven and the new earth.

These seven plot points are the major movements of God's story. Every plot movement in the Bible's overarching story points in some way to Jesus. Since Jesus came to lead us into all-of-life discipleship, not just a one-time conversion, this storyline is essential to know. You can fully understand and follow Jesus and what he calls us to only in light of this grand, creation-fall-restoration story.[30] Again, do not worry if you do not understand every detail in this story. Let it serve as a starting point.

CHAPTER 2

Jesus in History

Key Theme: Jesus was a real historical person, and most of the key elements of his life have been acknowledged and accepted by historians.

W e want to start with the question of historical truth. It's important for thinking people who approach the question of faith to be able to honestly ask, "Was Jesus a real person in history?," "Do we have good reason to believe that the things the Bible describes actually happened?," and "What facts do we know, independent of the Bible, that show us whether or not the core things in the Bible about Jesus are true?" The following six points provide an informed perspective on the historical evidence.

1. Jesus is a historical figure. In fact, there is very good evidence for Jesus *outside* the Bible. We can know, even today, that the things described in the Gospels have an objective basis in history.

Ancient non-Christian historians like Josephus and Tacitus record Jesus as a historical person. The popular archaeology journal *The Biblical Archaeology Review* asked the question, "Did Jesus Exist? Searching for Evidence beyond the Bible."[31] It is a good, scholarly article, and it addresses a question many people want to know. In this article, Lawrence Mykytiuk summarizes the evidence about Jesus from sources outside the Bible:

1. **He existed as a man.**
2. **His personal name was Jesus.**
3. **He was called *Christos* in Greek, which is a translation of the Hebrew word *Messiah*.**
4. **He had a brother named James.**
5. **He won over both Jews and Greeks.**
6. **Jewish leaders of the day expressed unfavorable opinions about him.**
7. **Pilate rendered the decision that he should be executed.**

8. His execution was specifically by crucifixion.

9. He was executed during Pontius Pilate's governorship over Judea (26-36 CE).

Why is it important to non-Christians and Christians to have historical evidence for Jesus from outside the Bible? Which point from the list is most surprising to you?

_____

_____

_____

2. The world's leading expert on Jesus and his kingdom today is N.T. Wright, who summarizes the scholarly consensus about him among historians: "Jesus' life, his announcement of God's kingdom, his radical re-definition of that kingdom, and his death on a Roman cross—we can be certain of all that. Few serious historians of any background or belief would deny those facts."[32]

Why would it be important to know that these basic facts about Jesus are well established and affirmed by the best historical scholars in the world today?

_____

_____

_____

_____

3. The Bible teaches that those who believe in Jesus should have a healthy reverence for Christ and be able to give the reasons for their faith. Believers are to defend their convictions with gentleness and respect to non-believers.

> 1 Peter 3:15 - But in your hearts revere Christ as Lord. Always be prepared to give an answer to everyone who asks you to give the reason for the hope that you have. But do this with gentleness and respect.

Why are gentleness and respect important when sharing one's faith?

_____

_____

_____

_____

4. Our faith is not a blind faith but an informed faith. Our faith has good evidence and reason to back it up. For example, Luke wrote the Gospel of Luke to tell people about Jesus. But he wrote it only after researching the evidence.

> Luke 1:1-4 - Many have undertaken to draw up an account of the things that have been fulfilled among us, just as they were handed down to us by those who from the first were eyewitnesses and servants of the word. With this in mind, since I myself have carefully investigated everything from the beginning, I too decided to write an orderly account for you, most excellent Theophilus, so that you may know the certainty of the things you have been taught.

Why does having an informed faith matter, and why do you think Luke investigated for himself?

_____

_____

_____

_____

5. Paul was an early believer in Jesus and a leader of the Christian faith. He explained to a Roman official named Festus what it meant to believe in Jesus. Paul was very intelligent, and Festus thought Paul might be insane to believe in Jesus. Paul reminded him of the historical evidence for Jesus as a reason for him to believe.

Acts 26:24-26 - At this point Festus interrupted Paul's defense. "You are out of your mind, Paul!" he shouted. "Your great learning is driving you insane." "I am not insane, most excellent Festus," Paul replied. "What I am saying is true and reasonable. The king is familiar with these things, and I can speak freely to him. I am convinced that none of this has escaped his notice, because it was not done in a corner."

Have you ever considered someone else to be unreasonable or out of their mind for their faith? Why is it important to be grounded in what is true and reasonable?

_____

_____

_____

_____

6. The faith we follow is focused upon the resurrection of Jesus from the dead. The Bible teaches that the resurrection is a historical truth and that many witnesses attested to it. As you read the following passage, note both the importance of the resurrection and the Apostle Paul's mention of eyewitnesses. Most of them were still living twenty-five years after the resurrection—and Paul was implying that the people in Corinth could (did) talk to them.

1 Corinthians 15:3-6 - For what I received I passed on to you as of first importance: that Christ died for our sins according to the Scriptures, that he was buried, that he was raised on the third day according to the Scriptures, and that he appeared to Cephas, and then to the Twelve. After that, he appeared to more than five hundred of the brothers and sisters at the same time, most of whom are still living, though some have fallen asleep [died].

What would your reaction be if you could talk to eyewitnesses of Jesus' resurrection today—just like these people were able to do then?

_____

_____

_____

Summary

Atheists and leaders from other religions (like Judaism, Buddhism, and Islam) have proposed alternative theories to the resurrection. Scholars have investigated them all, and none have been found to be a good alternative explanation. No theory makes as much sense as the reality of the resurrection.[33]

The eyewitnesses of the resurrection were closest to the facts. They truly believed it. We know from history that their beliefs were so strong that they did not just claim that Jesus rose from the dead, they radically altered their lives, lived through awful persecution, and many died terrible deaths as martyrs rather than giving up their faith in the resurrection. The earliest eyewitnesses bet their lives that Jesus' resurrection pointed to a better life after death.

The resurrection of Jesus is also the best explanation for the start of Christianity and the early church. Something caused the explosion of this new religion into the world. It started in Jerusalem, where the evidence for the resurrection was best known, and it spread to the outer reaches of the Roman Empire.

The evidence for Jesus and his resurrection is strong. Those with faith should also know that the evidence provides factual support for what they believe in their hearts—that the Bible accurately reflects the historical truth about Jesus.

Have you ever altered your life because of a conviction based on objective evidence? Why is this so powerful?

_____

_____

Jesus in History

We want to give you a deeper overview of the evidence for Jesus in this chapter. I have spent many hours researching these things at advanced levels. I have also visited Israel more than ten times, where I personally investigated the places, artifacts, and backgrounds found in the Bible.

I am a lot like John the Baptist: When I have doubts, I find it helpful to review the factual basis for my faith (Luke 7:19ff). The historical, geographical, and archaeological evidence I present below has been formative for me, and I think it will be for you too as you seek to know the objective facts behind the historical claims of Jesus and the Gospels.

In what follows, I will be summarizing the evidence and presenting simply that which is presented more comprehensively by various scholars.[34] There are some websites and books that I recommend to serious readers who want to investigate further:

- Reasonablefaith.org – William Lane Craig is one of the world's leading experts on the historical evidence for Jesus.
- Craigkeener.com – Craig Keener is one of the world's leading experts on miracles and the evidence for Jesus.
- Peter Williams, *Can We Trust the Gospels* (Crossway, 2018).
- Craig Evans, *Jesus and His World: The Archaeological Evidence* (Westminster, John Knox Press, 2013).
- Craig Evans, *Jesus and the Remains of the Day* (Hendrickson Publishing, 2015).
- Craig Keener, *Christobiography: Memory, History, and the Reliability of the Gospels* (Eerdmans, 2019).
- R. Steven Notley, *In The Master's Steps: The Gospels in the Land* (Carta, Jerusalem, 2014).

The evidence for Jesus and the Gospels is very solid, much more so than the average person realizes.

The Archaeological, Historical, and Geographical Evidence

There is a lot of evidence in Israel for what the Bible teaches about Jesus. As mentioned above, I have led many trips to Israel (as the pictures below will demonstrate). In the following pages, I will show you ten major archaeological and geographical backgrounds behind the life of Jesus.

The first followers of Jesus in history marked the key locations from Jesus' life. Some places still have inscriptions about Jesus in the stone from the late first century (e.g., Capernaum) and the late second century (e.g., Nazareth). We know how these places were marked because the early historian Eusebius (260-339 CE) identified many of these locations from earlier times in his writings. We also have the ancient travelogue of Bordeaux Pilgrim, a woman named Egeria, and early church leaders Cyril and Jerome from the same times.[35] They tell us about many locations in Israel.

Many of the major sites from the life of Jesus were made into church buildings when Christianity was first legalized (in the early 300s). Constantine was the Roman emperor who became a Christian and who made Christianity legal at that time. Helena (ca. 250-330 CE) was Constantine's mother and an important person to note as we retrace the steps of Jesus. She helped her son embrace Christianity, and then used her power to ensure that this new faith spread. When her son made Christianity legal, she traveled to Palestine. There, with the support of her son's officials, she helped organize the construction of many church buildings at the locations from the life of Jesus that had been identified and revered by the earliest Christians. This action was a wonderful gift to us because the church buildings became permanent markers, ensuring that people through the centuries would know the precise locations of many of the events from Jesus' life.

Other places—such as the Temple Mount, the Kidron Valley, and the Jordan River—did not need to be marked by church buildings. These locations are well-known to anyone familiar with the area, both in ancient and modern times.

1. Jesus' Birth in Bethlehem and King Herod

Bethlehem is just about six miles outside Jerusalem. It was the birthplace of Jesus (Matthew 2:1; Luke 2:4-8). Modern Bethlehem is located in the same location as in New Testament times. The ancient sites for both the "Shepherd's Field" and the birth of Jesus have been marked from early times.

The Shepherd's Field

There were very few good fields in the area outside the ancient village of Bethlehem for sheep to graze on grass. The places marked from the earliest time is now part of the modern city of Bethlehem. The picture to the right is one of the key places marked from ancient times as the Shepherd's Field.

Church of the Nativity

Several beautiful church buildings have been built in this area. From the earliest times, followers of Jesus marked the location of the Church of the Nativity as the place where Jesus was born. Archaeologist Jim Flemming describes it this way:

> Under the apse at the Church of the Nativity in Bethlehem shown at right, there is a cave. The Protoevangelium of James, the gospel from the 2nd century A.D. says the baby was born in a cave. The gospels do not mention the word stable. They simply say the baby was laid in a manger. Almost all mangers were in caves.[36]

It was built here by Helena in the early 300s to mark the spot which had long been considered the place Jesus was born.

Remnants of Herod's Herodium Palace today

King Herod's Tomb

The Place of the Manger

In the time of Jesus, animals were kept in caves, and the manger Jesus was placed in would have been located in one of those caves. The Church of the Nativity includes a shrine to mark the location of the ancient cave (see above) thought to be the birthplace of Jesus. There is a star that marks the traditional spot where the manger may have been placed.

King Herod

The Bible describes how Jesus was born during the reign of King Herod. This notoriously paranoid ruler of Israel tried to kill the baby Jesus by killing all the babies in Bethlehem. Herod is well-known to us not only by written historical records, but also from buildings he left behind. A great builder, Herod designed many palaces, and the remnants of some of the palaces are still in existence. For example, just outside of Bethlehem is his palace called Herodium.

In 2007, something very interesting and surprising happened at Herodium. Archaeologists found the tomb of King Herod himself.

2. Jesus' Dedication at Birth and Time in the Temple in Jerusalem at Age 12

After Jesus was born in Bethlehem, his parents had him circumcised in the Jewish temple on the eighth day according to Jewish law (Luke 2:22-24). The only event about Jesus recorded in the New Testament between his birth and the beginning of his ministry at around the age of thirty was his visit to the temple when he was about twelve. Today, the temple is the largest and most important archaeological site from the time of Jesus. It was destroyed by the Romans in 70 CE, but the base, the retaining wall, and the grounds remain to this day.

Look closely at the recent picture below to see if you can locate the retaining walls of the ancient Temple Mount. They frame the area where Muslims erected the Dome of the Rock (the gold dome in the middle) in the late 600s. The lower part of the retaining walls and the area up top (the Temple Mount) maintain the basic structure and appearance from ancient times.

The Retaining Wall of the First Century Temple Today

From the replica of first-century Jerusalem below, notice the temple. Shortly after Israel established control of Jerusalem in 1967, the government commissioned that a replica be made of ancient Jerusalem from the first century (i.e., the time of Jesus), because that was the last time until 1967 that the Jewish people controlled Jerusalem. This was also the last time Jewish people had control over the temple. Below the replica is a picture of the model they created. Notice the prominence of the temple, which in the first century was a marvel to behold (Matthew 24:1-3).

Notice the rendition of what the temple looked like in the picture below.

Recent rendering of the temple from Jesus' time

Trust and Follow Jesus

In the picture to the right, you will see the steps up to the temple that were uncovered recently. These ancient steps lead up to a gate in the corner (where the people are gathered). In Jesus' time, this gate led directly into the temple.

The gate was the remnant of the Beautiful Gate (Acts 3:10) that Jesus walked through. Thomas Friedman wrote a book called *From Beirut to Jerusalem* several years ago. In that book, he tells the story of this gate and astronaut Neil Armstrong.

When American astronaut Neil Armstrong, a devout Christian, visited Israel after his trip to the moon, he was taken on a tour of the Old City of Jerusalem by Israeli archaeologist Meir Ben-Dov. When they got to the Hulda Gate, which is at the top of the stairs leading to the Temple Mount, Armstrong asked Ben-Dov whether Jesus had stepped anywhere around there.

"I told him, 'Look, Jesus was a Jew,'" recalled Ben-Dov. "These are the steps that lead to the Temple, so he must have walked here many times." Armstrong then asked if these were the original steps, and Ben-Dov confirmed that they were.

"So Jesus stepped right here?" asked Armstrong.

"That's right," answered Ben-Dov.

"I have to tell you," Armstrong said to the Israeli archaeologist, "I am more excited stepping on these stones than I was stepping on the moon."[37]

The Huldah Gate from the first century temple

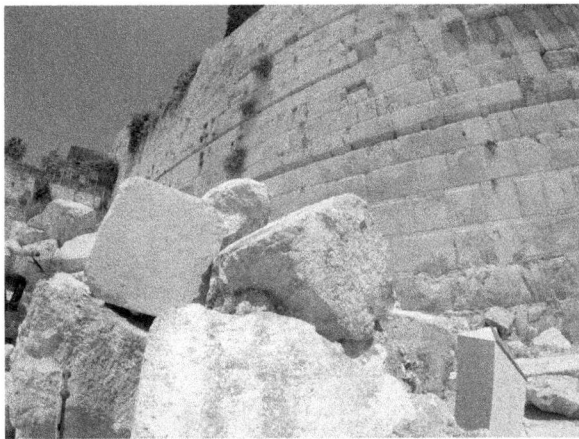

The stones from the temple knocked
down by the Romans in 70 CE

The Jordan River

Note in the picture to the left where a group of us have gathered on the threshold of the door that would have led up to the temple in the time of Jesus.

In 2000, the Jerusalem Archaeological Park opened. The Israeli Antiquities Authority had supervised the excavation of the remnants left under centuries of rubble from the destruction of the temple in 70 CE. For the first time in almost 2,000 years, we were able to see the first-century pavement beside the temple. Jesus, when asked about the temple, told his disciples it would be destroyed and not one stone would be left; they would all be thrown down (Matthew 24:1-3). The stones cast down by the Romans, as Jesus prophesied almost 2,000 years ago, were recently revealed from underneath 1,900 years of rubble.

3. Jesus' Baptism in the Jordan River and Preparation in the Judean Desert

The geography of the Gospels fits the exact geography we find in Israel. As we follow the life of Jesus from Bethlehem to Jerusalem, we travel to the next two places mentioned prominently as Jesus began his public ministry. These are the Jordan River and the Judean Desert.

John the Baptist baptized people in the Jordan River, not far from Jerusalem (about 20 miles) and near Jericho. The location shown on the previous page is the direct access point from Jerusalem. John baptized people at or near this location.

After his baptism, Jesus went into the Judean Desert, where he fasted and prayed for forty days (Luke 4:1-2). The mountain in the background is called "Temptation Mountain." It may have been at a place like this where Jesus was tempted by the devil in the Judean Desert.

Temptation Mountain in the Judean Desert

4. Jesus' Ministry in Galilee (North of Jerusalem)

The Bible tells us Jesus started his public ministry following his baptism and temptation and spent a lot of time in the northern part of Israel, a region called Galilee. Jesus and his

The Sea of Galilee

Marking the towns of first-century Galilee

disciples often fished on the Sea of Galilee. Not only was it a great place to fish back then, but it continued to be a site of commercial fishing for two millennia. The most populous fish is a form of tilapia.

Several close towns on the northern edge of the Sea of Galilee are mentioned in the Gospels (see Northern Galilee in the picture to the left). They have been uncovered by archaeologists exactly where the Bible says they were. Below is a picture of markers to each town that Israeli archaeologists have placed in the ground for scholars and tourists. Each marker points to places mentioned in the Bible from about 2,000 years ago. Archaeologist James Fleming has told me they have identified 23 of the 27 towns in Galilee mentioned in the Gospels.

Examples of geographical confirmation such as these are abundant in Israel.

5. Jesus' Life and Ministry in Nazareth

Nazareth was Jesus' home when he was growing up. It was a very small town in the first century and was located in a basin surrounded by hills. It is estimated that 150 to 300 people lived there. Many homes were built in caves with a few stone homes and a synagogue built nearby. Today, it is a city of roughly 100,000 residents.

Nazareth Village recreates life in ancient Nazareth

I have spent a good amount of time in Nazareth, sifting through the archaeological records and talking to the resident archaeologist. One of the homes became a place where Christians came to worship from the very beginning. It was revered as the home of Mary. From a very early time, there was a mark on a pillar in the home, in Greek, that mentioned Mary (see lower right).

According to the curator, archaeologists are 90 percent certain that this is the house Jesus grew up in. The evidence is indeed impressive, with both the early church building and the inscription marking the location.

It was in a synagogue in Nazareth where Jesus' public ministry was formally announced in Luke 4. From Nazareth, Jesus moved to Capernaum, which served as a home base for his public ministry.

6. Jesus' Ministry Base in Capernaum

Matthew 4:13 tells us that when Jesus' cousin, John the Baptist, was arrested, Jesus moved to Capernaum. It became the central place out of which he developed his ministry. Capernaum was on the Sea of Galilee and not very far from Nazareth (about 30 miles or 48 kilometers away). In the 1960s, archaeologists excavated a large part of this ancient town.

The picture to the left is an archaeologist's drawing of Capernaum in the first century. This site is considered one of the top ten archaeological discoveries in Israel.[38]

In Capernaum, archaeologists have located a house which was likely the home of Peter's mother-in-law.[39] The Gospel of Matthew describes how Jesus healed her at her home (8:14-15). After the excavation was finished, a church building was constructed over the site. The church has a glass floor so people can see the remnants of a home that was turned into a small church in the last part

Capernaum in the first century

of the first century, within the lifetime of people who lived when Jesus lived.

The first picture is the church building from a distance, and the second is a close-up view of the remnants of a church building that goes back to the end of the first century.

Another important site has been found in Capernaum. The Gospel of John describes a pivotal sermon Jesus preached in the synagogue in Capernaum (6:59). At the end of the sermon, most people left Jesus because they did not like what he said. The base of the synagogue from the first century is still in existence and is marked by archaeologists for tourists today.

7. Jesus in Jerusalem (South)

The New Testament records that Jesus often spent time in Jerusalem teaching. It was the Jewish center of the world. About one-third of the Gospels focus on Jesus' time in Jerusalem at the end of his life. It was in this city that Jesus suffered and died. In the aftermath of the 1967 Arab-Israeli war, much of the ancient city of Jerusalem was excavated, resulting in multiple archaeological finds. The excavations correspond with the locations we read about in the New Testament. Let us look at five.

Base of synagogue where Jesus actually taught

Pool of Bethesda

Pool of Siloam

The Kidron Valley

The Pool of Bethesda

The Pool of Bethesda was where Jesus healed a man who had been an invalid for 38 years (John 5). Archaeologists have long known the exact location, and many tours of Jerusalem start at this spot.

The Pool of Siloam

In 2006, an important water pipe started leaking in Jerusalem. In the course of making repairs, the workmen found an ancient pool. Archaeologists investigated and confirmed that they had found the original Pool of Siloam. This is the place the blind man traveled to after Jesus made mud and put it on his eyes (John 9:7). "Go and wash in the Pool of Siloam," Jesus said, which the man did and was cured.

The Kidron Valley

The Kidron Valley is mentioned repeatedly in the Bible, and it exists today exactly where the Bible indicates. You will see from the picture on the left the Kidron Valley to the left of the temple retaining wall. In Jesus' time, the Kidron Valley was located just outside the city.

The Garden of Gethsemane

It is recorded in the Bible that Jesus left the place of his final Passover feast (the "Last Supper") and went across the Kidron Valley to an olive grove

The Garden of Gethsemane

(John 18:1). As we discover, the Garden of Gethsemane is a real place still in existence on the other side of the Kidron Valley. Even the olive trees remain. The roots of these trees have been tested, and the archaeologists in Israel claim that some of the trees have descended from trees that were living at the time of Jesus.

Where Judas killed himself

The Potters Field

Even the field where Judas hanged himself has likely been discovered. The Field of Akeldama (Acts 1:19) is thought to be located to the upper right of the hospital in the picture to the right (in the area of the trees).

Courtyard outside Caiaphas's house

Pavement beside Caiaphas's house from Jesus' time

8. Jesus' Trials and Caiaphas and Pilate

Jesus was arrested on the night of his betrayal and taken to trial. The first trial took place in the house of the high priest Caiaphas (Matthew 26:57; John 18:25-27). Caiaphas's house is the place where Jesus was tried, where Peter warmed himself by the fire, and where Peter denied he knew Jesus three times. Archaeologists believe they have found the ancient house. The courtyard has a statue, as an image of what it would have been like at that time, made to commemorate the denial.

The courtyard was located beside a road remaining from the first century. The road and stones on which Jesus would have walked are still in place.

Not only that, but the prison or torture chamber where Jesus would have been held during the night of his trial has also been known from ancient times. In the early centuries, a Christian pilgrim to the Holy Land etched a cross inside of the prison hole, where it opens to another room above.

The Bible describes how Jesus was beaten in front of Caiaphas and then was sent to the Romans to be tried by Pontius Pilate (Matthew 26:3; 27:2; John 18:13-28). In 1990, when workers were widening a road in Jerusalem's Peace Forest, they stumbled across an unusually large burial site. Inside, archaeologists found the family tomb of Caiaphas, the high priest who presided over Jesus' Jewish trial.[40] The tomb had been buried for many centuries and had been lost from history. Scientists examined the box and bones and determined that they were those of a sixty-year-old man believed to be Caiaphas, the Jewish high priest who condemned Jesus.

The two main characters who were instrumental in Jesus' trial and condemnation to death were Caiaphas (for the Jews) and Pontius Pilate (for the Romans, the occupying power in Israel). Pilate's title was Prefect of Judea. Not a lot was known about Pilate, and for centuries, there were no inscriptions of him to be found. Then, in June 1961, a group of Italian archaeologists uncovered a limestone block with a dedication from Pontius Pilate, Prefect of Judea, confirming the biblical account.

After Jesus was condemned by Caiaphas and Pilate, he was forced to carry his cross. Another man, Simon of Cyrene, was later compelled to carry it for him (Matthew 27:31-32; Mark 15:20-21; Luke 23:26). This is likely because Jesus himself was too weak from the scourging to carry it at that point. In an interesting twist of history, in 1941, two Jewish archaeologists (Eleazer Sukenik and Naham Avigad) seem to have found the family tomb of the man who carried the

Caiaphas' family ossuary found in 1990

Dungeon in which Jesus was likely held

Pilate Inscription

cross. They found it during World War II, catalogued it, published the find in a scholarly journal, and then placed it in the storeroom of a museum in Israel. Because it was not a highly noted find (the war was underway and the discovery was published in an elite journal), few people noted it. The key ossuary sat unknown in the storeroom for about 60 years before everything was republished in 2003.[41] Then, the broader scholarly world realized that the family tomb of Simon of Cyrene had very possibly been found.

The inscriptions on the ossuaries in this family tomb combine Jewish-style and Greek-style names. Some of the particular names were very uncommon in ancient Israel, but especially common in the region known as Cyrenaica (eastern Libya), whose main city was Cyrene.[42] The faint text on the ossuary, from the time of Jesus says, "Alexander, son of Simon." Mark 15:30 describes Simon's role as he carried Jesus' cross:

> A certain man from Cyrene, Simon, the father of Alexander and Rufus, was passing on his way in from the country, and they forced him to carry the cross.

Scholars conclude that everything about this artifact seems to fit with the individuals named in Mark 15:21. It is from the correct historical and geographical context (first century Jerusalem), and the family origin reflected in the inscriptions is accurate (Cyrenaic). The combination of names, one rather rare in a Jewish context (Alexander), and the description of the correct familial relations (Alexander, son of Simon) point to the men described in the Bible.

By these discoveries, three of the actual people involved in Jesus' trial and journey to crucifixion described in the Gospels are confirmed. And remember that these are just some of the examples of the many archaeological discoveries that corroborate what the Gospels teach.

9. Jesus' Cross

Crucifixion was the common means used to implement the death penalty for Jews by Romans in the first century. Although the practice was widely described in the literature from the time, it was not until 1968 that the first remnants of a crucified person were found. While working in Jerusalem, construction workers uncovered a tomb from the first century. Inside the tomb, they found an ankle bone from a skeleton that had a nail embedded into the bone. The nail had not been extracted because it had been driven into a knot in the wood and was difficult to pull out.

We now know that wood was not easy to find in Jerusalem in the first century, so they often used the same tree for different crucifixions. The criminal would carry the cross beam, which would be placed on one of the trees by the side of the road used for crucifixion.[43] The picture to the right is a re-creation by archaeologists of a cross probably like the one upon which Jesus was crucified.[44]

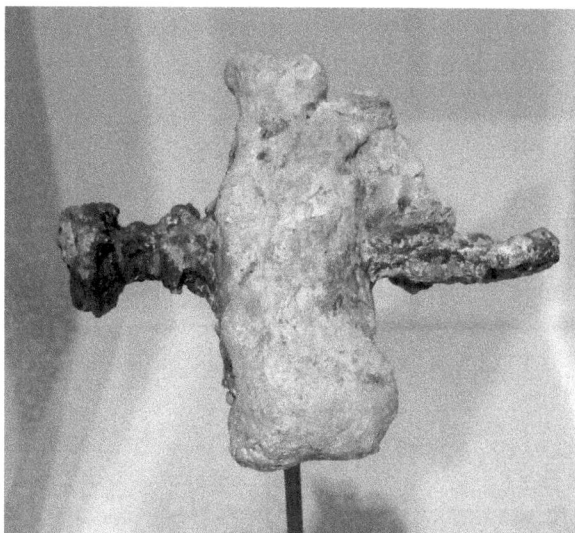

A crucifixion nail in an ankle from first-century Jerusalem

An example of what the cross looked like

10. Jesus' Burial and Resurrection

The Bible describes the death, burial, and resurrection of Jesus as the heart and core of the Christian faith. According to the Christian faith, Jesus was crucified and died on the cross for our sins. By his death and resurrection, he paved the way for us to be made right with God. It is natural to wonder how it happened and if it could have truly happened as the Bible describes. Notice a tomb from Jesus' time in the picture at the top left. The tomb was accidentally found when the Israelis were building a road and is no different from how the Bible describes Jesus' tomb.

The picture to the left shows the interior of first-century tombs.

There are two possible locations in Jerusalem where scholars believe Jesus could have been crucified and buried. One location is the "Garden Tomb," a beautiful tomb located near a place that looks somewhat like a skull. This seems

to match the description of the place where Jesus was crucified, called the "place of the skull" ("Golgotha," Mark 15:22).

This tomb was found in the late 1800s, and it seems to match what the Bible describes, especially the rocks that have the appearance of the skull, along with a beautiful tomb, a garden, and a well to hold water for the garden.

The Garden Tomb gives us an excellent sense of what the crucifixion and burial site would have been like. But the best ancient tradition points us to a different location which has been revered as the place of Jesus' death, burial, and resurrection.

Early Christians built a monument at the place where they believed Jesus was crucified and buried. In fact, an ancient Roman Emperor built a pagan temple at this location to stop Christians from meeting here. But when Christianity became legal in the Roman Empire, one of the first church buildings in Israel was built over that location. The ancient church is called "Church of the Holy Sepulchre."

Church of the Holy Sepulchre built over the tomb of Jesus

First-century tomb inside the
Church of the Holy Sepulchre

The dark picture to the left is a first-century chamber within a tomb, located in the Church of the Holy Sepulcher. Jesus would have been placed within a tomb chamber, something like this one.

There is an ancient tradition that the exact location of Jesus' tomb was marked. Today, there is a huge monument within the church built over the marked tomb. People will line up for hours to go in to see the possible tomb of Jesus.

The purpose of this short survey is to give you a taste of the objective evidence for Jesus and the events described in the Gospels. The historical basis of the resurrection is particularly important for Christian faith.

The central fact presented in the New Testament for the truthfulness of Jesus is his resurrection from the dead. If he was raised from the dead, then it is the most important event in history and most consequential miracle in the Bible. It means Jesus' core promises are true. It means that his sacrifice on the cross really did forgive us for our sins. It means that, for us as well, death is not the end. Jesus' kingdom is real, and we can live with God after death.

Belief in the resurrection was the core belief of the earliest witnesses in the Bible as 1 Corinthians 15:3-7 shows us:

For what I received I passed on to you as of first importance: that Christ died for our sins according to the Scriptures, that he was buried, that he was raised on the third day according to the Scriptures, and that he appeared to Cephas, and then to the Twelve. After that, he appeared to more than five hundred of the brothers and sisters at the same time, most of whom are still living, though some have fallen asleep. Then he appeared to James, then to all the apostles.

The resurrection is the key reason the church started meeting on Sunday—the day of the week on which Jesus rose from the dead (Mark 16:2). His resurrection was expressed in the earliest accounts of Christian conversion through baptism by immersion in water, a re-enactment in water of the burial and resurrection of Jesus. Jesus' resurrection and return are also in mind during the memorial known as Christian communion, during which bread and wine help Jesus' followers remember his death, as they "proclaim the Lord's death until he comes" (1 Corinthians 11:26; cf. Matthew 26:29). The resurrection was also the foundational belief of the earliest Christian writers in the period after the New Testament was written.

Atheists and leaders from other religions (like Judaism, Buddhism, and Islam) have proposed alternative theories to the resurrection. These theories have all been investigated by scholars, but none have been found to be plausible explanations. No theory makes as much sense as the reality of the resurrection.[45]

The eyewitnesses of the resurrection were closest to the facts. They truly believed it. We know from history that their beliefs were so strong that they did not just claim that Jesus rose from the dead. Rather, they allowed the event to radically alter their lives, as they endured awful persecution, and they often died terrible deaths as martyrs, rather than give up their faith in the resurrection. The earliest eyewitnesses bet their lives that Jesus' resurrection pointed to a better life after death.

The resurrection of Jesus is also the best explanation for the start of Christianity and the early church. Something caused the explosion of this new religion. Christianity started in Jerusalem just weeks after Jesus' public crucifixion just outside the city. Within a relatively short time, the religion spread beyond where the evidence for the resurrection was best known, to the outer reaches of the Roman Empire.

The evidence for Jesus and his resurrection is strong. Those with an informed faith believe that the evidence provides factual support for what they believe in their hearts. We believe that Jesus is who the Bible says he is, and the facts confirm it.

Do we believe God exists? Does the broader story of the Bible make sense? Do we personally believe that our sin is real? Are we willing to believe that our sin is a barrier to a relationship with God? Do we sense the presence of God's Spirit bringing personal conviction on this issue? Does Jesus' death for our sin make sense in our personal life?

These are questions that will require reflection. They also require spiritual conviction—a sense that God is somehow present, authenticating the message of Jesus and the resurrection. The Bible teaches that God's invisible Spirit opens the eyes of a human heart to these truths. I have been personally convinced by both the evidence and a sense that God's Spirit authenticated it in my inner being. I pray that the same thing will happen to you as you work through this material.

Conclusion

There is a key word that captures what many people experience when they travel to Israel. The word is *verisimilitude*, a term coined by archaeologists. The New Testament scholar Craig Evans describes how *verisimilitude* works in his book, *Jesus and His World: the Archaeological Evidence*:

> There is also a very important argument in favour of the general reliability of the New Testament Gospels, and that concerns what is called verisimilitude; that is, *what the Gospels describe matches the way things really were in early first-century Jewish Palestine.* The New Testament Gospels and Acts exhibit a great deal of verisimilitude. They speak of real people (such as Pontius Pilate, Herod Antipas, Annas, Caiaphas, Herod Agrippa I and II, Felix and Festus) and real events (deaths of John the Baptist and Agrippa I). They speak of real places (villages, cities, roads, lakes and mountains) that are clarified and corroborated by other historical sources and by archaeology. They speak of real customs (Passover, purity, sabbath, divorce law), institutions (synagogue, temple), offices/officers (priests, tax collectors, Roman governors, Roman centurions) and beliefs (of Pharisees, and Sadducees; interpretation of Scripture).[46]

I hope it is now easy to understand the word *verisimilitude.*

When I take people to Israel, there is often a moment when it suddenly hits them—that what the Bible describes matches what we will see in front of us. It is just as you would expect it to be if the Gospels are telling us the truth about Jesus.

This brings us back to what we mean when we say that we hold to an *informed faith*. The factual evidence may not prove to everyone beyond doubt that Jesus was who the Gospels say that he was; but the facts do provide solid, objective evidence for those of us who say that we believe in Jesus. We can support our belief by solid evidence.

The path recommended by God is solid evidence and good thinking, coupled with the internal, spiritual conviction of Jesus' reality within each of us. It is holistic and includes the mind. That is the path we seek to follow in this book.

Is there anything that stands out to you from this section that you would like to note and discuss?

_____

_____

_____

_____

_____

_____

CHAPTER 3

Scripture

Key Theme: God inspired the Bible and gave it to us for our guidance.

Once we know that Jesus existed and that there are good reasons to consider the Gospel accounts about him are accurate, we're ready for the next step. In this section, we want to look at what Jesus claimed about his teachings.

Again, we are on solid ground to assume based upon historical evidence that the Gospels accurately present Jesus. That's because in everything we can look at objectively in history, we find that the Gospels are accurate. So we are going to assume the continued accuracy of the accounts as we look at what Jesus said in his teachings.

The written records of Jesus' teachings are important. Especially if Jesus expected his apostles and followers to carry on his teachings and to make other followers (disciples), it was necessary to write them down. These teachings became part of the Bible.

Before we look at these teachings, it is helpful to understand how people looked at Scripture in Jesus' time. Knowing this will help us determine how Jesus' teachings would have been understood and preserved for us.

Scripture in Jesus' Time

Contrary to what most people think, everyday people in Jesus' time were typically literate. Historians have learned that first-century Jewish people had tremendous respect for Scripture. They believed God had commanded them to teach the Old Testament writings (the first part of the Bible) to their children, *so children were required to learn to read and write.* Josephus was a historian living at that time, and he wrote about Jewish people and their children. He said that God's law "orders that (children) shall be taught to read and shall learn both the laws and the deeds of their forefathers."[47] This meant that the average Jewish person at that time could read. So even though Jesus lived 2,000 years ago, both Jesus and the people of his time regularly discussed the meaning of the Scriptures (this reality is reflected in the Gospels in the New Testament).

Jewish people not only read, but they also made sure the Scriptures were accurately passed down. The Old Testament is the record of God and the Jewish people from the time of Moses (from the mid-1400s BCE to 1260 BCE) up until the last books of the Old Testament (around 400-165 BCE). Recent discoveries like the Dead Sea Scrolls at Qumran in Israel show us how careful the people were to preserve the teachings of the Old Testament. The people at Qumran lived before and during the time of Jesus, and they would check every small detail of Scripture to make sure it was accurately copied; then, they would check and re-check it. They were accurate and neat in all their copying work, as my picture of a scroll of Isaiah from 150 BCE shows below. Notice the clear and neat free-hand writing.

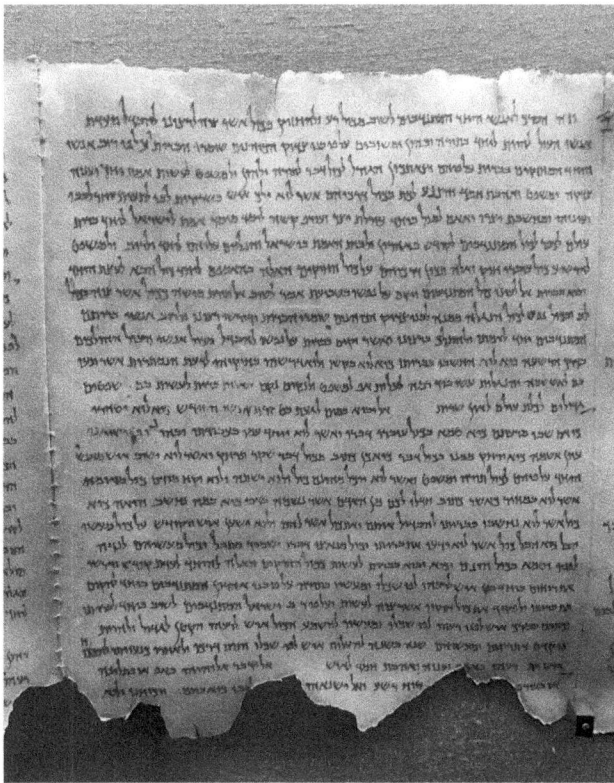

They would even take ritualistic baths after their work, to ensure that their work was consecrated to God, and that they were faithful scribes, accurately copying God's words.

It's also important to know that people in the time of Jesus widely relied upon the educational method of memorization. Jewish boys had an established practice of reading and memorizing portions of the Old Testament starting at five or six years of age.[48] Some teachers even had the entire Old Testament committed to memory. They didn't have printing presses, and the work of copying was a specialized, religious work (for people like those at Qumran).

It was their practice to memorize important teachings—the Scriptures and the teachings in the synagogue. There is an entire Jewish tradition (the oral interpretation of the Law by leading rabbis) that was very active in the time of Jesus. These teachings were passed on for hundreds of years and were only written down around 200 BCE. The important teachings of their leaders were memorized and carefully passed down from generation to generation. That is what they did to ensure accurate record keeping.

I say this to point out that when Jesus gave his teachings, he gave them to people who were trained to write down and memorize the teachings of their rabbis (religious leaders). As a well-known teacher, Jesus' teaching would have been immediately written down and memorized by his disciples.

Furthermore, many parts of Jesus' teachings were structured so that they could be easily memorized. Take the Sermon on the Mount, Jesus' most famous teaching on moral issues, as a case in point (Matthew 5-7). It was structured like the teaching of philosophers in the Roman world, whose teachings were summarized in a form that was easily memorized. From the sayings at the beginning of the Sermon on the Mount to the introduction proper (Matthew 5:17-20) to the first six contrasted teachings through to the conclusion (Matthew 7:20-28), the structure was designed to make it easy to memorize.

The Jewish practice of preserving teachings intact like those found in the Gospels would have been commonplace. From the earliest times, the memories of Jesus' life and teaching would have been considered sacred and been memorized and written down.[49] In this way, the earliest disciples would have naturally ensured that Jesus' words and deeds were accurately established. This perspective is a key to understanding the development of the Christian Scriptures.

We will focus on Jesus and his teachings through the creation of the Gospels and the rest of the New Testament Scriptures in this chapter. Those who have questions about which books should be considered Scripture and the reliability of the manuscripts will find the material by scholars Craig Blomberg and Michael Kroger to be helpful, along with information that can be found at Renew.org.[50]

1. How do these historical facts help us when it comes to the question of whether there could have been good written records of Jesus' teachings?

2. Jesus promised that God was with his disciples ensuring that they had an accurate recounting of what Jesus said and did. God promised that the Holy Spirit (God's invisible presence) would guide the apostles and help them to remember everything, to make sure it was recorded accurately. Notice the promise:

> John 14:24-26 - These words you hear are not my own; they belong to the Father who sent me. All this I have spoken while still with you. But the Counselor, the Holy Spirit, whom the Father will send in my name, will teach you all things and will remind you of everything I have said to you.

In what way does this passage give us additional perspective on how the apostles could accurately record Jesus' teachings?

_____

_____

3. Jesus said that people should believe in him, but even more, he said that he spoke for God. God, Jesus said, would use Jesus' words as the basis for our judgment at the end of time:

> John 12:47-49 - If anyone hears my words but does not keep them, I do not judge that person. For I did not come to judge the world, but to save the world. There is a judge for the one who rejects me and does not accept my words; the very words I have spoken will condemn them at the last day. For I did not speak on my own, but the Father who sent me commanded me to say all that I have spoken.

According to this passage, who gave Jesus his words and how will Jesus' words be used on the final day of judgment?

_____

_____

_____

_____

4. What is your personal reaction to what you just read? Explain.

_____

_____

_____

_____

5. Jesus acknowledges that many people call him "Lord," which is a word that means "master and God." According to Jesus, saying he is "Lord," is only meaningful if we hear his words and put them into practice.

> Luke 6:46-49 - Why do you call me, "Lord, Lord," and do not do what I say? As for everyone who comes to me and hears my words and puts them into practice, I will show you what they are like. They are like a man building a house, who dug down deep and laid the foundation on rock. When a flood came, the torrent struck that house but could not shake it, because it was well built. But the one who hears my words and does not put them into practice is like a man who built a house on the ground without a foundation. The moment the torrent struck that house, it collapsed, and its destruction was complete.

How can it be that if we hear and put Jesus' words into practice it is like building a house with a good foundation?

_____

_____

_____

_____

6. Jesus committed his teachings to the apostles. He then gave them the job of teaching people to obey everything Jesus taught.

> Matthew 28:18-20 - Then Jesus came to them and said, "All authority in heaven and on earth has been given to me. Therefore go and make disciples of all nations, baptizing them

in the name of the Father and of the Son and of the Holy Spirit, and teaching them to obey everything I have commanded you. And surely I am with you always, to the very end of the age."

Does Jesus teach us to learn everything he commanded or to obey everything he commanded—and what is the difference?

_____

_____

_____

_____

7. Paul was an apostle of Jesus and he taught people that Scripture is our inspired guide.

2 Timothy 3:16-17 - All Scripture is God-breathed and is useful for teaching, rebuking, correcting and training in righteousness, so that the servant of God may be thoroughly equipped for every good work.

Which of the four purposes of Scripture described in this passage is the most difficult use of Scripture to apply to yourself today?

_____

_____

_____

_____

8. Paul proceeded, in the following verses after 2 Timothy 3:17, to describe the presence of God and Jesus under the banner of "The Word," meaning that the teaching of Jesus through the apostles is very much "Jesus' Word."

2 Timothy 4:1-4 - In the presence of God and of Christ Jesus, who will judge the living and the dead, and in view of his appearing and his kingdom, I give you this charge. Preach

the word; be prepared in season and out of season; correct, rebuke and encourage—with great patience and careful instruction. For the time will come when people will not put up with sound doctrine. Instead, to suit their own desires, they will gather around them a great number of teachers to say what their itching ears want to hear.

What happens to make us gravitate to teachers who say what "our itching ears want to hear," and how do you envision stopping yourself from doing that?

_____

_____

_____

_____

9. We believe, based upon history, that the Bible contains accurate teachings. The Bible also says that God guided the process of creating prophecies in Scripture.

2 Peter 1:19-21 - We also have the prophetic message as something completely reliable, and you will do well to pay attention to it, as to a light shining in a dark place, until the day dawns and the morning star rises in your hearts. Above all, you must understand that no prophecy of Scripture came about by the prophet's own interpretation of things. For prophecy never had its origin in the human will, but prophets, though human, spoke from God as they were carried along by the Holy Spirit.

What do you think it means that people were "carried along by the Holy Spirit" to write what they did and, again, how does that give people extra confidence in the teachings of Scripture?

_____

_____

_____

_____

10. The following passage is a very important guide for us today. It describes the people of Berea (a town in the ancient world) as being noble. They were noble because they examined the Scriptures to see if what was being taught was true. We want to be noble in the same way that they were noble.

> Acts 17:10-12 - As soon as it was night, the believers sent Paul and Silas away to Berea. On arriving there, they went to the Jewish synagogue. Now the Berean Jews were of more noble character than those in Thessalonica, for they received the message with great eagerness and examined the Scriptures every day to see if what Paul said was true. As a result, many of them believed, as did also a number of prominent Greek women and many Greek men.

What would it mean to be a Berean today, and how do you feel about aspiring to be one?

_____

_____

_____

_____

Scripture

1. Jesus Believed in the Inspiration and Authority of the Hebrew Bible

As we will see, Jesus believed in and fully accepted the Old Testament, from the story of creation until the last Jewish prophet, Malachi. Jesus' attitude is important for us to keep in mind because we do not have the ability to go back much further than the Dead Sea Scrolls (200-150 BCE) or the Septuagint (270 BCE) to explore the texts and textual accuracy of the Old Testament. We know that they are generally historically accurate, [51] but we do not have access to the earliest Old Testament texts.[52] Jesus guides us because he believed that they were accurate, inspired, and historical representations of what God did and said for the Israelites. [53]

Jesus not only believed in the inspiration of the Old Testament and its teachings; he personally followed the Old Testament and upheld it in discussions. His belief in the inspiration of the Old Testament is demonstrated on multiple occasions when he quoted it as historical fact. For example, he referenced Sodom and Gomorrah as historical towns in Matthew 10:15, and he referenced Jonah and the people of Nineveh as historically accurate representations in Matthew 12:40. He used the Old Testament as his source for truth against Satan in his temptations in the desert (Luke 4:1-13), and he used it in debate with his opponents, pointing out how the reason they erred is that they did not uphold its teaching (Mark 12:24).

Jesus specifically taught the abiding validity of the Old Testament Scriptures, as long as they were interpreted in the light of how he, himself, fulfilled it and showed its true meaning.

For truly I tell you, until heaven and earth disappear, not the smallest letter, not the least stroke of a pen, will by any means disappear from the Law until everything is accomplished (Matthew 5:18).

Jesus showed that the Old Testament pointed to himself, beginning with Moses and the prophets (Luke 24:25-27). Stated another way, Jesus saw himself as the point of the Old Testament. We will talk more about this below, but Jesus was clear that the Old Testament could only be accurately interpreted through a proper understanding of himself and how he fulfilled its teachings.

This is important because if Jesus believed in the Old Testament writings, then those who have made the decision to trust and follow him will believe in their basic integrity. We have copies of the texts Jesus trusted in and upheld. There is archaeological and historical evidence for much of what is reported in the Old Testament, but, as mentioned above, there is little explicit evidence on the transmission of the Old Testament text from before 300 BCE. If we have confidence in Jesus and his views, then we can have confidence in the Old Testament.

2. Jesus Said His Teachings Finalize the Hebrew Bible

Jesus went further than fulfilling Old Testament teachings and instructing how to interpret the Law. As the promised Messiah, Jesus claimed that his teachings and his words were to be the foundation of life. He repeatedly described himself as the bridge between God and the human race:

I am the bread of life. Whoever comes to me will never go hungry, and whoever believes in me will never be thirsty (John 6:35).

I am the light of the world. Whoever follows me will never walk in darkness, but will have the light of life (John 8:12).

Jesus answered, "I am the way and the truth and the life. No one comes to the Father except through me" (John 14:6).

Jesus described himself and his teachings this way:

Jesus cried out, "Whoever believes in me does not believe in me only, but in the one who sent me. The one who looks at me is seeing the one who sent me. I have come into the world as a light, so that no one who believes in me should stay in darkness. If anyone hears my words but does not keep them, I do not judge that person. For I did not come to judge the world, but to save the world. *There is a judge for the one who rejects me and does not accept my words; the very words I have spoken will condemn them at the last day.* For I did not speak of my own, but the Father who sent me commanded me to say all that I have spoken. I know that his command leads to eternal life. So whatever I say is just what the Father has told me to say (John 12:44–50).

In this way, Jesus makes it clear. He and his teachings are the final authority and the criteria by which God will evaluate our lives. He is not just the promised Messiah, the king of Israel. He is not just a good teacher of the Old Testament. He and his teachings are the standard upon which we are to build our lives. It is the standard that God will use to determine our eternal destiny. There are no more sober words in all of human history.

3. Jesus' Written Teachings Became the New Testament

Jesus came into the world—he lived, taught, raised up disciples, and died. After he died, the Bible says he rose from the dead and ascended back into heaven. Just before his ascension back to heaven, Jesus committed his words and teachings to his followers, the apostles. The apostles were commissioned by him to help other people trust and follow Jesus. In other words, they were commissioned to make disciples. Jesus told them to baptize everyone who wanted to be a disciple and to teach the new disciple to obey all of his commandments.

Then Jesus came to them and said, "All authority in heaven and on earth has been given to me. Therefore go and make disciples of all nations, baptizing them in the name of the Father and of the Son and of the Holy Spirit, and *teaching them to obey everything I have commanded you.* And surely I am with you always, to the very end of the age" (Matthew 28:18-20).

Jesus also promised that God was guiding the apostles, ensuring they accurately recalled everything through the Holy Spirit. Notice the following promise:

These words you hear are not my own; they belong to the Father who sent me. All this I have spoken while still with you. *But the Advocate, the Holy Spirit, whom the Father will send in my name, will teach you all things and will remind you of everything I have said to you* (John 14:24–26).

According to Jesus, the Holy Spirit would ensure that the disciples would be properly taught and would remember everything he told them. God did not just rely on the memory practices of the Jewish people. He guided them and protected the accuracy of Jesus' teachings by his Holy Spirit.

This is why the first Christians devoted themselves to the apostles' teaching: they were not just the apostles' teachings, but they were the inspired teachings of Jesus himself!

They devoted themselves to the apostles' teaching and to fellowship, to the breaking of bread and to prayer (Acts 2:42).

Jesus Christ and his words were God's *final* message for the human race:

In the past God spoke to our ancestors through the prophets at many times and in various ways, but in these last days he has spoken to us by his Son, whom he appointed heir of all things, and through whom he made the universe (Hebrews 1:1-2).

This is why the writers of the New Testament urged Christians to uphold and defend these teachings from then on. God would provide no new gospel, no other path, and no other way (Galatians 1:8). In the book of Jude, it is described this way:

Dear friends, although I was very eager to write to you about the salvation we share, I felt compelled to write and urge you to contend for the faith that was once for all entrusted to God's holy people (Jude 3).

We never wish to be contentious or harsh toward sincere people. We always want to show respect and gentleness (1 Peter 3:15). Yet it ought to be emphasized that Jesus gave us only one path to God (John 14:6). Those who seek truth need to take his words with utter seriousness.

Scriptures such as these explain why those who believe in and follow the Bible are naturally inclined to reject any inspired teachings that are alleged to come after the time of the apostles. Stated differently, there is a fundamental contradiction between these passages and the claims of inspiration found in the Qur'an or the Book of Mormon (or other religious texts like them).

Five Beliefs about Jesus in the Qur'an That Contradict the Bible

- Jesus was not crucified for our sins (Sura 4:157).
- Jesus was not the Son of God (Sura 19:34-35; 9:30).
- Jesus was not God in the Flesh (Sura 3:59).
- Jesus should not be worshiped (Sura 5:116).
- Jesus is not part of the Trinity (Sura 4:171).

Five Beliefs of Latter-Day Saints (Mormons) That Contradict the Bible

- Jesus is one of many gods in the universe (Abraham 4:1).
- Latter-Day Saints can become gods themselves (Doctrine & Covenants 76:50-58, 95, 132:15-23, 29, 37).
- No virgin birth—God literally had sex with Mary to conceive Jesus (1 Nephi 11:18-21; Alma 7:10).
- Jesus and the devil (Satan) are brothers (Moses 4:1-4).
- The faith was not delivered "once for all" as Jude 3 says, it needs additions (Namely, the Book of Mormon, Doctrine and Covenants, and Pearl of Great Price).

4. The Bible Combines the Hebrew Bible (Old Testament) with Jesus' Teachings (New Testament)

It was natural then that the writings of the apostles and those closely associated with them quickly assumed the status of inspired Scripture.[54] Even as the writings of the New Testament were being completed, the Apostle Peter referred to Paul's writings as "Scripture" (2 Peter 3:15-16). And in 1 Timothy 5:18, two texts, one from the Old Testament and the other from the Gospel of Luke, are both introduced by the phrase "the Scripture says." In this way, God ensured there was a written record of Jesus' teachings—given through the apostles—and made available for all people in an objective form. The recognition of these books as the authoritative standard that we now call the New Testament occurred as the apostles' teachings spread throughout the Greco-Roman world.

As the Bible teaches, humanity has both the Old and New Testaments as its guide. Both parts are inspired and authoritative. Consider 2 Timothy 3:16-4:4, which approves both the Old Testament writings and the apostolic message:

All Scripture is God-breathed and is useful for teaching, rebuking, correcting and training in righteousness, so that the servant of God may be thoroughly equipped for every good work. In the presence of God and of Christ Jesus, who will judge the living and the dead, and in view of his appearing and his kingdom, I give you this charge: Preach the word; be prepared in season and out of season; correct, rebuke and encourage—with great patience and careful instruction. For the time will come when men will not put up with sound doctrine. Instead, to suit their own desires, they will gather around them a great number of teachers to say what their itching ears want to hear. They will turn their ears away from the truth and turn aside to myths.

There are important principles about the role of Scripture mentioned in this passage that will be helpful for us to keep in mind.

The two parts of the Bible are described in this passage. In this context, the phrase "all Scripture" is a reference to the Old Testament. And the phrase "preach the word" is a reference to the teachings of Jesus (that will be collected later into the New Testament). Survey the following diagram that shows an overview of both the Old Testament books (with the star of David icon) and the New Testament books (with the cross).

BOOKS OF THE BIBLE

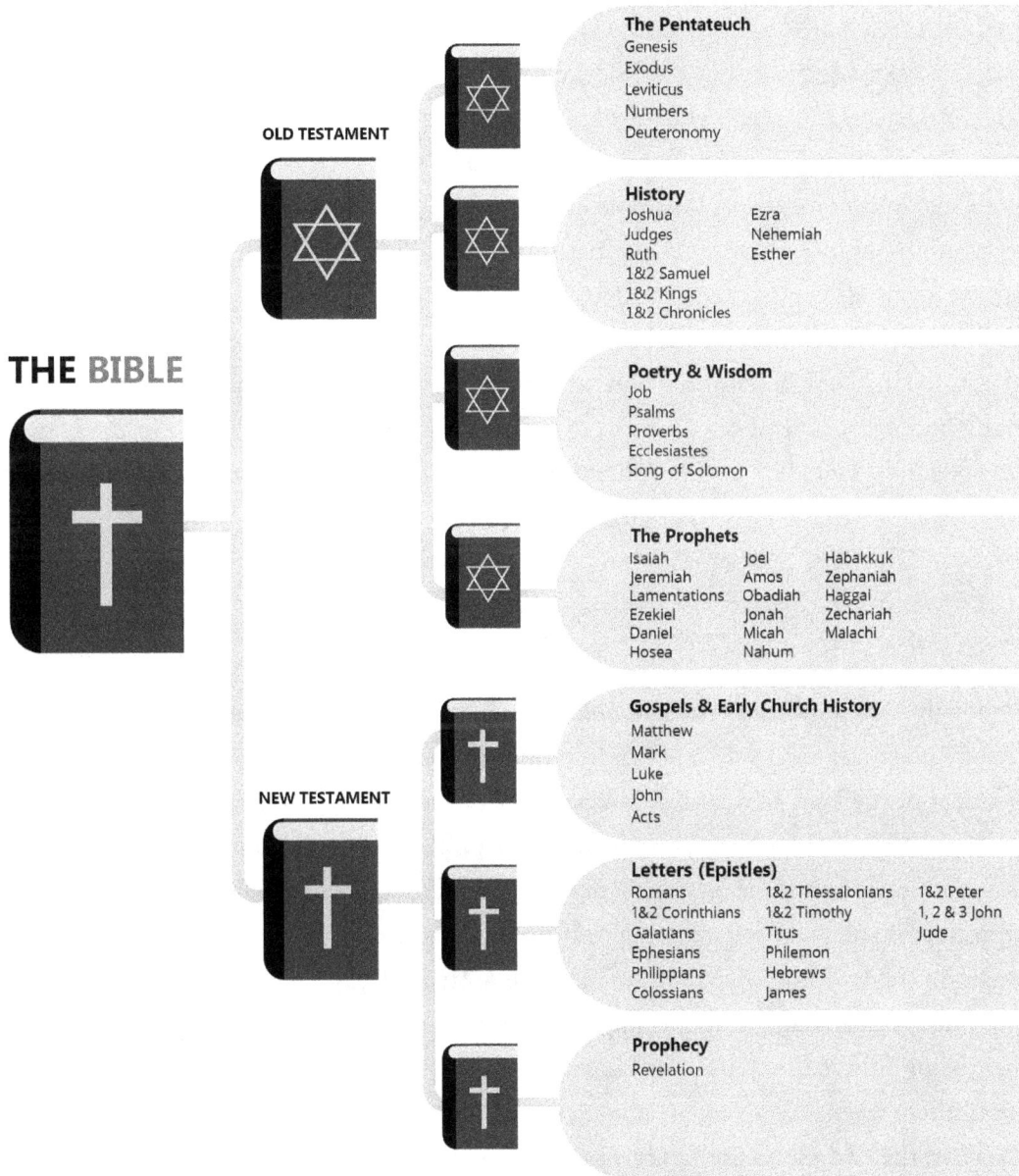

THE BIBLE

OLD TESTAMENT

The Pentateuch
Genesis
Exodus
Leviticus
Numbers
Deuteronomy

History
Joshua   Ezra
Judges   Nehemiah
Ruth   Esther
1&2 Samuel
1&2 Kings
1&2 Chronicles

Poetry & Wisdom
Job
Psalms
Proverbs
Ecclesiastes
Song of Solomon

The Prophets
Isaiah   Joel   Habakkuk
Jeremiah   Amos   Zephaniah
Lamentations Obadiah   Haggai
Ezekiel   Jonah   Zechariah
Daniel   Micah   Malachi
Hosea   Nahum

NEW TESTAMENT

Gospels & Early Church History
Matthew
Mark
Luke
John
Acts

Letters (Epistles)
Romans   1&2 Thessalonians   1&2 Peter
1&2 Corinthians 1&2 Timothy   1, 2 & 3 John
Galatians   Titus   Jude
Ephesians   Philemon
Philippians   Hebrews
Colossians   James

Prophecy
Revelation

If we refer back to the description on the inspiration of the Bible in 2 Timothy, some important points stand out. These highlights are worth noting.

First, the authoritative Scripture mentioned in this passage is primarily the Old Testament. It continues to have an abiding validity for the church today, as it did for the early church. This is why God commended those who examined the Old Testament Scriptures to determine the truthfulness of the Christian faith (Acts 17:10-12). The Apostle Paul told the early Christians in Rome to look to the Old Testament because, "Everything that was written in the past was written to teach us, so that through endurance taught in the Scriptures and the encouragement they provide we might have hope" (Romans 15:4). Paul also told the Corinthians that the events of the Old Testament serve as an example and contained principles to guide Christian lives (1 Corinthians 10:1-11).

There is even more. A Christian cannot properly understand many things about their relationship with God and the true nature of the faith without the Old Testament. How can we know all that we need to about humankind's origins, life in this world, the nature of God's love, God's providential care, etc., without the Old Testament? As Robert Woodrow says, "The New Testament claims and presupposes the faith of the Old. For this reason, many important aspects of Christian thought are not explicitly developed in the New but are taken for granted."[55] For the Christian then, there is an explicit sense in which the Old Testament remains the Word of God.

5. The New Testament Has a Higher Authority Than the Old Testament

Although both testaments have an abiding validity, this is not to say that both testaments are of equal authority. With the coming of Jesus and his teachings, along with the establishment of the New Covenant, the teachings of the Old Testament must be subjected to the higher light of the New Testament. The Apostle Paul in 2 Timothy 4:1-4 makes this relationship clear: it is the preaching of the apostolic "word," or message about Jesus, which supplements and gives full meaning to the Old Testament. This is also what Jesus regularly taught in the Gospels (Matthew 26:56; Luke 4:21; 24:27).

There are some key teachings in the Old Testament that have changed as a result of their being fulfilled by Jesus. An understanding of these teachings is particularly important in three ways:

First, the Old Covenant (and its sacrificial system) has passed away and become obsolete. It has been replaced by the superior priesthood and covenant of Jesus (Hebrews 7:11-14; 8:6-13). In this way, Jesus' "once for all sacrifice" has replaced the various Jewish ceremonial sacrifices (Hebrews 9–10). There is no longer an abiding validity for the temple (Acts 7:47-49), animal sacrifices, the tabernacle, or any other Old Testament liturgical requirement (Hebrews 9:1-10). These elements of Jewish worship and practice have been made obsolete.

Second, through Christ, God has opened the way for people of all ethnic backgrounds. A person no longer has to follow specific Jewish regulations to be accepted by God. As the Apostle Paul said, both Jews and non-Jews (Gentiles) are made one in Christ.

> For he himself is our peace, who has made the two groups one and has destroyed the barrier, the dividing wall of hostility, by setting aside in his flesh the law with its commands and regulations. His purpose was to create in himself one new humanity out of the two, thus making peace, and in one body to reconcile both of them to God through the cross, by which he put to death their hostility (Ephesians 2:14-16).

Laws about circumcision (Galatians 1:6-9; 5:4), keeping the Sabbath (Saturday) as a special day of rest (Romans 14:5-6), and other ethnic distinctions between Jew and non-Jew have been removed as requirements for God's people.[56] Consequently, Gentile Christians are not under Old Testament teachings that require circumcision of newborn males, rejection of certain meat (such as pork), Sabbath observance, and the like.

Third, Jesus Christ is the interpretive key to understanding the full meaning of the Old Testament (Matthew 5:17-20). He is central to Israelite history (Galatians 3), worship (Hebrews 7:26-28), and prophecy (e.g., the book of Revelation). He is the essential thread for all of God's plans, from the beginning to the end of time. And he is the end or goal of the Law (Romans 10:4).

Therefore, the Christian takes the Bible, containing both the Old and New Testaments, as their standard of faith. But in doing this, the Christian looks closely at Jesus, knowing that he is God's highest light and final message—the interpretive key for all Scripture (Hebrews 1:1–2).

Five Examples of Jewish Commandments in the Old Testament Not Applied to Gentile Christians:

- Observe the Sabbath (rest and worship on Saturday; see Exodus 20:8-10).
- Circumcise baby boys (Genesis 17:11).
- Don't eat pork (Leviticus 11:8).
- Don't eat shellfish (Leviticus 11:10).
- Don't blend fabrics (Leviticus 19:19, 27).

6. The Bible Is Complete and No Books Can Be Added

Jesus entrusted his teachings to the apostles. The writings of the apostles (and those closely associated with them) were combined with the writings of the Old Testament to form the *canon*.[57] The canon is a technical term that means "the list of books contained in Scripture, the list of books recognized as worthy to be included in the sacred writings of a worshiping community."[58] Or, again, "the list of the writings acknowledged by the church as documents of the divine revelation."[59] It is important to understand the process by which books became part of our modern Bible.

The books in the New Testament were all written before the end of the first century (100 CE).[60] Soon, however, these writings were not the only ones being circulated in the churches. In order to protect the original disciples from false teaching after the death of all the apostles, the early leaders had to delineate those writings that were authoritative from those that were not. By 170 CE (at the latest), the concept of the New Testament canon was firmly established, and the main contents were set in place.[61] The early Christians recognized as authoritative those books that met three key criteria:

1. The authoritative book had to be written by apostolic authors (or by those closely associated with apostles).
2. The book had to teach the orthodox faith of the apostles.
3. The book had to have been widely accepted in the earliest churches from the beginning.[62]

As the early church clarified the final list of authoritative books, they affirmed that the church itself had been established by words and works of Jesus as communicated by the apostles (Ephesians 2:20). The written works associated with the apostles were the objective norm by which the church was to measure and evaluate itself.[63] Though the concepts and the main contents of the canon were established hundreds of years earlier, it wasn't until 367 CE that the final list of books, which comprise our modern Bible, was agreed upon.

In doing this, the early church recognized that Christians and churches are subject to the objective record of the apostles' teachings as their final authority. This is why no ancient church can claim to have an authority over the Bible or equal to the Bible. The apostolic teaching (recorded in the Bible) created the church; no church or church authority created the Bible. In a very important article summarizing the Protestant and evangelical understanding against the Roman Catholic and Orthodox view, German scholar Oscar Cullmann pointed to the ultimate authority of the Bible. This highly respected scholar summed up the ultimate authority of the Bible over all other churches with these words: "The early church did not fix a norm for others, but for itself, and committed the church for all future centuries to this norm."[64] In affirming which books were authoritative and inspired, the early church recognized that, without a superior written norm, it could not keep itself or the apostolic teachings pure. One of my professors summed up the authority of the Bible over any church or ancient or modern form of Christianity with these words:

> By accepting the norm of Scripture, the church declared that there was a standard outside herself to which she intended to be subject for all time . . . . The church can fall into error and needs the Bible to measure herself by. In turn, the church serves the canon by continuing in the truth and faithfully proclaiming the Word of God.[65]

Under God's hand, the apostolic teachings and the Old Testament writings were fixed as the "canon." Thus, they are the foundational documents and the standard for the church of all time.[66]

Five Beliefs Based upon Later Church Tradition but Not Taught in the Canon of the Bible:

- *The Pope* – There are no passages in the Bible about the pope or his role in establishing doctrine.
- *Purgatory* – There are no passages about Christians spending time in purgatory paying for sins which Jesus' sacrifice hasn't already paid for.
- *Penance and Indulgences* – There is nothing about adding human works to the cross of Jesus to help others spend less time in purgatory.
- *A Celibate Priesthood* – There is nothing about church leaders (e.g., priests) being forbidden to marry.
- *Sacramental System, Mary, and the Saints* – There is nothing about sacraments playing a role in salvation apart from faith, or that Mary and other saints have merit so they can receive prayers and intercede to God on behalf of the living.

7. The Bible Has Been Reliably Passed Down

It is one thing to state that the Bible is the Christian's source of authority, but is what we have today the same Bible as it was written back then? Many people wonder if this collection of books is still reliable. Has it come down to us as it was originally written? Have these documents been changed or corrupted by churches, religious people, or other influences after the time of the apostles?

Fortunately, there are encouraging answers at hand. We can trust that on all points of substance the Bible has come down to us as it was originally written. This is true in regard to both the Old Testament Scriptures and the New.

First, consider the Old Testament text. These books were written over a long period of time and hundreds of years before Christ.[67] The entire Old Testament textual tradition before the time of Jesus is difficult to assess because we have little hard evidence. But we know that Jesus believed that the Old Testament was inspired and fully trusted in the Old Testament text.[68]

Somewhere around 270 years before the time of Christ, the Hebrew Scriptures were translated into Greek, and this version, known as the Septuagint, became exceedingly popular, especially later during the first century. Ancient copies of parts of the Septuagint have been preserved, and they provide support for the Old Testament text.[69] Of greater interest for Old Testament scholarship, however, are the Hebrew manuscripts because Hebrew is the original language of most of the Old Testament. Up to the end of World War II, the oldest known complete manuscript of the Old Testament was dated at 900 CE.[70] This meant that there was a significant gap between the time when the Old Testament was written and the oldest Hebrew manuscripts available for scholarly study. There was suspicion in some places that the text may have been corrupted.

No one could have anticipated the great discoveries at Qumran (near the Dead Sea in modern Israel) at the end of World War II. A Bedouin shepherd boy stumbled upon jars of ancient manuscripts in a group of long-abandoned caves.[71] Many of the manuscripts he found were older than the oldest manuscripts previously known by more than 1,000 years.[72] Scholars had known that great care had been taken to ensure the preservation of the Old Testament text in as pure a form as possible. It still came as a pleasant surprise to see the net result of the tremendous care that had been exercised over this thousand-year period.[73] Though there were some variations, the major doctrines and important teachings of the Old Testament were not distorted or changed in any way. Old Testament scholar Gleason Archer summarizes what we have learned:

> Because of their faithfulness, we have today a form of the Hebrew text which in all essentials duplicates the recension which was considered authoritative in the days of Christ and the apostles, if not a century earlier. And this in turn, judging from Qumran evidence, goes back to an authoritative revision of the Old

Testament text which was drawn up on the basis of the most reliable manuscripts available for collation from previous centuries. These bring us very close in all essentials to the original autographs themselves and furnish us with an authentic record of God's revelation.[74]

In commenting on the whole treasury of Old Testament manuscripts, Hebrew and otherwise, Old Testament scholar R.K. Harrison summed up the matter in this way:

> In the light of present knowledge concerning the conditions under which the ancient scribes made copies of biblical manuscripts, it is nothing short of miraculous that so few mistakes were made in the transmission of the text.[75]

On the basis of current evidence, we can see how God has protected the reliability of the fundamental teachings of the Old Testament and preserved the Old Testament text. For those who want to study the reliability of the Old Testament, the respected scholar Walter Kaiser has written a book titled *The Old Testament Documents: Are They Reliable and Relevant?*[76] He presents all the background evidence that supports the authenticity of these older writings.

Likewise, the evidence for the reliability of the New Testament is convincing and extensive.[77] The books in the New Testament were all written between 50 and 95 CE. The early Christians recognized that only certain books had divine authority. These books were considered to be inspired by God and to be the final standard for orthodox Christianity. Again, to be in the New Testament, each book met three key criteria: 1) each had apostolic authors (or writers closely associated with apostles), 2) each taught the orthodox faith of the apostles, and 3) each had been widely accepted in the churches from the beginning.[78] We can have confidence that they have come to us without any substantive change in the way they were originally written because of two additional means:

1. Preserved ancient manuscripts from the earliest times
2. The quotations of the New Testament, which are found in the writings of the church Fathers (those who lived in the period immediately after the originals were written).[79]

The three criteria listed above forever established which books belong in the New Testament and which do not. Because these criteria locate the New Testament books in the first century, the canon is "closed," meaning that books have not been added to the New Testament since ancient times. The scholar F.F. Bruce, in his book *The Canon of Scrip-*

ture, discusses the background material on this point at length.[80] Let us now turn to the two sources which demonstrate that the manuscripts of the Bible have not been materially altered.

A. Ancient Manuscripts

Every book of the Bible was written and then copied by hand. The number of ancient copies of the New Testament text is substantial. We have fragments and copies of the Scriptures that go back very close to the time of the originals. For example, recently a fragment of the Gospel of John was uncovered which scholars date around 130 CE (about forty years after the original was written). Another significant set of manuscripts called the Chester Beatty Papyri has been discovered, containing a much larger number of New Testament passages. These manuscripts are dated at 155 CE. These recent discoveries were supplemented by the discovery of the Bodmer Papyri II, dated at 200 CE.

These are just a few examples of the great abundance of very early manuscripts in existence that are available to be examined. In fact, there are over 24,000 complete or partial handwritten manuscripts of the New Testament. The complete copies include Codex Sinaiticus, dated at 350 CE (discovered in the 1840s); Codex Vaticanus, dated at 350 CE; and Codex Ephraemi, dated 400 CE.

Compare the manuscript evidence for the New Testament with other ancient books:

Work Written	When	Earliest Copy	Time Lapse	Number of Ancient Copies
Herodotus	488-428 BCE	900 CE	1,300 years	8
Thucydides	460-400 BCE	900 CE	1,300 years	8
Aristotle	384-322 BCE	1100 CE	1,400 years	49
Caesar	58-50 BCE	900 CE	950 years	10
Tacitus	100 CE	1100 CE	1,000 years	20
Livy	17 CE	900 CE	900 years	20
The New Testament	50-95 CE	130 CE	35 years	24,300+

The New Testament has far more support for its authenticity than other books from the ancient world. Though hand-copied manuscripts contain minor textual variations, we know the New Testament today is an accurate reflection of the earliest ancient text. By comparing existing copies of the Bible with these old manuscripts, scholars and historians affirm that the textual variations do not materially affect any significant teaching in the Bible.[81]

However, some people might think that minor textual variations are a significant fact and would compromise the credibility of the New Testament. The minor variations are things like a change in the order of words (from "Jesus Christ" to "Christ Jesus"), dropping a word (from "Jesus Christ" to "Christ"), or spelling something in a slightly different way (like English variations of "Smith" and "Smythe"). Yet, all the important variations are listed in the footnotes of the major modern Bible translations; no one tries to hide them because they do not have a significant impact. They change no major doctrine of Christianity.

B. The Early Christian Writers

Writings from the earliest Christian leaders outside the Bible also support the reliability of the Bible. These are leaders who wrote about the Christian faith in the period immediately following the apostles, and in one case, during the time when a book of the New Testament was still being written (Revelation). The men who wrote these books are known as the "church Fathers." Their works were typically produced between 90 CE and 160 CE, and they quote from most of the New Testament books.

Early writings, such as those by Ignatius (115 CE) and the Didache (125 CE), describe the beliefs and practices of the early church in great detail. As we read their writings, we discover that they were quite familiar with the New Testament, and they provide another rich information source by which modern scholars can compare the modern Bible with the ancient Greek text and confirm its accuracy. By reviewing these writings, the historical accuracy and authenticity of the Bible manuscripts have been firmly established.

With so many ancient sources and manuscripts of this sort in existence, scholars have been careful to compare them to make sure that no significant changes have crept into the text of the modern Bible. Few of us can speak authoritatively on this topic, but Princeton's Bruce Metzger was one who could. His authority in this regard was second to none. Here is what he had to say about the reliability of the New Testament manuscripts:

> There are no doctrines in the church which are in jeopardy because of variants . . . . The variations, when they occur, tend to be minor rather than substan-

tive . . . . We can have great confidence in the fidelity with which this material has come down to us, especially compared with any other ancient literary work.[82]

This is why informed Christians can read the New Testament with confidence, knowing that it is a reliable representation of the original documents. In ensuring that we have reliable manuscripts by which to translate the Bible in modern times, God has safeguarded the truth about Jesus Christ and the way of salvation.

The Inspiration of Scripture

Now that we understand how God has providentially protected Scripture up to the present time, we are in a better position to appreciate how the Bible is to be the standard for matters of life and doctrine. Paul's words to his apprentice Timothy make clear what is to be our standard:

> But as for you, continue in what you have learned and have become convinced of, because you know those from whom you learned it, and how from infancy you have known the Holy Scriptures, which are able to make you wise for salvation through faith in Christ Jesus. All Scripture is God-breathed and is useful for teaching, rebuking, correcting and training in righteousness, so that the servant of God may be thoroughly equipped for every good work (2 Timothy 3:14-17).

According to this passage, and commensurate with countless other passages, Scripture finds its origin in God (Matthew 5:18; Hebrews 1:1-2; 1 Peter 1:10-11, etc.). It is God who inspired and "breathed into" it. There are three important truths about Scripture found in this passage and others.

The first and most important truth is that the purpose of Scripture is to "make us wise for salvation through faith in Christ Jesus" (2 Timothy 3:15). Scripture was given to guide people to salvation and the related way of life, both corporately and individually. The Bible was not primarily intended as a detailed guide in astronomy, geology, geography, or science. My seminary professor Clark Pinnock offered important insight in this regard:

> Their treasure and their wisdom are oriented to presenting Jesus Christ, the wisdom and the power of God. We should never define biblical authority apart from this stated purpose or apply to it standards of measurement that are inappropriate. God speaks through the Bible, not to make us scholars and scientists,

but to put us in a right relationship with God and to give us such a religious understanding of the world and history that we can grasp everything else better . . . . The Scriptures teach firmly, faithfully, and without error that truth which God wanted put into the sacred writings for the sake of our salvation.[83]

The Christian looks to the Bible as their infallible guide to salvation and the Christian life. I. Howard Marshall carries the thought to its logical conclusion.

If we look again at 2 Timothy 3:15, we find that the stated purpose of the Scriptures is to provide the instruction that leads to salvation through faith in Jesus Christ, and this is then detailed in terms of teaching, reproof, correction and training which will enable the man of God to be fully equipped for every good work. The purpose of God in the composition of the Scriptures was to guide people to salvation and the associated way of life. From this statement we may surely conclude that God made the Bible all that it needs to be in order to achieve its purpose. It is in this sense that the word "infallible" is properly applied to the Bible; it means that it is "in itself a true and sufficient guide, which may be trusted implicitly."[84]

The Bible is then taken by Christians to be God's inspired guidebook. It infallibly teaches us how to be saved and how to live as Christians.

A second truth inherent in God's inspiration of Scripture is his utilization of human beings. To be sure, the ultimate author of Scripture is God, but he communicates through people and in human ways. According to 2 Peter 1:20-21, "No prophecy of Scripture came about by the prophet's own interpretation of things. For prophecy never had its origin in the human will, but prophets, though human, spoke from God as they were carried along by the Holy Spirit." In light of this, the proper view about the origin of Scripture holds that in writing Scripture, humans were carried along by the Spirit to write the things of God. In this way, God used human minds, human language, and even individual human styles.

A third truth from 2 Timothy 3:16 is that Scripture was given to be our supreme authority. It was given for "teaching, rebuking, correcting, and training in righteousness," so that God's people could be equipped and trained to live faithfully in his ways (2 Timothy 3:16-4:4). Consequently, we must be very careful to follow only what God established in the Bible. This passage and others warn that Christians can fall into error, and they need Scripture to keep them on the right path.

The Bible is God's platform and foundation for us. It guides us in the ways of Jesus and shows us where it is spiritually and theologically safe to walk. It provides both a map of where to go and a barrier or wall of God's boundaries. God gave the Bible to be the charter document for his people. We must learn it, follow it, and live by it. It is our job as those who are a part of God's church to uphold this objective standard of God's truth against all attacks and onslaughts. The Bible stands ever over us—a safeguard against human self-will, and a witness for or against us as we choose whether or not to walk in the ways of Jesus.

Unfaithfulness to the Bible is why Jesus denounced the religious leaders of his day. They had replaced the teachings of Scripture with the traditions of fallible human beings:

> Thus you nullify the word of God for the sake of your tradition. You hypocrites! Isaiah was right when he prophesied about you: "These people honor me with their lips, but their hearts are far from me. They worship me in vain; their teachings are merely human rules" (Matthew 15:6-9).

In this way, the writings of the Bible are the standard for our doctrine, practice, and lifestyle. The Bible guides us as individuals and as church leaders. The Bible is our final, reliable, and ultimate authority.[85] We call it God's infallible Word.

8. We All Must Learn the Bible for Ourselves

Many of the teachings in Scripture are clear. In fact, most Bible scholars believe the central and most important teachings of the Bible are abundantly clear. Most of those who genuinely and diligently search the Scriptures and apply a prayerful attitude should come to understand the central teachings of the Bible and be able to see how to apply those teachings to their lives.[86] Mark Twain once said, "Most people are bothered by those passages of Scripture which they cannot understand: but as for me, I have always noticed that the passages of Scripture which trouble me most are those *which I do understand*."[87] Most would agree that living in the light of the core teachings of the Bible is much harder than understanding them. For example, it is not natural to love your enemies and forgive those who hurt you. Twain was right.

At the same time, many parts of the Bible are hard to understand. The Bible itself comments that some passages are difficult and can be twisted (2 Peter 3:16). These sections require special help. In a way, Bible study and Bible application are like an art. We become better at this art through practice as well as when we have teachers who can show us the way and offer special tools to help. This is one of the reasons God has given the Bible to the church, not just the individual. In the church, there are teachers, scholars, and elders who can guide us and show us how to study and apply the Bible.

Too many people have opinions about the Bible because of what teachers, preachers, and religious groups say about the Bible. Too few people have opinions about the Bible because of what they have studied for themselves *in the Bible*. This makes Christianity seem very confusing. The truth of the matter is that the major doctrines of the Bible are not too difficult to understand when we carefully study the Bible for ourselves.

As the people of Jesus' time modeled, we too must get to know Scripture. The major difficulties do not come from what the Bible says, but from how different traditions, people, and groups have put their own slants on what the Bible says. At the same time, there is far more agreed-upon clarity about the core teachings of the Bible than the average person may realize. This is why there is such broad acceptance of things like the Apostles' and Nicene Creeds (faith statements from the earliest times). The Bible can be a deep well where mature theologians dive deep and barely touch the bottom, but it can also be a pool, shallow enough that infants may explore, but never drown.

The Bible describes the Jewish people in the ancient city of Berea as the ideal role models for us. They were compared to the Thessalonians in the book of Acts, and unlike the Thessalonians, they carefully looked into the Scriptures to see what was true, so that they could know the way of God and properly follow him for themselves. They are highly commended for seeking to know the truth of Scripture and searching out the true meaning.

> Now the Berean Jews were of more noble character than those in Thessalonica, for they received the message with great eagerness and examined the Scriptures every day to see if what Paul said was true (Acts 17:11).

Yes, we may need teachers and aids to help us. Yes, there are often complex issues involved. And yes, different well-studied and highly educated Christians understand some things in different ways. But like the Bereans, if we want to be noble in God's sight, we must examine the Scriptures in all things to determine the truth for ourselves.

Years ago, I lived and worked during the summer at my home in Calgary, Alberta, Canada, while I carried on a serious relationship with a young lady who lived in Memphis, Tennessee. We had met at college one year earlier. At that time, phone calls were very expensive and email hadn't been invented, so we often wrote letters to each other. I would look forward to getting her letters when the mail arrived. I read them and enjoyed them very much. I still have them, even though it was over forty years ago.

I would open the letter and read it over, often several times in a row. By these letters, I got to know her and learned more and more about her. In fact, by her letters, she was present to me. I experienced her presence, even though she was over 2,000 miles away. I not only came to know her better, but I came to develop a deeper relationship with her. By the relationship we developed through letters, I came to love this woman in deeper and deeper ways. Our relationship strengthened so much that by the time we met up again, after an absence of three months, I asked her to marry me and she became my wife four months later.

In many similar ways, the Bible is like a letter to us from God. By reading the Bible, we can learn more and more about God. He can literally become present with us when we study it! By seeking him out through Scripture, we can not only know him better, but also develop a relationship with him. Then, the more and more we study, we will come to know, experience, and love him in deeper and deeper ways.

This is a fundamental part of what it means to know God personally. And in the end, knowing him is the ultimate purpose and meaning behind the Bible. God made the Bible to be inspired and authoritative because its teachings are the primary foundation by which we develop a relationship with him. And there is nothing as important as that.

Is there anything that stands out to you from this section that you would like to note and discuss?

_____

_____

_____

_____

_____

_____

CHAPTER 4

God Is Holy

Key Theme: The Bible shows that because God is holy, our core problem is our sin, which separates us from God. We must own our sin and repent of it by faith.

Now that we know how Scripture came to us and the good reasons to believe it was reliably guided by God, we are ready to look at the core problem that exists between human beings and God. It begins with an understanding of what it means for God to be holy.

When we describe God as "holy," it means God is "pure, free from every stain, wholly perfect and immaculate in every detail."[88] To say God is holy means no sin, wrongdoing, evil, or anything bad exists in him. "God is light; in him there is no darkness at all" (1 John 1:5).

God's holiness explains why human beings are separated from God and destined to face punishment if they are not rescued. Because God is holy, he must insist that all of his creatures be like him, lest his own holiness, dignity, honor, and sovereign rule of the universe be diminished. This makes him very different than humans. He is high, dignified, lofty, and worthy of profound reverence.[89]

The creation story is a model of the entire human race, not solely Adam and Eve. It tells us what's wrong with humanity. We cannot handle the pull of sin, selfishness, and evil our ancestors brought into human experience by choosing to eat from the tree of the knowledge of good and evil.

Because of this choice, God had to separate himself from us. Holiness means God cannot have anything to do with sin. Sin cut humans off from God and eternal life with him (the tree of life). We have been sentenced to physical and spiritual death.

The Bible teaches that God made Adam and Eve, the first humans, to live in an innocent state in the Garden of Eden. But they also had an enemy. Satan was there, as a snake, to tempt Adam and Eve to sin and turn away from God, to which they succumbed. Now, we are all separated from God, gravitating to sin and living life without trusting and following him.

1. When God created humans in the Garden of Eden, he wanted to keep them from the autonomous knowledge of good and evil. It was necessary to establish a boundary. Influenced by Satan (as a snake), Adam and Eve disobeyed.

Genesis 2:16-17 - And the Lord God commanded the man, "You are free to eat from any tree in the garden; but you must not eat from the tree of the knowledge of good and evil, for when you eat of it you will surely die."

Genesis 3:1-5 - The serpent was the shrewdest of all the wild animals the Lord God had made. One day he asked the woman, "Did God really say you must not eat the fruit from any of the trees in the garden?" "Of course we may eat fruit from the trees in the garden," the woman replied. "It's only the fruit from the tree in the middle of the garden that we are not allowed to eat. God said, 'You must not eat it or even touch it; if you do, you will die.'" "You won't die!" the serpent replied to the woman. "God knows that your eyes will be opened as soon as you eat it, and you will be like God, knowing both good and evil."

Genesis 3:6-10 - The woman was convinced. She saw that the tree was beautiful, and its fruit looked delicious, and she wanted the wisdom it would give her. So she took some of the fruit and ate it. Then she gave some to her husband, who was with her, and he ate it, too. At that moment their eyes were opened, and they suddenly felt shame at their nakedness. So they sewed fig leaves together to cover themselves. When the cool evening breezes were blowing, the man and his wife heard the Lord God walking about in the garden. So they hid from the Lord God among the trees. Then the Lord God called to the man, "Where are you?" He replied, "I heard you walking in the garden, so I hid. I was afraid because I was naked."

Genesis 3:22-23 - Then the Lord God said, "Look, the human beings have become like us, knowing both good and evil. What if they reach out, take fruit from the tree of life, and eat it? Then they will live forever!" So the Lord God banished them from the Garden of Eden, and he sent Adam out to cultivate the ground from which he had been made. (NLT)

How did Adam and Eve sin? How did God ensure that Adam and Eve would eventually die?

_____

_____

_____

2. When Adam and Eve sinned, God said that they would die. Humanity is now separated from God and in Satan's kingdom. The following passage describes the state of humanity after Adam and Eve's fall into sin. We now come into this world as people who are "spiritually dead."

> Ephesians 2:1-4 - As for you, you were dead in your transgressions and sins, in which you used to live when you followed the ways of this world and of the ruler of the kingdom of the air, the spirit who is now at work in those who are disobedient. All of us also lived among them at one time, gratifying the cravings of our sinful nature and following its desires and thoughts. Like the rest, we were by nature objects of wrath.

In what ways does Satan influence the world? How does he influence you?

_____

_____

_____

3. Many of us do not know what is sinful in God's eyes.

> Galatians 5:19-21 - The acts of the flesh are obvious: sexual immorality, impurity and debauchery; idolatry and witchcraft; hatred, discord, jealousy, fits of rage, selfish ambition, dissensions, factions and envy; drunkenness, orgies, and the like. I warn you, as I did before, that those who live like this will not inherit the kingdom of God.

We must accept what God calls sin and not let the world define right and wrong for us. As you review that list, notice how it ends with a sober warning: *those who live in these ways will not inherit God's eternal kingdom!* Look at each item in the list below again:

- *Sexual immorality* = any sexual activity except between a male and a female in marriage. This means that sex before marriage, sex outside of marriage, and homosexual sexual unions are sinful (Romans 1:26-27)
- *Impurity and debauchery* = a wild, party lifestyle
- *Idolatry* = worshiping other gods like money, success, and admiration from others
- *Witchcraft* (*pharmakeia* in Greek) = drugs, spells, and contacting the dead
- *Hatred, discord* = bitterness and strife

- *Jealousy* = bad attitudes because you want for yourself what others have
- *Fits of rage* = angry outbursts and uncontrolled episodes
- *Selfish ambition* = focused concern about yourself to the exclusion of others
- *Dissensions, factions* = divisiveness and causing trouble between people
- *Envy* = a bad attitude toward people because you want what they have
- *Drunkenness* = getting intoxicated with alcohol and getting intoxicated with marijuana
- *Orgies* = partying and involvement with promiscuous sex
- *And the like* = other things that reflect selfish sin . . .

Can anyone be left out of this list of sins? What areas surprise you that God says are sinful?

_____

_____

_____

4. Humans, by nature, are separated from God because of our sin, and we need God to save us because we cannot save ourselves from brokenness.

> Isaiah 59:2 - Your iniquities have separated you from your God; your sins have hidden his face from you, so that he will not hear.

a. Sin separates us from God.

HUMANS   GOD

God—He is holy and he is love.

Humans—God made humans in his image, but we do sinful, wrong things.

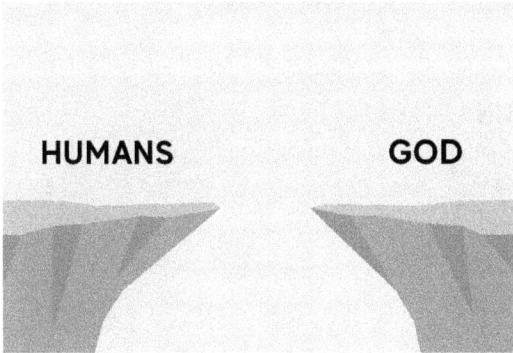

God and Humans—are separated because God is holy and humans act out their sinful nature.

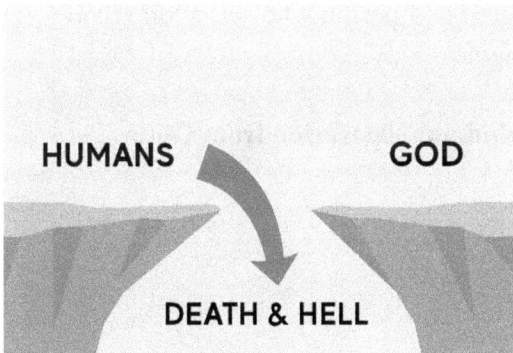

Human Deeds—We are lost (to death and hell) and separated from God because of our sin. Only God can take away our sin. Unless God saves us, we are lost.

b. In order for a human to have a relationship with God, the wall must be broken down and sin must be forgiven.

Romans 3:10-12 - As the Scriptures say, "No one is good—not even one. No one has real understanding; no one is seeking God. All have turned away from God; all have gone wrong. No one does good, not even one."

a. Who has sinned? Everyone! Notice the graphics below which represent different levels of sin that different people commit in their lives.

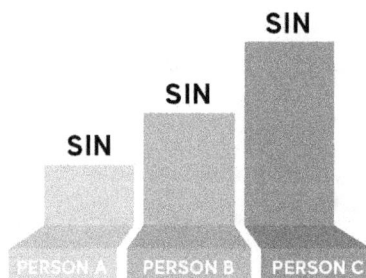

b. Who is further away from God: a person who sins a little or a person who sins a lot? All are equal, all lost.

How do these passages affect your perspective on sin and our separation from God?

_____

_____

_____

5. Our separation from God is the most serious of all the problems we face. It is our core problem as human beings. Sin often involves the affections of our hearts or the neglect of things we should do but do not.

The sins of the heart are described in 2 Timothy 3:1-5. Notice how this can include religious people.

> But mark this: There will be terrible times in the last days. People will be lovers of themselves, lovers of money, boastful, proud, abusive, disobedient to their parents, ungrateful, unholy, without love, unforgiving, slanderous, without self-control, brutal, not lovers of the good, treacherous, rash, conceited, lovers of pleasure rather than lovers of God—having a form of godliness but denying its power. Have nothing to do with such people.

Sins of neglect are described in James 4:17:

> If anyone, then, knows the good they ought to do and doesn't do it, it is sin for them.

Do these passages convict you of your sin struggles? In what areas?

_____

_____

_____

6. There is good news—God loves us and wants to forgive us of our sin. He wants us to rely on him and to help us repent and turn to Jesus so that our sins can be forgiven.

We do this by faith as we believe what God says in the Bible about sin. Repentance = a change in the way we feel and think that leads to a change in what we do.

- Sin is powerful. It easily entangles our lives.
- Sin is pleasurable; that's why we sin.
- Sin is deceitful.
- Sin is my responsibility: I cannot blame others for my sin because I am accountable for my life.
- We can overcome sin with the help of Jesus Christ and the power of his Spirit.

2 Corinthians 7:10-11 - Godly sorrow brings repentance that leads to salvation and leaves no regret, but worldly sorrow brings death. See what this godly sorrow has produced in you: what earnestness, what eagerness to clear yourselves, what indignation, what alarm, what longing, what concern, what readiness to see justice done. At every point you have proved yourselves to be innocent in this matter.

What would it look like if your faith in Jesus led you to repent the way this passage describes?

_____

_____

_____

7. Repentance is important because we will all be raised up and stand before God for a final judgment of our lives. We want to repent before our lives end, when we'll give an account

of our sinful actions to God. Those who do not repent and put their faith in Jesus will go to hell.

> 2 Corinthians 5:10 - For we must all appear before the judgment seat of Christ, so that each of us may receive what is due us for the things done while in the body, whether good or bad.

> Mark 9:46-48 - And if your foot causes you to stumble, cut it off. It is better for you to enter life crippled than to have two feet and be thrown into hell. And if your eye causes you to stumble, pluck it out. It is better for you to enter the kingdom of God with one eye than to have two eyes and be thrown into hell, where "the worms that eat them do not die, and the fire is not quenched."

What will happen to those who do not repent? What kind of help do you need, if you are to repent?

_____

_____

_____

God Is Holy

The Bible's Creation Account

When God first created humans, they were beings who had not yet experienced sin and who dwelled in his presence in Eden. Scholars debate the extent to which the biblical accounts of creation and the Garden of Eden are literal or symbolic.[90] No doubt there are elements of both. Those who believe in the reliability of the Bible take different approaches on this point, while affirming that there is no final conflict between the facts of science and the Genesis record.[91]

Ever since Charles Darwin published *On the Origin of Species* in 1859, there has been a conflict between many scientists and Christians over the theory of evolution and a literal reading of Genesis 1–3. In light of this conflict, too many people think we cannot turn to the Bible to understand the roots of humanity. The majority of well-informed believers, however, who wade through scientific findings and biblical interpretation believe the two actually complement each other. For example, there are multiple responsible, possible harmonies between Genesis 1 and the evidence for an old earth: [92]

1. **The Appearance of Age** – The belief that the earth was created in six literal 24-hour days, but that it was created with *the appearance of age.* The earth looks much older than it is because God created a mature earth (analogous to how God created Adam).
2. **The Re-created World** – The belief that the earth was created over billions of years, but that Genesis 1 describes a re-creation event where God re-created the earth and made humanity.
3. **Six Days to Reveal Creation** – The belief that the days of creation are not describing how long it took God to create the world, but the six separate days in which God revealed how he created the world to the author of Genesis. Stated differently, it took

God six days to tell the author how he made creation. The days describe what God revealed each day to Moses; they do not describe how long it took for God to create it.

4. **Six Days as a Symbolic Structure** – The belief that the creation account is simply a symbolic, ancient, figurative framework for creation. The Genesis account uses the artistic structure of six days as a framework for God's symbolic description of creation.

5. **The Day-Age Theory** – The belief that the word for "day" in Genesis 1 should be understood to mean "age" or "undefined period of time." Understood that way, the "days" match the old-earth evidence, for example, from the fossil record. In my opinion, scientist Hugh Ross has done the best job of showing how theology and science work together in his book, *Navigating Genesis: A Scientist's Journey Through Genesis 1-11.*[93] I highly recommend it.

As further support for the Day-Age Theory, it ought to be noted that the Hebrew word for day is "yom," a word that can be translated as "day" or "age." The days-as-ages roughly correspond to the broad periods of creation activity found in the fossil evidence. Understood this way, there is good, general concordance between the order of creation and the facts of science. [94] The following chart has been created to show how this theory makes sense both from a biblical and a scientific point of view and it is used with permission from Reasons to Believe.[95]

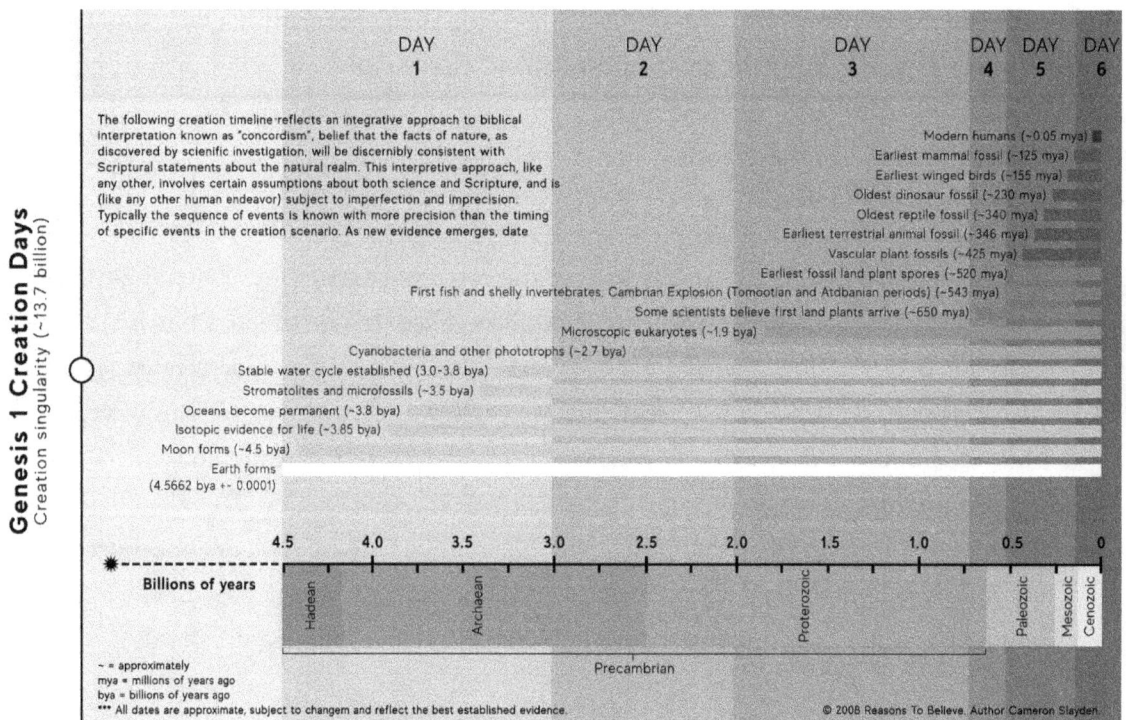

Trust and Follow Jesus

The Day-Age view fits well with the scientific evidence for an old earth. According to this view, God created many life forms over the millions of years of earth history. Some fulfilled their divine purpose and then died off. As an example, the dinosaurs were created, lived on planet earth, and then became extinct (see www.reasons.org for more information on dinosaurs and related issues). In more recent times, God created human beings, an event the Bible clearly teaches. After that, God's creation activities ceased.

My point is not to strictly advocate for this one understanding that resolves the suggested conflict between science and the Bible. There are numerous theories that address it. My point is that conservative biblical scholars and well-respected scientists can join together to 1) uphold the infallibility of the Bible (in Genesis in particular and the Bible as a whole) and 2) uphold the scientific facts of our world.

The goal of explaining the Day-Age Theory and other ways of linking the facts of science to the Bible is to put that potential conflict to the side so we can focus on the real point of the early chapters of Genesis: the creation and nature of human beings in relationship to God. Our ancestors, the Bible tells us, were created by God to be close to him, but they chose sin and set humanity on a perilous journey.

The Garden of Eden

The primary purpose of the account of Adam and Eve in Eden is to show the original intimate relationship between a loving God and a sinless people, and then humanity's fall into sin.[96] This is the main point we will focus on.

The writer of Genesis wants to display that God, in his love, provided for all of the man's needs in the Garden of Eden.[97] Whenever Eden is referred to in the Bible, it is pictured as a wonderful place: a fertile area, a well-watered oasis with large trees, etc. (Isaiah 51:3; Ezekiel 31:9).[98]

God created the man first and placed him in the garden (Genesis 2:7-8). God spoke directly to the man, known to us as Adam (which literally means "man" in Hebrew), and described for him the gracious provisions he had provided in the garden (2:16). The Lord created the man to work and care for the world, and he was specifically assigned to these roles in the Garden (2:15). At this point, it was joyous labor. Commensurate with man's rule over the earth was man's dominion over the earth's creatures. Therefore, God brought the animals to the man to see what the man would name them (2:19-20). The man named each of the animals, and in doing so, took up his leadership role.[99]

There was something lacking though. God noticed that the man was lonely, and so he stated, "It is not good for man to be alone. I will make a helper suitable for him" (2:18).

God then created woman (2:21-24). The narrative brilliantly depicts God's loving and miraculous creation: he took a part of the man and transformed it into a partner for him. When Adam realized God had created such a wonderful helpmate for him, he exclaimed "This is now bone of my bones and flesh of my flesh; she shall be called woman, for she was taken out of man." Several writers have commented on the creation of Eve, but the best words belong to Matthew Henry:

> Not made out of his head to top him, nor out of his feet to be trampled upon by him, but out of his side to be equal with him, under his arm to be protected, and near his heart to be loved.[100]

No doubt, this was the most loving and perfect gift God could provide. Genesis is written to show his provision for the man's every need. This is the way that God intended it to be between himself and humankind (2:9; 3:22).

The Cosmic Decision

Let's go back to the Garden of Eden. Like all truly meaningful relationships, it was necessary to establish boundaries. Adam and Eve were not programmed like computers; the last thing God wanted to do was compel their love for him. He gave them one restriction: They could not eat the fruit of the knowledge of good and evil:

> And the Lord God commanded the man, "You are free to eat from any tree in the garden; but you must not eat from the tree of the knowledge of good and evil, for when you eat from it you will surely die" (Genesis 2:16-17).

These words were serious; if the man and woman chose to violate this one term of the relationship, disaster would ensue (Genesis 3:2-3).

Soon, a new character entered the scene. According to a literal interpretation of the story, he was a serpent (3:1). In reality, however, he was much more than a serpent: he was crafty, he could speak, and he subtly twisted God's words. A later biblical author would refer to this serpent as the devil, or Satan—enemy of both man and God (Revelation 12:9; 20:2). At this point, however, neither Eve nor Adam realized his true nature.

The serpent began by talking to the woman. He used three devices in an attempt to make her doubt God's words and turn her against God.

Now the serpent was more crafty than any of the wild animals the Lord God had made. He said to the woman, "Did God really say, 'You must not eat from any tree in the garden?'" The woman said to the serpent, "We may eat fruit from the trees in the garden, but God did say, 'You must not eat fruit from the tree that is in the middle of the garden, and you must not touch it, or you will die.'" "You will not certainly die," the serpent said to the woman. "For God knows that when you eat from it your eyes will be opened, and you will be like God, knowing good and evil" (Genesis 3:1-5).

First, the serpent twisted God's words to make it look as if God was overbearing and unreasonable. He implied that God told them they could not eat from *any* tree in the garden (3:1), when really there was only one tree whose fruit they could not eat. When that ploy didn't work, Satan contested God's truthfulness, by saying God's promised punishment would not happen (3:4). Thirdly, he accused God of bad motives. According to the serpent, God wanted to keep Adam and Eve from being "gods," unfairly wanting them to be his perpetual inferiors (3:5).

It didn't take long for the serpent's deception to have an impact on the woman. She started contemplating the fruit. She noticed it was good for food and pleasing to look at (3:6). More importantly, it could give her wisdom, perhaps even wisdom to make her a "god," independent just like the Lord God. The woman gave in to the temptation and ate the fruit.

During the whole scene, the man had been passively at the woman's side (3:6). He was the one to whom God had given the restriction directly. It was his responsibility to exercise leadership in this situation. He instead remained passive and listened to the discussion between his wife and the serpent without saying anything. Finally, after the woman ate the fruit, the man chose to follow her example by eating it himself.

Things changed instantly. Whereas previously the couple had been naked without concern (a metaphor for their innocence), they instantly realized they were naked and were full of shame (3:7). They covered themselves, and then they hid (3:7, 10). Denial, deception, and blame entered human history for the first time. They were guilty.

God confronted the man first, and the man in turn blamed the woman. He also indirectly blamed God, because it was God who created her to be his companion. He referred to her as "the woman *you* put here with me" (3:12). Then, when God spoke to the woman, she denied her responsibility by blaming the serpent. Neither of them admitted to having committed an act of rebellion against God. The repercussions would be far-reaching and universal for the human race.

The Knowledge of Good and Evil

One of the most important elements in this account is the tree of the knowledge of good and evil and what it represented. Its fruit gave those who ate it the knowledge of good and evil, in the same way that eating from the tree of life gave eternal life as long as they had access to its fruit (3:22). But what was it to have the knowledge of good and evil?

There are two important keys to understanding this phrase from the Bible. First, Eve believed that this knowledge would enable her to become "like God" (3:5-6). Indeed, God and the heavenly hosts affirmed that after the couple had the knowledge of good and evil, they were somehow "like one of us" (3:22). Second, in Ezekiel 28, the king of Tyre was compared to Adam and Eve when he became prideful and thought of himself as being wise "as a god" (28:6, 15-17). What do these two passages show us? In choosing to eat the fruit from the tree of the knowledge of good and evil, Adam and Eve wanted to be more than creatures of God—they wanted to be god-like, prideful, and independent moral beings.[101]

By choosing the knowledge of good and evil over living in submissive trust as creatures under God, Adam and Eve chose foolish human pride. They wanted to make their own moral choices, without guidance from God. Their action was a decision to *try* to be more than what they were—created beings who were made from the dust of the earth. They wanted to be morally god-like and independent. As Gordon Wenham puts it, this knowledge of good and evil for human beings "leads to human autonomy and an independence of the Creator incompatible with the trustful relationship between man and his Maker."[102]

Instead of a humble trust in God, their pride fully asserted itself. They foolishly believed they could be more than created beings who are by nature dependent on God. They did not simply make a bad choice; they deliberately usurped God's place and rebelled against him. This independent capability is fine for God, but it is too much for a created being.

This kind of defiant "self-rule" is the essence of what the Bible calls "sin." Sin results from the desire to be morally god-like, to be one's own ruler, and to make decisions in defiance or disregard of God's will. It is a violation of a trustful relationship between the Creator and his creation. The Genesis account unveils humanity's pattern of sin. It is a model of the underlying factors when a person disobeys God. The crux of it all is the prideful human aspiration for "self-rule."

Satan typically uses three ploys to entice humans into this prideful state of self-rule and sin:

- He makes God out to be overly strict and unrealistic (by exaggerating the difficulty of God's way).
- He prompts us to foolishly think there will be no consequences for sin.
- He entices us to think we can live for ourselves and be god-like.

Then, after Satan entices humans into sin, we typically respond in ways similar to Adam and Eve:

- We feel a sense of shame in our inner self, that something is wrong with us.
- We seek to cover or hide the shame we feel.
- We become afraid of God and hide from him.
- We blame others for our actions.

In this way, the biblical account of Adam and Eve is also the account of the human race and our own individual experience with sin and a lost relationship with God.

God Is Holy

God is revealed through the Bible to be a good, loving God, but he is also much more than most people understand. God is holy.[103] For God to be holy means God is "pure, free from every stain, wholly perfect and immaculate in every detail."[104] To say God is holy means no sin, wrongdoing, evil, or anything bad exists in him. "God is light; in him there is no darkness at all" (1 John 1:5).

Isaiah was an Old Testament prophet who had a vision of God. In Isaiah 6:1-5, we see how he learned what it meant to say *God is holy*.

> I saw the Lord, high and exalted, seated on a throne; and the train of his robe filled the temple. Above him were seraphim, each with six wings: With two wings they covered their faces, with two they covered their feet, and with two they were flying. And they were calling to one another: "Holy, holy, holy is the Lord Almighty; the whole earth is full of his glory." At the sound of their voices the doorposts and thresholds shook and the temple was filled with smoke. "Woe to me!" I cried. "I am ruined! For I am a man of unclean lips, and I live among a people of unclean lips, and my eyes have seen the King, the Lord Almighty."

God then used an angel to show Isaiah how God would take away his sin.

> Then one of the seraphim flew to me with a live coal in his hand, which he had taken with tongs from the altar. With it he touched my mouth and said, "See, this has touched your lips; your guilt is taken away and your sin atoned for" (Isaiah 6:6-7).

God's holiness explains why there is a veil between humans and God. It explains why human beings are separated from God and destined to die. Because God is holy, he must insist that all of his creatures be like him, lest his own holiness, dignity, honor, and sovereign rule over the universe be diminished. This makes him very different than humans. He is high, dignified, lofty, and worthy of profound reverence.[105]

The story of Adam and Eve's fall is a model of the entire human race, not solely Adam and Eve. It tells us what is wrong with all of us. We cannot handle the pull of sin, selfishness, and evil our ancestors brought into human experience when they chose to eat from the tree of the knowledge of good and evil.

Because of this choice, God had to separate himself from us. Holiness means God cannot have anything to do with sin. Sin cut humans off from God and eternal life with him (i.e., the tree of life). We have been sentenced to physical and spiritual death.

> Genesis 3:19 – By the sweat of your brow you will eat your food until you return to the ground, since from it you were taken; for dust you are and to dust you will return.

> Genesis 3:22-23 – And the Lord God said, "The man has now become like one of us, knowing good and evil. He must not be allowed to reach out his hand and take also from the tree of life and eat, and live forever." So the Lord God banished him from the Garden of Eden.

From this point forward, the Bible narrates the often sad story of human beings losing their way and it reveals how sin and rebellion against God have harmed us.[106] We lost our paradise kingdom with God and now live in Satan's kingdom of darkness. As God warned Adam and Eve, humans now come into the world separated from God and destined for death, physically and spiritually.

Our Spiritual Disease

Sin is not as much a single act of rebellion toward God and how he told us to live as it is an ongoing attitude of rebellion or seeking to be our own gods. It is where we tell God that we will live life on our terms, not his.

Our condition is best thought of as a spiritual disease. Everyone struggles with their own sinful nature. It is most blatant in people like alcoholics, drug addicts, and murderers. But even those who do not manifest the extreme forms of the disease still have it. Gossip, pride, and materialism are subtle but equally pervasive signs of our depraved condition. The most profound sign of the disease appears in those who live as though God does not exist and that they are not answerable to him.

The first human beings, our ancestors, did not trust what God said, nor did they want to maintain their relationship with him. Because of their rebellion, God was forced to cast them out of the garden and away from the closeness of his presence. Since then, there have been great difficulties for the human race. We were made for a relationship with God and for a paradise kingdom. But it was lost and a new kingdom emerged by default.[107]

The kingdom which emerged is the kingdom of darkness, where Satan has a hold on the human race. From this time onward, two kingdoms existed side by side—God's and Satan's. The story of the Bible, as we will see, is the story of the eventual triumph of God's kingdom and the destruction of Satan's kingdom.

We must see ourselves in the story. Whose kingdom are we in?

A Morality Inventory

We might find it helpful to compare ourselves to this summary of God's law in the Old Testament. Make a mental list of the sins you have committed in each of the following areas. Place an X beside each commandment after you have thought about it.

1. HAVE NO OTHER GODS. (Do you put anything before God?)
2. DO NOT WORSHIP IDOLS. (Do you live for money, fame, or other gods?)
3. DO NOT TAKE GOD'S NAME IN VAIN. (Do you misuse God's name, for example, in swearing?)
4. KEEP THE SABBATH HOLY. (Do you reserve a day off each week just for God?)
5. HONOR YOUR FATHER AND MOTHER. (Do you honor your father and mother, treating them with respect?)

6. Do not murder. (Few of us have murdered, but Jesus teaches in Matthew 5:21-22 that hatred can be like murder. Do you harbor hatred for others?)

7. Do not commit adultery. (Have you had sexual relations outside marriage? Do you lust after people?)

8. Do not steal. (Have you taken things that were not yours?)

9. Do not give false testimony. (Have you spoken about people in untrue ways?)

10. Do not covet the possessions of others. (Do you want and crave what others have?)

If we are honest, we must admit we have failed to uphold at least some of these commandments.

The Galatians 5:19-21 Moral Inventory

Here is another inventory for you to examine yourself by from Galatians 5:19-21. This list focuses more on the outward passions that express the sinful nature.

> The acts of the flesh are obvious: sexual immorality, impurity and debauchery; idolatry and witchcraft; hatred, discord, jealousy, fits of rage, selfish ambition, dissensions, factions and envy; drunkenness, orgies, and the like. I warn you, as I did before, that those who live like this will not inherit the kingdom of God.

As you review the list, notice how it ends with a sober warning: *those who live like this will not inherit God's eternal kingdom!* Look at each item in the list below again:

- *Sexual immorality* = any sexual activity except between a male and a female in marriage. This means that sex before marriage, sex outside of marriage, pornography, and homosexual sexual relationships are sin.
- *Impurity and debauchery* = a wild, party lifestyle
- *Idolatry* = worshiping other gods (e.g., when we make money, success, or admiration from others into our ultimate pursuit)
- *Witchcraft* (*pharmakeia* in Greek) = drugs, spells, and contacting the dead
- *Hatred, discord* = bitterness and strife
- *Jealousy* = bad attitudes because you want what others have
- *Fits of rage* = angry outbursts; uncontrolled episodes
- *Selfish ambition* = focused concern about yourself to the exclusion of others

- *Dissensions, factions* = divisiveness and causing trouble between people
- *Envy* = bad attitudes toward people because you want what they have
- *Drunkenness* = getting intoxicated with alcohol (by extension, this would include getting intoxicated with drugs)
- *Orgies* = partying and involvement with promiscuous sex
- *And the Like* = other things that reflect selfish sin

Isn't it true that this list seems to capture everyone?

As the Bible says in Isaiah 59:2, "Your iniquities have separated you from your God; your sins have hidden his face from you, so that he will not hear." Romans 3:23 puts it succinctly: "For all have sinned and fall short of the glory of God."

These lists have only focused on the evil things we have done (doing what the Bible says not to do). We could also add the things we have not done which the Bible tells us to *do*; for example, the Bible teaches about how we are to love our enemies and help those who are poor or marginalized. James 4:17 lays our responsibility clearly before us: "if anyone, then, knows the good they ought to do and doesn't do it, it is sin for them." Most of us must admit we have not loved our fellow human beings as we should.

Are You a Sinner?

Let us suppose that you consider yourself a fairly good person, sinning only three times a day. You commit just one sin in the morning, one during the day, and one at night. That sounds like a pretty good person! But let's think for a moment. If you started sinning when you were 10 and kept it down to three sins a day until you were 70, you would have committed *65,700 sins*! If God is fair and just, your actions would still require a very severe punishment. Our sins should cause us great concern because God is holy, and we are unholy.

A story is told of famous English philosopher G.K. Chesterton, who once responded to a series of articles in a well-known newspaper. The series was titled, "What Is Wrong with the World?" Chesterton sent a short letter to the editor that said the following:

Dear Sir: Regarding your article, "What Is Wrong with the World?" I am. Yours truly, G.K. Chesterton

There is no one who is truly good. The Apostle Paul described what human beings are like in the face of God's holiness:

As it is written: "There is no one righteous, not even one; there is not one who understands; there is no one who seeks God. All have turned away, they have together become worthless; there is no one who does good, not even one" (Romans 3:10-12).

We understand spiritual reality when we fully realize how sinful we are.

God's Holiness and Human Sin

There are very important consequences that result from the biblical teaching about God's holiness and human sin.

1. Humanity Is Separated from God by Nature and Is Part of Satan's Kingdom.

The first and most important consequence since the time of Adam and Eve is that, by nature, we are separated from God. God is holy; we are all sinners. Every person comes into the world and naturally gravitates to sin in thought, word, and deed (Romans 5:12). We now come into this world as people who are "spiritually dead."

As for you, you were dead in your transgressions and sins, in which you used to live when you followed the ways of this world and of the ruler of the kingdom of the air, the spirit who is now at work in those who are disobedient. All of us also lived among them at one time, gratifying the cravings of our flesh and following its desires and thoughts. Like the rest, we were by nature deserving of wrath (Ephesians 2:1-3).

Let us state it again: we are all spiritually dead, separated from God by nature. We must start with this understanding, or we will not appreciate our need for reconciliation. As human beings, we all find ourselves in the same situation: following the ways of the world, living in a kingdom ruled by Satan, pulled by cravings we struggle to control, and separated from God.

2. We Will All Be Subject to God's Judgment at the End of Our Lives.

In his popular book, *The 7 Habits of Highly Effective People*, Stephen Covey asks his readers to think about the day of their death.[108] Covey rightfully teaches that we can only live properly in the present if we begin with the end in mind. The Bible teaches a similar concept, but it focuses on what happens *after* our death: the Day of Judgment. We do not like to think about death and judgment, but they will come, more quickly than we might think.

The Bible teaches that Jesus Christ will come back to the earth and bring history to an end. Once he comes back, or if we die first, our eternal fate has been set. There will be no second chances. God will judge us and fix our eternal destiny. The book of Romans describes it this way:

> For we will all stand before God's judgment seat. It is written: "'As surely as I live,' says the Lord, 'every knee will bow before me; every tongue will confess to God.'" So then, each of us will give an account of himself to God (Romans 14:10-12).

At this judgment, God will call us to account for everything we have done. We will even have to give an answer for every careless word we have spoken (Matthew 12:36).

3. God Will Punish Those Who Did Not Receive His Forgiveness.

Our separation from God is the most serious problem we face. It is our core problem. Jesus inspired the Apostle Paul to describe our condition in the book of Ephesians 5:3-6:

> But among you there must not be even a hint of sexual immorality, or of any kind of impurity, or of greed, because these are improper for God's holy people. Nor should there be obscenity, foolish talk or coarse joking, which are out of place, but rather thanksgiving. For of this you can be sure: No immoral, impure or greedy person—such a person is an idolater—has any inheritance in the kingdom of Christ and of God. Let no one deceive you with empty words, for because of such things God's wrath comes on those who are disobedient.

In the next chapter, we will learn about God's offer of forgiveness for our sins through his Son, Jesus Christ. But apart from Jesus, we face the frightening prospect of eternal punishment. We will be eternally cut off from God and punished for our sins. This is described in 2 Thessalonians 1:8-9:

> He will punish those who do not know God and do not obey the gospel of our Lord Jesus. They will be punished with everlasting destruction and shut out from the presence of the Lord and from the glory of his might.

Jesus himself said, "Whoever rejects the Son will not see life, for God's wrath remains on him" (John 3:36).

The path to forgiveness through Jesus Christ is essential. The alternative is unthinkable. But until we understand that we are lost in sin, we will not appreciate our need for salvation.

God Is Both Holy and Loving

It is important to understand that holiness is an integral part of God, but his love is just as dominant. God is our ultimate king, and he is a good, good King. When God revealed and described himself in the Bible, a major theme was his goodness.

Moses was a leader of the Israelites. He wanted to see God's glory, so God revealed himself. Moses stood in the cleft of the rock, and God covered him for a time, then allowed Moses to see his back, but not his face. After this, God came and proclaimed his name to Moses:

> And [the Lord] passed in front of Moses, proclaiming, "The Lord, the Lord, the compassionate and gracious God, slow to anger, abounding in love and faithfulness, maintaining love to thousands, and forgiving wickedness, rebellion and sin. Yet he does not leave the guilty unpunished; he punishes the children and their children for the sin of the parents to the third and fourth generation" (Exodus 34:6-7).

When Moses heard God's self-description, he bowed to the ground at once and worshiped.

This self-description by God is one of the most important statements in the Bible. In fact, some scholars believe that these two verses serve as the theme of the entire Old Testament! This proclamation by God is recalled and re-emphasized throughout the later history of the Israelites (Numbers 14:18; Nehemiah 9:17; Psalm 86:15; 103:8; 145:8; Joel 2:13; Jonah 4:2), so it is helpful to stop and consider God's self-described character. There are seven character traits mentioned:

1. **God Is Compassionate.** This Hebrew word is used to portray the compassion a mother has for her child. God has the compassion for his people that a mother has for her newborn.

2. **God Is Gracious.** This word depicts a yearning toward or a longing for. God yearns toward and longs for his people.

3. **God Is Slow to Anger.** Because of his intense love for his people, God is slow to become angry with them. God's anger surfaces slowly and only after explicit and/or enduring provocation.

4. **God Is Abounding in Love.** This is love that endures. God's love for his people cannot be exhausted. He will not easily give up on his people.

5. **God Is Faithful.** This word is used to describe steadfastness and firm commitment. God is faithful to his people, and his faithfulness is something a person can depend on.

6. **God Is Forgiving.** This word depicts something that is lifted up or removed. In this relationship, God is willing to lift up and remove the sins of his people.

7. **God Punishes the Guilty.** Though God is full of persistent love, he is also a being who sets boundaries. As the creator, sustainer, and ultimate judge of the human race, God puts limits on the extent of rebellion and evil he will allow his people to commit. When God's boundaries are violated, he acts firmly. God's punishment can affect his people for generations. Like a married person who severs the marriage relationship because of their partner's continued unfaithfulness, God will not tolerate ongoing unfaithfulness and rebellion by his people.

Most people do not have this full description in mind when they think of God. He is typically thought of as either a harsh, judging taskmaster or as a kindly, indulging "everything is okay with me" grandfather. This is not how God, as King, described and revealed himself to the Israelites.

Given the full picture of God, we can understand that he loves us, but we must turn from our sin. It is the love of God that gives us hope and a belief that things can be made right. We know God to be compassionate, gracious, slow to anger, etc., but we also must turn from our sin.

Repentance

The word in the Bible used to describe turning away from sin and turning to God is *repentance*. Repentance is a change in the way we *think* that leads to a change in what we *do*. We must repent and turn from our sins and turn toward God.

Repent, then, and turn to God, so that your sins may be wiped out, that times of refreshing may come from the Lord (Acts 3:19).

Repentance is important to God, because God is not just loving; he is also holy. To be holy means God is pure, separate, and without sin. A holy God cannot embrace sin or call it acceptable.

REPENTANCE = A CHANGE IN THE WAY WE THINK THAT LEADS TO A CHANGE IN WHAT WE DO.

We are naturally estranged from God because of our sin. We don't just commit a few sins; we often unconsciously develop sinful mindsets and habits. God's holiness will not allow him to accept us in this sinful state. Every single sin separates us from him. That is why we need to turn from our sinful ways and trust Jesus to take away our sin. One of Jesus' apostles described it this way: "I preached that they should repent and turn to God and demonstrate their repentance by their deeds" (Acts 26:20).

Is there anything that stands out to you from this section that you would like to note and discuss?

_____

_____

_____

_____

_____

CHAPTER 5

God Is Love

Key Theme: Jesus showed God's love when he came to rescue us by dying on the cross and rising from the dead. We are to respond and place our faith in him.

In the last chapter, we focused on God's holiness. We are now ready to focus on God's love. It's only in the light of God's holiness that God's love can truly be seen. This is why John 3:16 would win, hands-down, in a contest to discover the most known and loved verse of Scripture:

John 3:16 - For God so loved the world that he gave his one and only Son, that whoever believes in him shall not perish but have eternal life.

God did not want human beings to be cut off from him because of his holiness, so in his love, God found a way to take away human sin. In Jesus, God entered into our world to die for us and save us through costly, sacrificial love.

John 3:17 - For God did not send his Son into the world to condemn the world, but to save the world through him.

Romans 5:8 - But God demonstrates his own love for us in this: While we were still sinners, Christ died for us.

Let's look at a list of important contrasts. This short list will help us understand how God is different than people presume. Our natural inclination is to think that as sinful people, we must approach God, earn our way, make sacrifices, and suffer for God. We think that if we do this, then somehow God might accept us. This concept is at the heart of all false religious beliefs. The Bible reveals a different kind of God.

Natural Human Thought	Biblical Teaching
Humanity approaches God	God approaches humanity
Humans suffer for God	God suffers for humanity
God receives human gifts	God gives his own Son
Sinners reconcile themselves to God	God reconciles sinners

Jesus' Life and Death and Resurrection

The Bible records how Jesus came into the world, lived, and taught us God's ways. In Chapter 2, we presented a brief overview of Jesus' life—from his birth in Bethlehem to his death and resurrection in Jerusalem. It's important to remember Jesus' whole life, not just his birth, the cross, and the resurrection.

Jesus did many good things. He lived as our role model and an ideal human. He healed people, cast out demons, and came as humanity's teacher. The Apostle Peter summarized Jesus' life with these words:

> Acts 10:36-39 - You know the message God sent to the people of Israel, announcing the good news of peace through Jesus Christ, who is Lord of all. You know what has happened throughout the province of Judea, beginning in Galilee after the baptism that John preached—how God anointed Jesus of Nazareth with the Holy Spirit and power, and how he went around doing good and healing all who were under the power of the devil, because God was with him. We are witnesses of everything he did in the country of the Jews and in Jerusalem.

All of these things are part of the gospel, the Good News about Jesus. We will look at Jesus' kingdom and teaching and what it means to be his disciple in an upcoming chapter, but for our purposes here, we want to focus on what Peter described next and how Jesus came to save us. He died and rose again, and he provides us with the forgiveness of sins.

> Acts 10:39-43 - They killed him by hanging him on a cross, but God raised him from the dead on the third day and caused him to be seen. He was not seen by all the people, but by witnesses whom God had already chosen—by us who ate and drank with him after he rose from the dead. He commanded us to preach to the people and to testify that he is the one

whom God appointed as judge of the living and the dead. All the prophets testify about him that everyone who believes in him receives forgiveness of sins through his name.

Here is a summary of Jesus' life:

Jesus came as this Messiah, our King, and in him, the kingdom of God broke into this sinful world. Jesus came to reveal the true nature of God and to restore and redeem God's original intent for humanity. Jesus' mission led him to the cross, where he suffered and died to save all people, both the Jews and the Gentiles (those not physically descended from Abraham). After three days, Jesus rose from the dead, freeing us from Satan; then, he ascended into heaven. He is coming back again to fully restore God's kingdom. By repentance and faith in Jesus and his finished work on the cross, we can enter into his kingdom. He takes away our sin, gives us the gift of the Holy Spirit, and we are adopted into his Father's family. Our old identity is dead, and we are a new creation through the grace of God by faith in Jesus and what Jesus has done for us. We now live a new life, trusting and following him as his disciples. This teaching is called "the gospel," which means "the good news." It is the best news anyone can ever hear!

1. The Gospel. The word *gospel* is an important word to know. It means "good news." Because of Jesus' life, death, and resurrection, everything has changed for us. We live between Jesus' first coming—when he died for our sins, was raised from the dead, and ascended into heaven—and his second coming, when he will return to judge the living and the dead and establish his eternal kingdom.

In 1 Corinthians 15:1-6, as the Apostle Paul prepares to give us the gospel in summary form, he highlights several of the benefits of the gospel for us:

> 1 Corinthians 15:1-3 - Now I would remind you, brothers, of the gospel I preached to you, which you received, in which you stand, and by which you are being saved, if you hold fast to the word I preached to you—unless you believed in vain. For I delivered to you as of first importance what I also received . . . (ESV).

Paul's language is clear: believing, receiving, and standing in the gospel that has been preached to us saves us! Jesus and his work on the cross are the basis of our standing with God, and there is nothing more important! The passage goes on to summarize the core events of the gospel announcement:

> 1 Corinthians 15:3-6 - . . . that Christ died for our sins in accordance with the Scriptures, that he was buried, that he was raised on the third day in accordance with the Scriptures,

and that he appeared to Cephas, then to the twelve. Then he appeared to more than five hundred brothers at one time, most of whom are still alive, though some have fallen asleep (ESV).

Why is the gospel the ultimate Good News?

_____

_____

_____

2. The Atonement. The word _atonement_ means "at-one-ment," and it is a word that describes how Jesus makes us at-one-with-God.

Look at the following passages, which describe Jesus' atonement for us:

1 John 2:2 - [Christ] is the atoning sacrifice for our sins, and not only for ours but also for the sins of the whole world.

2 Corinthians 5:19-21 - For God was in Christ, reconciling the world to himself, no longer counting people's sins against them. And he gave us this wonderful message of reconciliation . . . . "Come back to God!" For God made Christ, who never sinned, to be the offering for our sin, so that we could be made right with God through Christ (NLT).

Romans 3:22-25 - We are made right in God's sight when we trust in Jesus Christ to take away our sins. And we all can be saved in this same way, no matter who we are or what we have done. For all have sinned; all fall short of God's glorious standard. Yet now God in his gracious kindness declares us not guilty. He has done this through Christ Jesus, who has freed us by taking away our sins. For God sent Jesus to take the punishment for our sins and to satisfy God's anger against us. We are made right with God when we believe that Jesus shed his blood, sacrificing his life for us (NLT).

How does Jesus provide for us so that we can experience atonement with God?

_____

_____

_____

3. Grace. This is the unearned gift of a right standing with God. It is his posture toward sinful people, which has been revealed in Jesus. In grace, God gives us the free gift of Jesus, whose life, death, and resurrection establish our right standing with God and save us from the eternal consequences of sin. By grace, we are free to receive God's offer of forgiveness and place our faith in Jesus.

Faith is more than a mere intellectual agreement with facts or a warm heart toward Jesus that is not faithful to him otherwise. It is both trust *and commitment to follow*. It is allegiance, loyalty, and faithfulness to Jesus: who he is, what he teaches, and what he has done for us. The Bible describes what this "by-grace-through-faith" salvation is.

> Ephesians 2:8-10 - For by grace you have been saved, through faith—and this not from yourselves, it is the gift of God—not by works, so that no one can boast. For we are God's handiwork, created in Christ Jesus to do good works, which God prepared in advance for us to do.

A.T. Robertson, an expert on New Testament Greek, describes it succinctly: "Grace is God's part, faith ours."[109]

What does "grace" mean to you:

_____

_____

What does "faith" mean to you:

_____

_____

4. Justice. To be "just" is to give the proper penalty for wrongdoing (or reward for doing right). The human mind will often ask, "How can a loving God send people to hell?" The Bible wants us to answer the deeper question: "How can a holy God not send everyone to hell?" Rephrased, this question is "How can a holy God save us?"[110] The holiness and love of God came together in the sacrifice of Jesus on the cross.

Bible scholar C.B. Cranfield puts it this way:

> For God simply to pass over sins would be altogether incompatible with his righteousness. He would not be the good and merciful God had he been content to pass over sins indefinitely, for this would have been to condone evil—a denial of his own nature and a cruel betrayal of sinners. God has in fact been able to hold his hand and pass over sins, without compromising his goodness and mercy, because his intention has all along been to deal with them once and for all, decisively and finally, through the cross.[111]

How does Jesus' sacrifice help us to understand both God's holiness and love?

_____

_____

_____

5. God's Forgiveness. We are saved by grace through faith, and this is both an event (our justification) and a process in which we learn to become more and more faithful (our sanctification). In other words, it continues from the time of our conversion through the end of our lives.

In the Bible, the word *walk* is a common metaphor for the basic direction of one's life. So a person with faith in Jesus "walks in the way of Jesus" or "walks in the light." One of the most helpful passages for dealing with sin in terms of walking is 1 John 1:5-9:

> God is light; in him there is no darkness at all. If we claim to have fellowship with him and yet walk in darkness, we lie and do not live out the truth. But if we walk in the light, as he is in the light, we have fellowship with one another, and the blood of Jesus, his Son, purifies us from all sin. If we claim to be without sin, we deceive ourselves and the truth is not

in us. If we confess our sins, he is faithful and just and will forgive us our sins and purify us from all unrighteousness.

What does this passage teach us to do to find ongoing forgiveness with God when we stumble and fall into sin as we seek to follow Jesus?

_____

_____

_____

Please review the diagrams on the next page as a summary of what it means to make the commitment to trust and follow Jesus.

How Faith in Jesus Renews Our Relationship with God

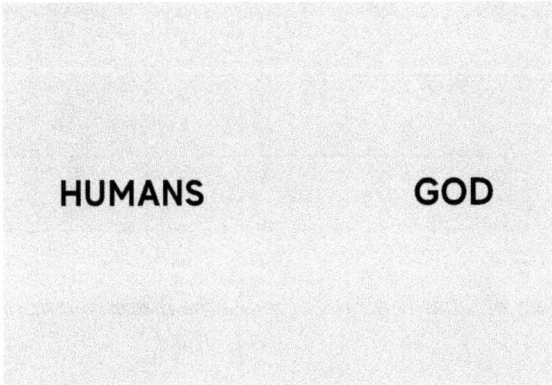

God—He is holy and he is love.

Humans—God made humans in his image, but we do sinful, wrong things.

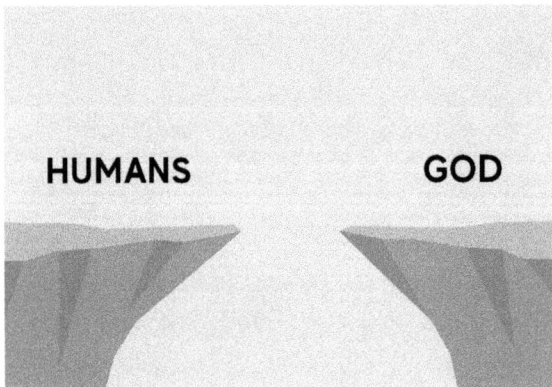

God and Humans—are separated because God is holy and humans sin—acting out their sinful nature.

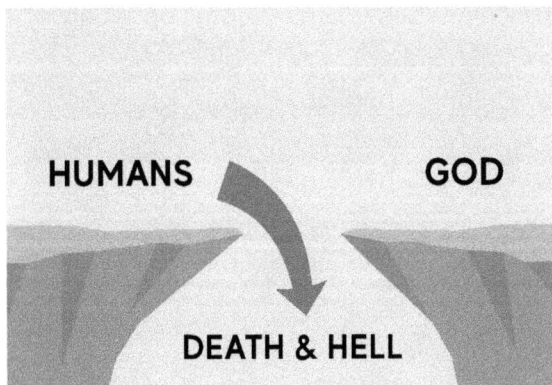

Human Deeds—We are lost (to death and hell) because of our sin—and all good deeds and attempts to make ourselves right with God fail. Only God can take away our sin. Unless God saves us, we are lost.

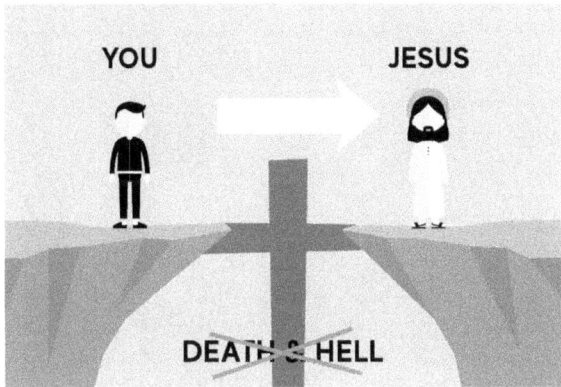

Jesus Christ—God so loved humanity that he sent Jesus Christ into the world to save us. Jesus showed the way by his teachings and life, and he paid for all our sins when he died on the cross, rose from the dead, and was enthroned as Lord and King. He makes a bridge for us and offers us the way to get right with God.

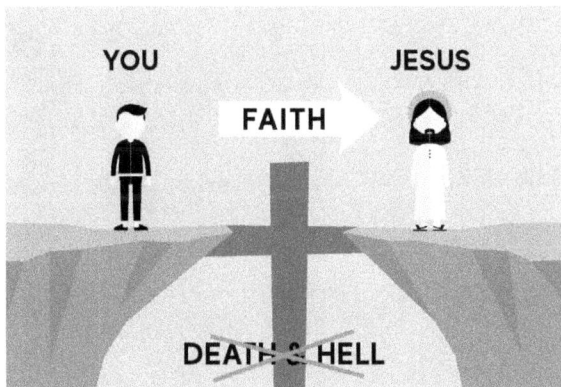

Faith—We must personally respond and place our faith in Jesus if we want to be right with God. This commitment of faith means we will turn from sinful lifestyles and trust and follow Jesus. We express this commitment to place our faith in Jesus by a verbal confession and water baptism.

Trust and Follow Jesus (Faith)—We live new lives where we trust and follow Jesus, as the Spirit leads, as disciples. A disciple follows Jesus, is changed by Jesus, and is committed to the mission of Jesus.

God Is Love

The Gospel

The word *gospel* is an important word to know. It means "good news." The gospel is, in the big picture, the storyline of the Bible we outlined for you in the introduction. But more specifically, the Bible speaks of this good news as the announcement that Jesus has overcome the curse and the consequences of sin through his life, death on the cross, and resurrection from the dead, and he has secured the gift of the Holy Spirit for us. His cross and resurrection are the basis by which our sins can be forgiven and we can be made right with God. His promised gift is the Holy Spirit, who enables our adoption into God's family and our empowerment for ministry. We respond in faith to these promises and to this amazing good news!

The key to understanding the gospel is recognizing that we live in an in-between-time. We live between Jesus' first coming, where he died, rose, and ascended, and his second coming, when he will return to judge the living and the dead and establish his kingdom as the Old Testament promised.

In 1 Corinthians 15:1-6, as he prepares to give us the gospel in summary form, the Apostle Paul highlights several of the benefits of the gospel for us:

> Now I would remind you, brothers, of the gospel I preached to you, which you
> received, in which you stand, and by which you are being saved, if you hold fast
> to the word I preached to you—unless you believed in vain. For I delivered to
> you as of first importance what I also received (ESV).

Paul's language is clear: what saves us is believing, receiving, and standing in the gospel that has been preached to us. Jesus and his work on the cross is the basis of our standing with God, and there is nothing more important! The passage goes on to summarize the core events of the gospel:

> Christ died for our sins in accordance with the Scriptures, that he was buried, that he was raised on the third day in accordance with the Scriptures, and that he appeared to Cephas, then to the twelve. Then he appeared to more than five hundred brothers at one time, most of whom are still alive, though some have fallen asleep (ESV).

The gospel focuses on Jesus the Messiah's death for our sin. But the full gospel is not only his death; it includes his burial, resurrection, and appearances to his followers, *and how all of it happened in accordance with the broader story of Scripture.* Our response to the Good News about what Jesus has done for us is to place our faith in him and receive it as God's grace—his gift to us.

Our friend Bill Hull describes what he calls the "gospel elevator speech."[112] He encourages every disciple to study the Scriptures and develop a brief description of the gospel to give to someone who asks you to summarize your faith as you ride on an elevator with them.

We believe there are five key components to a good gospel elevator speech:

- Jesus' identity — who he is (i.e., Messiah, Son of God, etc.)
- Jesus' work — what he did for us by his death for our sins and resurrection from the dead
- Jesus' invitation — what he offers to us and how we respond by faith
- Jesus' kingship — what responding to Jesus means for our lives here and now
- Jesus' future promise — what it means for our lives when we die

Upholding the Essential Elements

We must face a challenge of tolerance here full force. Many Bible believers want to embrace the spirit of our age and be tolerant, saying any belief in Jesus is good enough. Sometimes they will say, "The Jesus of Mormonism, the Jesus of the Qur'an, and the Jesus of the Bible are all the same." That cannot be true. The Jesus in Mormonism is the blood brother of Satan, and he is only one god among billions of gods in the universe. And the Jesus of the Qur'an is not the Son of God, and he did not die on the cross for our sins. So if it is just Jesus, then which Jesus are we talking about? We must get things right at this level—these are heaven and hell issues.

It is not the same Jesus, and it is not the same gospel.

Think of concentric circles with core truths in the middle, and moving outward, the truths become more personal.[113] Here is a diagram that will help you envision what we are describing:

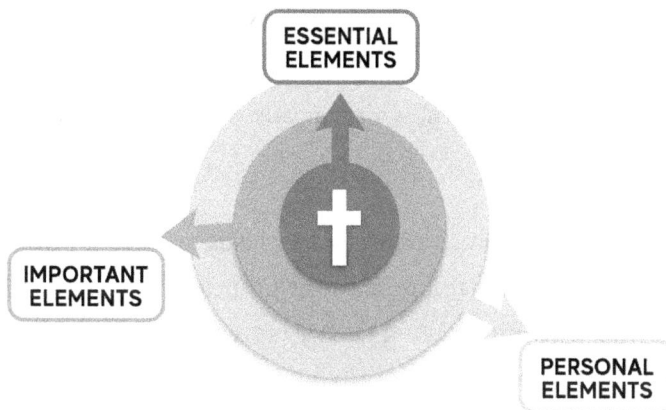

The essential and central issues in the Bible have to do with Jesus Christ, first and foremost. John 14:6 teaches us that Jesus "is the way, the truth and the life." The greatest reality in the Bible is that God sent Jesus Christ into the world to save us out of Satan's dark kingdom, transfer us into Jesus' kingdom, transform us in this life, and take us to the new heaven and new earth so that we can enjoy an eternal relationship with him forever in the next life (Colossians 1:13-14; John 3:16).

Essential truth is bedrock, foundational truth. The gospel and our faith response to Jesus' gospel are essential truths. The Bible says that we enter Jesus' kingdom when we turn from our sinful ways to place our faith in Jesus Christ.

Jesus and the gospel are the core and foundation of the faith.

Here is my summary of the gospel (Romans 1:16-17; 1 Corinthians 15:1-8; 2 Timothy 2:8; etc.):

The Good News is that God sent his one and only Son, Jesus the Messiah, to save us. Jesus became one of us, taught us how to live, and then . . .

- ► He died on the cross for our sins.
- ► He was buried.
- ► He rose on the third day, according to the Scriptures, and appeared to many witnesses.

- He ascended into heaven and sent his Spirit.
- Jesus has been enthroned as King of Kings and Lord of Lords.
- He is coming back to judge the living and the dead.
- But first, he invites everyone into his kingdom, where, by this gospel of grace, we are forgiven, made blameless, and empowered for a new life in this world and in the next.

> We respond to the gospel by faith, which means we trust and follow Jesus as his disciples in all things.[114]

Those who accept and commit themselves to Jesus and his gospel become disciples. Notice an essential element is our response to the gospel—we must respond with faith.

The Bible teaches that genuine, saving faith is more than mere intellectual agreement or simply emotional warmth toward God; it is living and active. Faith is surrendering our self-rule to God's rule through Jesus by the power of the Spirit. We surrender by trusting and following Jesus as both Savior and Lord in all things. Faith includes repentance, allegiance, loyalty, and faithfulness to him.[115] We summarize the nature of saving faith by saying that it means we trust and follow Jesus as his disciples. By this kind of faith, we become true disciples—people who follow Christ, are changed by him, and join his kingdom mission.[116]

There is so much that I could say about these essential elements. But we must state this clearly: "The gospel is the Good News—the best and most important announcement that anyone could ever hear."[117] Consider these things:

- This gospel is the central message of the holy Scriptures and the key to understanding them.[118]
- This gospel focuses on Jesus Christ, his person, his redemptive work on the cross, and his launching of the kingdom of God.
- This gospel declares the only way to know God is through Jesus Christ and his reconciling work on the cross.
- This gospel proclaims Jesus Christ as the living savior, king, teacher, life, and hope of all who put their trust in him. It tells us that the eternal destiny of all people depends on whether or not they are in right standing with God through Christ.

The gospel is so simple that small children can understand it, yet so profound that the wisest theologians will never exhaust its riches.

When we teach on these items, we carefully look at Scripture (there are ninety-two references to *the gospel* in the New Testament, with 1 Corinthians 15:1-8 and Galatians 1:6-10 being prominent among them). We may also find the Apostles' Creed to be helpful because it correlates to the gospel. It is the earliest Christian statement of faith outside the Bible. It was defined a long time ago by those who lived close in time to the apostles, and it has stood the test of time.[119]

We have to be straightforward and candid at this point. Here are some teachings that are common but should cause concern. The reason for concern is they are out of step with the teaching of the gospel. You will hear people say things like the following:

- "We are saved by being good people, whether or not you believe in Jesus."
- "People will be saved in other religions—they teach the same thing."
- "Muslims and Mormons believe in the same Jesus we believe in."
- "The Roman Catholic Church teaches the same thing about the gospel and salvation as Bible-believing evangelicals, even with doctrines like purgatory."

These are just samples of areas where different faiths *do not teach* the same gospel.[120] There are many cults and other groups that do this too. Jesus and the gospel are sacred to those who follow the Bible. Sometimes people come to genuine faith in Jesus through these groups, but it is in spite of what they add to the gospel, not because of how they add to it. The gospel must be important enough to us that we will state it and defend it from error.

The Atonement

From the beginning of time, the problem between God and his people has been sin. Sin can be defined as everything in daily life that is against or fails to conform to the character of God. This is usually demonstrated in an attitude of rebellion or disobedience. From the eight words used to describe sin in the Old Testament and the twelve in the New Testament, we gather that the foundational idea is that of lack of conformity to God's will. Sin is the failure to do what God would have us do. As Isaiah said, "Your iniquities have separated you from your God; your sins have hidden his face from you, so that he will not hear" (Isaiah 59:2).

God's reaction to sin is hard for many people to understand. We fail to understand because we do not appreciate God's holiness. To say that God is holy is to say that God is absolutely pure and separate from sin. Holiness cannot tolerate sin. A holy God must insist on holiness in others, lest his own dignity, honor, and sovereign rule of the universe be diminished. God's holiness requires that sin be punished and that divine judgment fall upon sinners (Exodus 34:7; Romans 1:18, 32). If God left sin and sinners alone, then he would fail to be a holy and just God.

Sin, therefore, is a serious matter to God. Sin destroys humanity's relationship with God. Ever since Adam and Eve sinned, God has been faced with a dilemma: he wants to be in relationship with his people, but that relationship is impossible because of sin. In his love, God decided to send his Son into the world to remove human sin, so that God and his people could be one. God's holiness made a penalty for sin necessary. God's love endured that penalty and made freedom from sin possible.[121] God prepared the Israelite people well in advance so they could understand how God's holiness required the sacrifice of Christ if people were to be forgiven.

In the Israelite covenant, God sought to help his people appreciate his holiness and understand the damage sin causes by the institution of a special tabernacle and a special priesthood.[122] As mentioned before, the priests had to meet specific qualifications, wear special clothes, and carefully follow ceremonial procedures. They were to represent God's holiness and to help the people understand sin and offer sacrifices for it. God described in detail the extent and exact nature of sin (Leviticus 8–16, etc.), and then he provided a sacrificial system to enable the people to atone for it.

To make atonement between a sinner and God, there had to be the loss of an animal's life and the shedding of blood. Consequently, numerous animal sacrifices were prescribed so that, after committing a particular sin, a person could kill an animal and have the animal's blood sprinkled before God in a ceremonial fashion.

God taught them that the only way sin could be removed was through the shedding of blood:

> For the life of a creature is in the blood, and I have given it to you to make atonement for yourselves on the altar; it is the blood that makes atonement for one's life (Leviticus 17:11).

By this, the Israelites became aware of God's holiness, the extent and nature of sin, as well as the necessity of a *blood sacrifice and the loss of life* to atone for sin.

The Old Covenant sacrificial system was set up, in part, as an educational foreshadowing or prefigure of what God would do in the sacrifice of Jesus Christ on the cross. By God's preordained plan, Jesus went to the cross as a willing sacrificial victim. Only the blood and life of God's Son could take away the sins of the whole world. The Old Testament sacrifices of goats and calves were miniscule imitations of the final and complete sacrifice of Jesus Christ.

> So Christ has now become the High Priest over all the good things that have come. He has entered that greater, more perfect Tabernacle in heaven, which was not made by human hands and is not part of this created world. With his own blood—not the blood of goats and calves—he entered the Most Holy Place once for all time and secured our redemption forever (Hebrews 9:11-12, NLT).

Only the sacrifice of Jesus' blood (Hebrews 9:24-28) could meet the demands of God's holiness and justice. Sin could be removed forever only by his sacrificial death. The basis by which we are made "at one with God" is what God provides through Jesus Christ.

Christ's sacrifice completely satisfies God's holy and righteous judgment of sin and sinners. As people, we all have done wrong. We have broken God's laws and God's heart. As it is written:

> There is no one righteous, not even one; there is no one who understands; there is no one who seeks God. All have turned away, they have together become worthless; there is no one who does good, not even one (Romans 3:10–12).

When Christ died on the cross, God was able to completely forgive our sin because the demand of his righteous judgment against us was put on Christ. As sinners apart from Christ, we all have real, objective guilt. Before God, we all stand guilty. Yet, when Christ died on the cross, he took away our sins:

> But he [Christ] has appeared once for all at the culmination of the ages to do away with sin by the sacrifice of himself. Just as people are destined to die once, and after that to face judgment, *so Christ was sacrificed once to take away the sins of many*; and he will appear a second time, not to bear sin, but to bring salvation to those who are waiting for him (Hebrews 9:26-27).

> He [Christ] is the atoning sacrifice for our sins, and not only for ours but also for the sins of the whole world (1 John 2:2).

> For God was in Christ, reconciling the world to himself, no longer counting people's sins against them. And he gave us this wonderful message of reconciliation. So we are Christ's ambassadors; God is making his appeal through us. We

speak for Christ when we plead, "Come back to God!" For God made Christ, who never sinned, to be the offering for our sin, so that we could be made right with God through Christ (2 Corinthians 5:19-21, NLT).

We are made right with God by placing our faith in Jesus Christ. And this is true for everyone who believes, no matter who we are. For everyone has sinned; we all fall short of God's glorious standard. Yet God, in his grace, freely makes us right in his sight. He did this through Christ Jesus when he freed us from the penalty for our sins. For God presented Jesus as the sacrifice for sin. People are made right with God when they believe that Jesus sacrificed his life, shedding his blood (Romans 3:22-25, NLT).

When Jesus was crucified, he provided the only possible way for sin to be removed. Only Christ could bear the penalty justice demanded. The human mind will often ask, "How can a *loving* God send people to hell?" The Bible wants us to answer the deeper question: "How can a *holy* God *not* send *everyone* to hell?" Put another way, the real question is, "How can a *holy* God save us?"[123] The holiness and love of God came together in the sacrifice of Jesus on the cross. Biblical scholar C.B. Cranfield puts it this way:

> For God simply to pass over sins would be altogether incompatible with His righteousness. He would not be the good and merciful God, had he been content to pass over sins indefinitely, for this would have been to condone evil—a denial of His own nature and a cruel betrayal of sinners. God has in fact been able to hold His hand and pass over sins, without compromising His goodness and mercy, because His intention has all along been to deal with them once and for all, decisively and finally, through the Cross.[124]

As sinners, we humans have no method of making right our sins against God. God had to take the initiative. Only Jesus—as fully human and fully God—could atone for the sins of human beings. Christ's death on the cross provided the complete ground and basis upon which God forgives, cleanses, and purifies people from wrongdoing.

As C.A. Dismore put it, "There was a cross in the heart of God before there was one planted on the green hill outside Jerusalem. And now that the cross of wood has been taken down, the one in the heart of God abides, and it will remain so long as there is one sinful soul for whom to suffer."[125]

Ransom

The Bible teaches that Satan gained a foothold in the human race when he first tempted Adam and Eve to rebel against God. Through their actions, the human race attached itself to the demonic order through a collective history of sin.

> We know that we are children of God, and that the whole world is under the control of the evil one (1 John 5:19).

> He who does what is sinful is of the devil, because the devil has been sinning from the beginning. The reason the Son of God appeared was to destroy the devil's work (1 John 3:8).

Did you notice that the Bible teaches that the "whole world" is under the control of the devil and that Jesus came to destroy his work? Through his death on the cross, Christ disarmed Satan and his powers and authorities in the spiritual realm.

> He canceled the record of the charges against us and took it away by nailing it to the cross. In this way, he disarmed the spiritual rulers and authorities. He shamed them publicly by his victory over them on the cross (Colossians 2:14-15, NLT).

Those who trust in Christ are released from the power of Satan. Through the cross of Christ and our steadfast faith in him, God will lead us to victory.

Without God's intervention, we are in grave danger, headed toward an eternal death because of the influence of evil forces we cannot handle. But God came into the world in the form of his Son. He was mistreated, mauled, and died. But he died that we might live, and he offers us life at a tremendous cost.

The good news is that when we trust in Christ, God literally moves us from Satan's kingdom into his own kingdom. We move from the side about to be defeated, punished, and destroyed as God's enemies, to those who are redeemed and victorious.

> For he has rescued us from the dominion of darkness and brought us into the kingdom of the Son he loves, in whom we have redemption, the forgiveness of sins (Colossians 1:13-14).

And they sang a new song, saying: "You are worthy to take the scroll and to open its seals, because you were slain, and with your blood you purchased for God persons from every tribe and language and people and nation" (Revelation 5:9).

By the cross, Satan has been defeated. Those who trust in Christ are set free, and they will reign victoriously (Revelation 12:10-11; 20:1-21:1).

Sincerity Vs. Truth

I often teach a class where I begin by asking everyone if they have a close relationship with anyone from another faith. Most people do. I then lead the class through an exercise where we try to determine the characteristics of people in other faiths.

We quickly determine that most people in other religions are as equally sincere as devout Christians. Those of us who know Buddhists, Muslims, Latter-Day Saints, or Hindus recognize their genuine zeal. In fact, the sincerity of some of these people puts many Christians to shame. Consider, for example, radical Muslims who are willing to commit suicide in an attempt to please God and enter paradise. Their sincerity also makes us ask, however, if they are right.

Unfortunately, zeal does not automatically make a person right. Before the discovery of bacteria, doctors did not wash their hands when dealing with sick patients. They sincerely did not believe in germs. That did not stop countless people from dying after the doctor's dirty hands gave them infections. Unfortunately, in the same light, the Bible tells us plainly that the sincerity of people will not bring salvation to them. Take the Jewish people as one example. The Bible explicitly states in Romans that their genuineness will not save them.

Dear brothers and sisters, the longing of my heart and my prayer to God is for the people of Israel to be saved. I know what enthusiasm they have for God, but it is misdirected zeal. For they don't understand God's way of making people right with himself. Refusing to accept God's way, they cling to their own way of getting right with God by trying to keep the law (Romans 10:1-3, NLT).

This passage makes it clear that salvation is based on what God has provided and the truth in Jesus Christ. We respect Jewish people and their right to practice their faith as they understand it. At the same time, we are concerned for them because we know that sincerity will not save. We hope and look to see many of them come to faith in Jesus as the Bible teaches (Romans 11:25). We also hope and pray that more and more people of all faiths will turn to Jesus with them.

Morality Vs. the Gospel

I then ask the class about the morals of people in other religious groups. Again, most of us who know sincere devotees of other religions have found them to be very moral people. Some adherents of other religions live better moral lives than many who claim to be Christians. But this too begs the question as to how we are saved.

Are we saved by good morals? Can a person's high moral standing take away the sins he or she commits? Some religions say "yes." But the Bible teaches that our good deeds do not undo our bad deeds. This makes sense when we realize that a bank robber's high moral conduct in regard to his wife does not take away from his just punishment for robbing a bank.

The Bible clearly addresses this issue in Romans 3:20 where it states that "no one can ever be made right in God's sight by doing what his law commands" (NLT). Again, the Bible describes those who think they can be made right with God, based on their obedience to law and moral commandments, with these words in Galatians 3:10-11:

> But those who depend on the law to make them right with God are under his curse, for the Scriptures say, "Cursed is everyone who does not observe and obey all the commands that are written in God's Book of the Law." So it is clear that no one can be made right with God by trying to keep the law (NLT).

No one will go to heaven by being good. According to the Bible, we will only go to heaven if our sin is taken away by what God has done for us in Jesus Christ.

In the end, salvation and forgiveness are God's prerogative. Only God determines whom he will forgive. Although, as humans, we think that sincere and good people should make it to heaven because of their worthiness, God does not save or forgive that way. In a real sense, none of us are worthy. Only Jesus is worthy. Forgiveness is based on Jesus' worthiness. Jesus and his cross are the grounds or basis by which God is compassionate and merciful. Without Jesus, there is no forgiveness; we remain in sin. The holy response to sin is justice and wrath. Justice is either absorbed by Jesus' death on the cross, or we must absorb it ourselves in hell as we deserve.

This is why the New Testament teaches that Jesus is the only way of salvation. As the Bible says, "It does not, therefore, depend on human desire or effort, but on God's mercy"

(Romans 9:16). In the end, the only thing that matters is *truth*. Which religion is the one grounded in truth? As Peter Cotterell puts it, that is the most important question between all religions:

> Truth is not a matter of pride or humility. It is a matter of fact. Islam says Jesus wasn't crucified. We say he was. Only one of us can be right. Judaism says Jesus was not the Messiah. We say he was. Only one of us can be right. Hinduism says that God has often been incarnate. We say only once. And we can't both be right.[126]

Christianity is unique in this regard. Not only does the Bible claim that the teachings about Jesus Christ are God's truth for the human race, but it claims that the only way of salvation is that which is provided for us by him.[127]

Grace

Grace is another important word. Grace is God's posture toward sinners that he loves. In grace, God gives us the free gift of forgiveness and eternal life through Jesus, whose life and death establish our right standing with God and save us from the eternal consequences of sin. The Bible teaches that we can only get right with God because of Jesus and the Good News of what he has done. By grace, we are free to receive God's offer of forgiveness and place our faith in Jesus.

God does not accept us because we are good people or because we do the right religious things. He forgives us because we place our lives, our future, and all of our hopes in his Son. When we rely on God's grace, looking away from ourselves in faith, God is pleased.

God gives his grace to all who place their faith in Jesus. By his Spirit, God leads us to Jesus (1 John 2:20, 27; John 16:7-11), and we must respond with faith. It is more than an intellectual agreement with facts. It is a warm, heartfelt trust and commitment to Jesus, who he is, and what he has done for us. The Bible describes in Ephesians 2:8-10 how this "by-grace-through-faith" pattern works for us:

> For it is by grace you have been saved, through faith—and this is not from yourselves, it is the gift of God— not by works, so that no one can boast. For we are God's handiwork, created in Christ Jesus to do good works, which God prepared in advance for us to do.

This passage is clear that we are not saved by our works. But as we trust and follow Jesus, relying upon his gift of salvation, the Bible tells us that we will begin to do what God created us to do, namely good works. God initiates this work by drawing us to himself. We respond in faith, and our transformed lives produce the fruit of good works. A.T. Robertson, an expert on New Testament Greek, puts it this way: "Grace is God's part, faith ours."[128] God initiates and draws us in, and as we respond with faith, the result is good works.

Do Vs. Done

Christian theologians describe the difference between Christianity and other world religions using the "do versus done" formula. All world religions differ with Christianity on the question, "How is a person made right?" Islam, Judaism, Buddhism, and other religions, including those others may consider Christian like the Latter-Day Saints, differ in their concepts of salvation and the afterlife, but they all agree that we get right by what we as humans *do*. Only Christianity teaches that we get right with God based on what Jesus Christ has already *done*. This doctrine is behind the biblical teaching that Jesus is "the way, the truth, and the life," and this is why "no one comes to the Father, except through [him]" (John 14:6).

In *What's So Amazing about Grace?*, Philip Yancey recounts the time that influential Christian writer C.S. Lewis was called upon to explain the uniqueness of Christianity among the world's religions:

> During a British conference on comparative religions, experts from around the world debated what, if any, belief was unique to the Christian faith. They began eliminating possibilities. Incarnation? Other religions had different versions of gods appearing in human form. Resurrection? Again, other religions had accounts of return from death.
>
> The debate went on for some time until C.S. Lewis wandered into the room. "What's the rumpus about?" he asked, and heard in reply that his colleagues were discussing Christianity's unique contribution among world religions. Lewis responded, "Oh, that's easy. It's grace." After some discussion, the conferees had to agree.[129]

The biblical concept of God's grace challenges our natural instinct; should we do something to gain a right standing with God? No. The Bible plainly teaches us God has freely offered his grace to us as a gift.

Is there anything that stands out to you from this section you would like to note and discuss?

_____

_____

_____

_____

_____

CHAPTER 6

Lord & King

Key Theme: True faith in Jesus means we have a faithful faith—that we both trust and follow Jesus as his disciples, surrendering to him as our Lord and King.

When Jesus came into the world, he came as God's promised Messiah to establish God's long-promised kingdom. The kingdom is both "the reign" of God and "the realm" in which God reigns.[130] Jesus established the kingdom of God by his life and ministry and by his death, burial, and resurrection.

Scripture teaches that Jesus is Lord—which means he is not just a human—he is also God with authority, control, and power over all.

Scripture teaches that Jesus is the Messiah—which means he is God's long-promised King.

Jesus promised his followers that he would return one day to fully remove the effects of the curse and usher in the new age where sin, death, pain, and sadness are gone forever. This is the blessed hope for all disciples of Jesus. Until that time, Jesus offers humans a standing invitation into his "already-but-not-yet" kingdom. He offers salvation to us by grace through faith. Grace is God's unearned favor where he offers us forgiveness and life in his kingdom, and we respond to his offer by faith, which is trusting and following Jesus. When Jesus comes back, he will judge those living as well as those who have died. Those who did not respond to God's gracious invitation to be redeemed in this life will be punished for their sins in hell. Those who trusted and followed Jesus will experience everlasting joy with God forever in the new heaven and the new earth.

Jesus spoke about the kingdom of God more than any other topic. His kingdom will be fully implemented over all creation when he returns—when everyone will say he is "Lord of lords and King of kings" (Revelation 19:16).

1. **The Already Kingdom.** When Jesus came, he announced his kingdom (Matthew 4:17). When a person turns to follow Jesus, they are added to God's kingdom. The Apostle Paul describes what kingdom life in this world is like in the book of Romans:

> Romans 14:17 - For the kingdom of God is not a matter of eating and drinking, but of righteousness, peace and joy in the Holy Spirit.

What would your life look like if you were to more fully experience the righteousness, peace, and joy of the kingdom through the Holy Spirit as described in this passage?

_____

_____

_____

2. **The Not-Yet Kingdom.** The kingdom has come, but it has not yet been fully revealed. When Jesus returns, it will be fully revealed to us. The following passage describes what will happen when Jesus returns:

> 1 Thessalonians 4:13-17 - Brothers and sisters, we do not want you to be uninformed about those who sleep in death, so that you do not grieve like the rest of mankind, who have no hope. For we believe that Jesus died and rose again, and so we believe that God will bring with Jesus those who have fallen asleep in him. According to the Lord's word, we tell you that we who are still alive, who are left until the coming of the Lord, will certainly not precede those who have fallen asleep. For the Lord himself will come down from heaven, with a loud command, with the voice of the archangel and with the trumpet call of God, and the dead in Christ will rise first. After that, we who are still alive and are left will be caught up together with them in the clouds to meet the Lord in the air. And so we will be with the Lord forever.

What is the order in which things will happen at the end of history?

_____

_____

_____

3. Final Judgment. After Jesus returns, all human beings will stand before God for a final judgment of our lives. Those who trusted and followed Jesus will have their names in the book of life—a record of the saved.

> Revelation 20:12-15 - And I saw the dead, great and small, standing before the throne, and books were opened. Another book was opened, which is the book of life. The dead were judged according to what they had done as recorded in the books . . . . Anyone whose name was not found written in the book of life was thrown into the lake of fire.

4. New Heaven and New Earth. Then, after the final judgment, Jesus will take those who had faith in him to the new heaven and new earth, where the complete rule and reign of God over all nature will be complete. The book of Revelation describes the final reign of King Jesus this way:

> Revelation 21:3-4 - And I heard a loud voice from the throne saying, "Look! God's dwelling place is now among the people, and he will dwell with them. They will be his people, and God himself will be with them and be their God. He will wipe every tear from their eyes. There will be no more death or mourning or crying or pain, for the old order of things has passed away."

What do you think a kingdom like the one described in Revelation 21 will be like?

_____

_____

_____

5. "Jesus is Lord." This was the earliest Christian confession. In the time of the Bible, a "lord" was someone with authority, control, or power over others.

> Philippians 2:9-11 - Therefore God exalted him [Jesus] to the highest place and gave him the name that is above every name, that at the name of Jesus every knee should bow, in heaven and on earth and under the earth, and every tongue acknowledge that Jesus Christ is Lord, to the glory of God the Father.

What does it really mean to say, "Jesus is Lord"?

_____

_____

_____

6. Disciple. It surprises many people to learn that the word *"Christian"* is used only three times in the Bible, but the word *"disciple"* is used about 270 times. In Matthew 4:19, Jesus says the following to two brothers, Peter and Andrew, while they are casting a net beside the Sea of Galilee:

> Matthew 4:19 - Come, follow me, and I will make you fishers of men (ESV).

If we use this verse as a framework for understanding discipleship, we find three important attributes of a disciple. A disciple is a person who:

1. Is following Jesus *(head)*,
2. Is being changed by Jesus *(heart)*, and
3. Is committed to the mission of Jesus *(hands)*.

Which part of this definition is hardest to live out and why?

_____

_____

_____

7. "Follow Me." John 14:23-24 connects our obedience to Christ with our hearts and affections:

> Anyone who loves me will obey my teaching. My Father will love them, and we will come to them and make our home with them. Anyone who does not love me will not obey my teaching.

Jesus lovingly rules our lives, and as he does, he replaces the falsehood we were handed from the world with his truth. In Mark 8:34-35, Jesus puts it starkly:

> Then he called the crowd to him along with his disciples and said: "Whoever wants to be my disciple must deny themselves and take up their cross and follow me. For whoever wants to save their life will lose it, but whoever loses their life for me and for the gospel will save it."

What kind of help do you need to truly trust and follow Jesus as these passages describe?

_____

_____

_____

8. "And I Will Make You." 2 Corinthians 3:17-18 promises that God is transforming us to be more and more like Jesus, described as moving from one degree of glory into another into his image.

> Now the Lord is the Spirit, and where the Spirit of the Lord is, there is freedom. And we all, who with unveiled faces contemplate the Lord's glory, are being transformed into his image with ever-increasing glory, which comes from the Lord, who is the Spirit.

What would it look like for your life to be truly transformed by the invisible Spirit?

_____

_____

_____

9. "Fishers of Men." Paul states it this way in 2 Corinthians 5:14-20:

> For Christ's love compels us, because we are convinced that one died for all, and therefore all died. And he died for all, that those who live should no longer live for themselves but for him who died for them and was raised again. So from now on we regard no one from a worldly point of view. Though we once regarded Christ in this way, we do so no longer. Therefore, if anyone is in Christ, the new creation has come: The old has gone, the new is here! All this is from God, who reconciled us to himself through Christ and gave us the ministry of reconciliation: that God was reconciling the world to himself in Christ, not counting people's sins against them. And he has committed to us the message of reconciliation. We are therefore Christ's ambassadors, as though God were making his appeal through us. We implore you on Christ's behalf: Be reconciled to God.

We want to become more and more like Jesus. His mission was to give his life to save us, and he focused his ministry on making disciples. Jesus' disciples followed him and focused on sharing the message of salvation and making disciples.

Why is it important for us to share how Jesus reconciles people to God?

_____

_____

_____

10. "A Faithful Faith." Some people think "faith" is just believing that Jesus died for them. They think it is simply mental assent. But saving faith involves both *trusting* and *following* Jesus. A recent summary shows that 76 percent of Americans claim to be a Christian.[131] James describes true discipleship by describing what faith really means:

> James 2:14-19 - What good is it, my brothers and sisters, if someone claims to have faith but has no deeds? Can such faith save them? Suppose a brother or a sister is without clothes and daily food. If one of you says to them, "Go in peace; keep warm and well fed," but does nothing about their physical needs, what good is it? In the same way, faith by itself, if it is not accompanied by action, is dead. But someone will say, "You have faith; I have deeds." Show me your faith without deeds, and I will show you my faith by my deeds. You believe that there is one God. Good! Even the demons believe that—and shudder.

What does it look like for you to show that your life is based upon faith by your deeds?

_____

_____

_____

Cultural Christianity	Biblical Disciple
I like the things of Jesus being part of my life.	Jesus is at the center of my life.
I have a life and Jesus is in parts of it.	I form my life around Jesus.
I believe that Jesus was a good man/teacher.	Jesus is my Savior, Lord, and King.
I was Christened/made a one-time decision.	I trust and follow Jesus daily.

Lord & King

In this chapter, we will get very practical as we discuss the New Testament teaching about Jesus as Lord and King of a kingdom. There are three key elements:

1. Jesus' kingdom is "Already, but Not yet."
2. Jesus rules over his disciples now.
3. Jesus rules his disciples through active faith.

The "Already" Kingdom

Jesus told those who were alive with him that "some who are standing here will not taste death before they see that the kingdom of God has come with power" (Mark 9:1). No one understood or foresaw that the kingdom of God would be established this way. Jesus explained how the kingdom came into the lives of his disciples with these words:

> Once, on being asked by the Pharisees when the kingdom of God would come, Jesus replied, "The coming of the kingdom of God is not something that can be observed, nor will people say, 'Here it is,' or 'There it is,' because the kingdom of God is in your midst" (Luke 17:20-21).

On another occasion in Jesus' life, he described the kingdom's presence with these words:

> After John was put in prison, Jesus went into Galilee, proclaiming the good news of God. "The time *has come*," he said. "The kingdom of God *has come near*. Repent and believe the good news!" (Mark 1:14-15).

The kingdom is both "the reign of God" and "the realm in which God reigns." Through Jesus, God rules over us as we trust and follow Jesus. The church is the community where Jesus' rule is most clearly manifest in the world.

The "Not-Yet" Kingdom

There are two "comings" of Jesus. The first coming was his birth, life, teaching, death, burial, resurrection, and ascension. The second coming will be when Jesus returns to the earth as the conquering Messiah, to judge the living and the dead at the end of time.

Although the kingdom has been present since the days of Jesus, it will not be fully consummated until he returns. Equal to the emphasis in the Bible on the "present kingdom" is the emphasis on the "future kingdom." In this sense, we still await the kingdom, even praying for it to come (Matthew 6:10). Paul encouraged the Thessalonian Christians to hold on to the faith in the midst of difficulty, for it showed their future destiny in the kingdom of God:

> All this is evidence that God's judgment is right, and as a result you will be counted worthy of the kingdom of God, for which you are suffering. . . . This will happen when the Lord Jesus is revealed from heaven in blazing fire with his powerful angels (2 Thessalonians 1:5-7).

God established his kingdom through Jesus, but the ultimate kingdom rule of God will not be made visible until Jesus returns. At that time, God will bring about the judgment of all human beings and take those who were loyal, faithful subjects of Jesus to be with him in a transformed eternity, where the complete rule and reign of God over all nature will be complete. Jesus described this reality in Matthew 25:

> Then the King will say to those on his right, "Come, you who are blessed by my Father; take your inheritance, the kingdom prepared for you since the creation of the world" (Matthew 25:34).

In this "eternal kingdom," Jesus will have a banquet with his subjects (Matthew 8:11). There will be no more crying, death, or tears, for the old order of this world will be gone (Revelation 21:3-6). Jesus gave his followers a foretaste of this new world order by casting out demons and healing the sick (Matthew 4:23). In the future kingdom, Satan and all evil will be banished (Revelation 19–22), and all the things that are out of keeping with God's best plan for humanity will be gone: sickness, disease, anything that harms, and death will be banished by the complete reign of God's kingdom (2 Peter 3:10-13).

Jesus Is Lord

Jesus is not only Messiah (King); he is also Lord. "Jesus is Lord" was the earliest Christian confession. Its root meaning is "ruler" or "sovereign," and for Christians, it means that Jesus wasn't just a man, but he was also God.

> For us, there is but one God, the Father, from whom all things came and for whom we live, and there is but one Lord, Jesus Christ, through whom all things came and through whom we live (1 Corinthians 8:6).

> For what we preach is not ourselves, but Jesus Christ as Lord, and ourselves as your servants for Jesus' sake (2 Corinthians 4:5).

Disciples of King Jesus

The primary evidence of Jesus' kingdom is given through the community of his people, who are most often referred to in the Bible as disciples. It surprises many people to learn that the word *Christian* or *Christians* is used only three times in the Bible, but the word *disciple* or *disciples* is used around 270 times.

The word *disciple* simply means "learner," "follower," or "apprentice."[132] One of the more comprehensive yet simple definitions of a disciple is presented in the book *DiscipleShift*.[133] As a co-author of that book, I have drawn heavily from it in the following material.

In Matthew 4:19, Jesus says the following to two brothers, Peter and Andrew, while they cast a net beside the Sea of Galilee:

> Come, follow me, and I will make you fishers of men (ESV).

In the most basic sense, his invitation is specific to these two men—men who worked as first-century fishermen. But the invitation Jesus makes to Peter and Andrew is also a more general invitation, one he gives to each of us as well.

If we use this verse as a framework and model for understanding discipleship, we can utilize three important attributes of a disciple.

1. "Follow Me"

The first two words of Jesus are a simple invitation. Jesus said, "Follow me." For us today, this invitation asks for our commitment to Jesus—his authority and his truth.

This could be described as a head-level item.

It's simple. Jesus leads, we follow. Following means that we recognize and affirm who Jesus is as Lord, King, and master of our lives. He's the one who initiates and guides. In turn, we respond to his leadership and direction. Following Jesus means acknowledging that Jesus is in front and we must place ourselves behind him. John 12:26 speaks of this process: "Whoever serves me must follow me; and where I am, my servant also will be."

Jesus is King and he is to rule our lives, and as he does, he gives us truth in place of the falsehood we were handed from the world. In Mark 8:34-35, Jesus puts it starkly:

> Then he called the crowd to him along with his disciples and said: "Whoever wants to be my disciple must deny themselves and take up their cross and follow me. For whoever wants to save their life will lose it, but whoever loses their life for me and for the gospel will save it."

Jesus is a light that illuminates our thinking, and we move from foolishness to wisdom as we spend time with him and his Word, the source of truth and wisdom. The invitation to follow him means learning and believing those truths. This leads to change at the headship (authority) and head (knowledge) level.

2. "And I Will Make You"

We can take the next five words in this verse to speak of a process of transformation. As Jesus works in our lives, he transforms us into people who become more and more like him. We like to say that discipleship involves Jesus molding our *hearts* to become more like his.

Jesus invites us to follow him and says he will make us fishers of men. In other words, a disciple of Jesus is *changed* by Jesus. Not only must we make a mental decision to follow Christ, but there must also be a process of transformation in which a work takes place in our heart and affections.

After Jesus invites Peter and Andrew to follow him, he hints at what he's going to do with them. We know from other passages of Scripture that disciples of Jesus are changed by Jesus, through the power of his Holy Spirit.[134] He transforms his disciples into something new, people who are different than they were when they first met him and started following him. Romans 8:29 tells us that we are being conformed into the image of Christ. In

2 Corinthians 3:17-18 we're promised that God is transforming us from one degree of glory into another as we are increasingly transformed into his image.

3. "Fishers of Men"

The final three words in this verse help us to describe action, something that affects what we live for and do. While our acceptance of Jesus begins in the head and extends to the heart, it naturally leads to a change in what we do with our *hands*. In other words, a disciple of Jesus is invited to join the mission of Jesus.

It is the greatest mission in the world.

We are called to join Jesus in his mission to love and reach a lost and hurting world. For their entire lives, Peter and Andrew had been fishers of fish. Fishing was all they knew. They would throw a net into the water, wait a while, and then haul out fish to sell at the market. Jesus was going to change all that. From now on, they were going to fish for men. Jesus was giving them a new purpose—living out his purpose by helping in God's work to bring people to salvation in him.

Being on a mission means we acknowledge that we're saved for God's kingdom purposes. Our mission is not simply to come to church each Sunday, to be nice to other people, or to cram a lot of biblical facts inside our heads. It's not even to give money to the church so the pastors can carry out the mission of Jesus. It's for every disciple to join in God's mission in this world, to participate with God's purposes in the world. The world is hurting and lost. People are dying and going to hell. We can give no greater gift of love than to share the Good News that brings people into a relationship with God through Jesus. Inspired by Jesus (literally), we seek to love people and tell them what we have found in him.

As we see, the third attribute of a disciple—that we are "fishers of men"—is a commissioning, a call to action. It speaks to us at the hands level: we use our abilities and what God has placed in our hands to serve Jesus.

Putting all three attributes together, we see that a disciple is a person who:

1. is following Jesus *(head)*;
2. is being changed by Jesus *(heart)*; and
3. is committed to the mission of Jesus *(hands)*.

We have found this to be a very helpful definition of a disciple, and this is what churches need to be seeking to make. Given the state of most churches in America today, this requires a shift from simply making converts to reaching people and discipling them. Our goal is to present people as mature in Christ (Colossians 1:28). When this is the goal, it changes everything.

The "By Grace, Through Faith" Formula

Another way of describing being a disciple of Jesus is to focus on living a new life lived by *faith*. We follow the lordship of King Jesus *by faith* and are saved by what Jesus accomplished in his life, crucifixion, resurrection, and ascension. All this is a gift to us from God. This is what the Bible teaches when it says that we are saved by grace.

Faith is the condition given by God in order to receive God's grace. The Bible describes the necessity of this response with clarity in Ephesians 2:8-9:

> For by grace you have been saved, through faith—and this is not from yourselves, it is the gift of God—not by works, so that no one can boast.

Recall the words of A.T. Robertson mentioned earlier: "Grace is God's part, faith ours."[135] Through Jesus, God provides us with everything we need. He gives us grace upon grace. Even our response of faith springs from and is empowered by God. Faith does not earn salvation; it *receives* the grace God offers.

Faith is our decision to believe and surrender to God through Jesus. The key element distinguishing cultural Christians from biblical disciples of Jesus is the nature of true faith. Biblical faith is a living, active thing. It leads to good works. It trusts and follows. It is known by its good works and obedient deeds. Likewise, when faith weakens or is not real, it is manifest in disobedience and sin.

Saving Faith Is a Faithful Faith

Some people think faith is just believing "Jesus died for me." They think it is simply mental assent, but saving faith is more than a mental assent to facts.[136] Faith includes facts, but it involves far more.

Saving faith is living and active. Faith involves our head, heart, and hands. It is what leads a disciple to follow Jesus, to be changed by Jesus, and to join the kingdom mission of Jesus. Faith is God's work within us, leading to good works, which God has prepared in advance for us to do (Ephesians 2:10).

We put it this way: true faith is trusting and following Jesus. Both trust and obedience are essential. The Apostle James teaches that faith without deeds is dead (James 2:26).

As one writer put it, "Faith obeys. Un-belief rebels. The fruit of one's life reveals whether that person is a believer or an unbeliever. There is no middle ground. Merely knowing and affirming facts apart from obedience to the truth is not believing in the biblical sense."[137]

Many times the Greek word for faith (*pistis*) is best translated as *faithfulness*. True faith includes faithfulness, which means we act on what we trust, that we live with integrity, and that we are trustworthy. It speaks of a life of obedience, one aimed away from sin and toward Jesus. Faith and faithfulness are the language of discipleship.[138]

The following material is adapted from *The Disciple Maker's Handbook*, which I co-wrote with Josh Patrick. I believe it will help us grasp what it means to follow Jesus in our current situation.

There are many people today who have a false security and a false assurance that they have a "real relationship with God" when, by biblical standards, they do not. Statistics show that some three-fourths of Americans claim to be Christian.[139] But claiming faith is different from living out our faith as a disciple. George Barna puts the problem this way: "Although most Americans consider themselves to be Christian and say they know the content of the Bible, less than one out of ten Americans demonstrate such knowledge through their actions."[140] The Apostle John described the problem as such:

> "We know that we have come to know him if we keep his commands. Whoever says, 'I know him,' but does not do what he commands is a liar, and the truth is not in that person" (1 John 2:3-4).

True disciple-makers are cognizant that millions of people today are cultural Christians without true, biblical faith. We say this not to condemn people or judge their sincerity, but because we love people and want to help them, as God guides us, to develop true faith.

One important point: we do not place our faith in faith. We place our faith in Jesus. He is the ground and the object upon which we focus. He works within us and creates this faithful faith (Philippians 2:13). Our decision to trust and follow him is the way God works through us to create this kind of faith (1 Corinthians 15:1).

Sin and Saving Faith

We are saved by grace through faith, and this is both an event (our justification) and a process (our sanctification). In other words, it *continues* from the time of our conversion to the end of our lives. The grace that made us right with God is the same grace that keeps us right with God. While we have been saved from the eternal consequences of our sin, our daily battle against our sin has just begun! After conversion, disciples need to learn *how* to deal with sin.

In the Bible, the word *walk* is a common metaphor for the "basic direction of one's life." Thus, when a Christian "walks in the way of Jesus" or "walks in the light," he or she is living with true faith as a disciple. This point is made clear in 1 John 1:5-9:

> This is the message we have heard from him and declare to you: God is light; in him there is no darkness at all. If we claim to have fellowship with him and yet walk in the darkness, we lie and do not live out the truth. But if we walk in the light, as he is in the light, we have fellowship with one another, and the blood of Jesus, his Son, purifies us from all sin. If we claim to be without sin, we deceive ourselves and the truth is not in us. If we confess our sins, he is faithful and just and will forgive us our sins and purify us from all unrighteousness.

There are three takeaways from this passage that help us maintain a healthy and balanced perspective:

First, this passage tells us that those with true faith will still struggle with sin. We will fall short. As James puts it, we all stumble in many ways (James 3:2). John declares in the passage above that if anyone claims to be without sin, Jesus' truth is not in that person (1:8). We must admit that sin is still a reality of our lives. I've noticed that this condition especially needs to be acknowledged and addressed by disciple-makers and church leaders. When we show transparency by speaking about our own struggle with sin, it helps those following us to realize that struggling with sin is a normal aspect of the Christian life.

I remember my early days as a believer when I was discipled by my French professor, and he shared some of his sin struggles with me. He talked about his pride and his battle against lust. One day, we were in a store and there was a magazine on the stand with a picture of a woman who was known for her nude scenes in movies. I started to say something negative in judgment about her, but Mac stopped me: "I would say the same thing, but I have found myself trapped in my own sinful and lustful thoughts far too often to be comfortable pointing my finger at others." His awareness of his own weakness and sin gave him humility toward others, and it was a concrete example of what it means to first take the plank out of my own eye before pointing out a speck in another's (Matthew 7:3).

The second takeaway in the passage is that Jesus' blood provides ongoing forgiveness throughout life. Grace isn't a one-time event. It continues with us always. In fact, it is evidence of God's grace that we grow in our awareness of our sin, leading to conviction. When this happens, we confess it, agreeing with God that sin is evil and choosing God and his promises to us in Jesus over the fading pleasure of sin. And God forgives us.

Disciple-makers may need to help their disciples learn how to do this as a regular habit in their lives and how to recover from a fall into sin. John tells us that Jesus' blood cleanses us from *all* unrighteousness (John 1:10). This means every sin you can imagine. Our confession is a sign that we hate and reject our sin and that we need a Savior who is greater. God often uses other disciples to help and encourage us in this battle (Hebrews 3:12-13). James says, "Confess your sins to each other and pray for each other so that you may be healed" (James 5:16).

The third takeaway from John's letter is that struggling with sin is different from giving in to a lifestyle of sin. If we purposefully and willfully embrace sinful lifestyles, we show that we are not in agreement with God. If we consistently love our sin, preferring it to God or justifying it as something God does not hate or judge, then there is a problem with our faith. Hebrews 10:26 warns about "deliberately continuing" in sin. Ongoing sinful patterns are inconsistent with true faith. If not addressed over time, such patterns can lead to a place where our faith is shown to be dead or, as some believe, faith becomes dead or nonexistent. 1 John tells us that we do not live by Jesus' truth when we "walk" or willfully live in the darkness of sinful lifestyle patterns. Biblical faith is alive. It is an active and repentant faith, present from the beginning of our relationship with Jesus until the end of our lives.

Conclusion

Discipleship and faith require nurturing and ongoing growth. To establish and develop this kind of faith, we must actively seek God, study the Bible, and be involved with others in the local church. We need to be discipled in the local church so that we are equipped to live as disciples with true faith.

At the end of his life, the Apostle Paul described the challenge this way: "I have fought the good fight, I have finished the race, I have kept the faith" (2 Timothy 4:7-8). If Paul said that he had to strive to keep the faith, then surely we will have to do the same.

Likewise, I am convinced that at the end of our lives, when we meet and bow before Jesus, we will be incredibly glad to have lived as disciples with a faithful faith. Jesus is the hope of the world, and discipleship in the local church is the fuel of that hope! It is the greatest cause on earth, and we get to be part of it.

Is there anything that stands out to you from this section that you would like to note and discuss?

_____

_____

_____

_____

_____

_____

CHAPTER 7

Commitment

Key Theme: We make the commitment to turn to Jesus and place our faith in him through repentance, confession, and baptism.

The central teaching of the Bible is God reclaiming his relationship with us through Jesus (John 3:16; Romans 3:24-26). Jesus came into the world to rescue us, to be sacrificed as a sin offering, to bring us into his kingdom, and to guide and rule over us until he returns. God invites all of humanity to place our faith in him (John 3:16-18).

This is what it means when the Bible says that we are saved "by grace through faith" (Ephesians 2:8-9). Grace is a "free gift"—the unearned, eternal blessing of God. The fact that Christ died does not save people in and of itself, but it provides the foundation upon which God, in full harmony with his holiness, is free to save those who have sinned against him.

The Apostle Paul described God's great gift in Titus 3:3-7:

> At one time we too were foolish, disobedient, deceived and enslaved by all kinds of passions and pleasures. We lived in malice and envy, being hated and hating one another. But when the kindness and love of God our Savior appeared, he saved us, not because of righteous things we had done, but because of his mercy. He saved us through the washing of rebirth and renewal by the Holy Spirit, whom he poured out on us generously through Jesus Christ our Savior, so that, having been justified by his grace, we might become heirs having the hope of eternal life.

This paragraph is a wonderful summary of the faith. It describes how God offers us his love, kindness, and mercy through Jesus. But we must respond to receive it, enter into his kingdom, and claim his promises. We do that through the faith commitment described in this passage.

1. Faith in Jesus. The core teaching of the Bible is that we are made right with God when we place our faith in Jesus. Review this summary of the core faith:

> Romans 3:22-26 - We are made right in God's sight when we trust in Jesus Christ to take away our sins. And we all can be saved in this same way, no matter who we are or what we have done. For all have sinned; all fall short of God's glorious standard. Yet now God in his gracious kindness declares us not guilty. He has done this through Christ Jesus, who has freed us by taking away our sins. For God sent Jesus to take the punishment for our sins and to satisfy God's anger against us. We are made right with God when we believe that Jesus shed his blood, sacrificing his life for us. God was being entirely fair and just when he did not punish those who sinned in former times. And he is entirely fair and just in this present time when he declares sinners to be right in his sight because they believe in Jesus (NLT).

Many people have found that a simple acronym helps bring the biblical concept of faith into proper focus:

F	—	forsaking
A	—	all
I	—	I
T	—	take
H	—	him

What does faith in Jesus look like for you?

_____

_____

_____

2. Confession, Repentance, and Baptism. Let's go back to the setting of Acts 2, where the Christian faith is being publicly explained for the first time after Jesus' resurrection. Picture Peter as he tells them that Jesus Christ is the promised Messiah. He tells a Jewish crowd that it was the

Jews themselves who cooperated with the Romans to put God's Messiah to death, but that God raised him from the dead. Peter tells them that Jesus Christ is now exalted at the right hand of God in heaven and that God is pouring out the Holy Spirit, as he promised long ago. Peter goes on to tell the people how they, too, can respond and place their faith in Jesus as Lord and Messiah.

> Acts 2:36-41 - "Therefore let all Israel be assured of this: God has made this Jesus, whom you crucified, both Lord and Messiah." When the people heard this, they were cut to the heart and said to Peter and the other apostles, "Brothers, what shall we do?"
>
> Peter replied, "Repent and be baptized, every one of you, in the name of Jesus Christ for the forgiveness of your sins. And you will receive the gift of the Holy Spirit. The promise is for you and your children and for all who are far off—for all whom the Lord our God will call." With many other words he warned them; and he pleaded with them, "Save yourselves from this corrupt generation." Those who accepted his message were baptized, and about three thousand were added to their number that day.

What do we need to do to express the commitment to place our faith in Jesus?

_____

_____

_____

3. Faith is expressed in a confession. In its irreducible essence, faith is quite simple. It is the pledge in one's heart to trust and follow Jesus as your Lord. The following passage shows the fundamental core of the conversion experience. This confession was usually made in the water, just prior to baptism, as a verbal expression of the commitment to place one's faith in Jesus.[141]

> Romans 10:9-11 - That if you confess with your mouth, "Jesus is Lord," and believe in your heart that God raised him from the dead, you will be saved. For it is with your heart that you believe and are justified, and it is with your mouth that you confess and are saved. As the Scripture says, "Anyone who trusts in him will never be put to shame."

When you declare that Jesus is Lord just before baptism, what are you saying?

_____

_____

_____

4. Faith is expressed in repentance. Repentance joins confession and baptism as an integral expression of saving faith. The Greek word in the New Testament for repentance, _metanoia_, literally means, "to have another mind" or "a change of mind" that leads to a change in behavior.[142] The Apostle Paul put it this way:

> Acts 17:30-31 - In the past God overlooked such ignorance, but now he commands all people everywhere to repent. For he has set a day when he will judge the world with justice by the man he has appointed. He has given proof of this to all men by raising him from the dead.

> Acts 26:20 - First to those in Damascus, then to those in Jerusalem and in all Judea, and to the Gentiles also, I preached that they should repent and turn to God and prove their repentance by their deeds.

Review the teaching in Chapter 3 on the sins listed in Galatians 5:19-21. What does it mean to personally show your repentance by your deeds as Acts 26:20 states?

_____

_____

_____

5. Water baptism in the Bible was intended to express faith in Jesus so we could receive the forgiveness of sins. Water baptism was the God-given vehicle, or method, by which people appealed to Jesus Christ by faith for salvation. Water baptism plays the role of unifying faith, confession, repentance, and the call of discipleship—together in a concrete moment of personal commitment.[143]

Faith was the essential human response, and baptism was the concrete method of expressing faith in a holistic way. For those who want to learn more about baptism, I recommend the short book that Tony Twist, David Young, and I wrote, *Baptism: What the Bible Teaches*.[144] In the following passages, please note how faith is the essential human response and how baptism expresses faith as the ceremonial aspect of a concrete commitment.

> Acts 22:14-16 - Then he said: "The God of our fathers has chosen you to know his will and to see the Righteous One and to hear words from his mouth . . . . And now what are you waiting for? Get up, be baptized and wash your sins away, calling on his name."

> 1 Peter 3:20-22 - God waited patiently in the days of Noah while the ark was being built. In it only a few people, eight in all, were saved through water, and this water symbolizes baptism that now saves you also—not the removal of dirt from the body but the pledge of a good conscience toward God. It saves you by the resurrection of Jesus Christ, who has gone into heaven and is at God's right hand—with angels, authorities and powers in submission to him.

What has/will it mean to you to express faith in Jesus in baptism so your sins can be washed away as Scripture teaches?

_____

_____

_____

6. Water baptism in the Bible expressed a personal commitment and was not for infants. The apostles described baptism as the point at which a person was saved because by doing that they were repenting and *pledging a good conscience to God* (Acts 2:38; 1 Peter 3:21). Romans 6:4-11 describes this pledge succinctly:

> Romans 6:4-11 - We were therefore buried with him through baptism into death in order that, just as Christ was raised from the dead through the glory of the Father, we too may live a new life . . . . In the same way, count yourselves dead to sin but alive to God in Christ Jesus.

The Bible teaches that a person enters into a saving relationship with God *only by their personal faith*.[145] Notice how the Apostle Paul contrasts the two systems:

> Colossians 2:12-13 - . . . having been buried with him in baptism and raised with him through your faith in the power of God, who raised him from the dead. When you were dead in your sins and in the uncircumcision of your sinful nature, God made you alive with Christ. He forgave us all our sins.

Baptism of infants/small children is common, but why does faith, repentance, and confession in this passage contradict this practice?

_____

_____

_____

7. Water baptism in the Bible was by immersion, which pictured burial and resurrection. The Greek word used in the New Testament for baptism is *baptizo,* which means "to dip, plunge, or to immerse."[146]

> Romans 6:3-5 - Or don't you know that all of us who were baptized into Christ Jesus were baptized into his death? We were therefore buried with him through baptism into death in order that, just as Christ was raised from the dead through the glory of the Father, we too may live a new life. If we have been united with him like this in his death, we will certainly also be united with him in his resurrection.

> Baptism, as a re-enactment of the death, burial, and resurrection of Christ, must be by immersion.

JESUS • DIED • RESURRECTED • BURIED

OLD LIFE • DIED WITH CHRIST • RAISED TO A NEW LIFE • BURIED WITH CHRIST

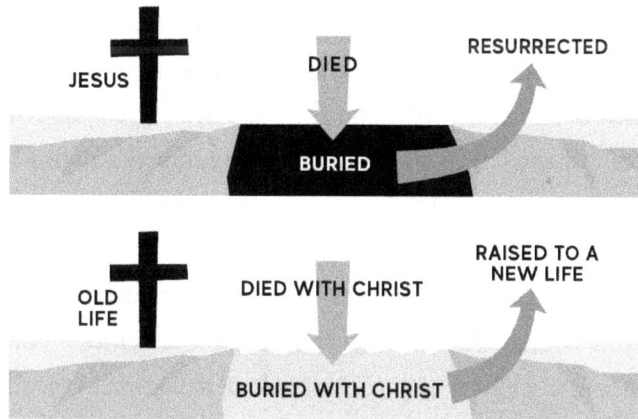

What does it mean for someone to die and be raised back to life with Christ in baptism?

_____

_____

_____

8. Making the commitment in our day. If we are seeking to follow the Bible, then we will teach that baptism is *the normative method* by which we make the commitment to turn from sin and place our faith in Christ. Baptism is given by God in the Bible as the prescribed way to do that for salvation.

Sometimes people use the "sinner's prayer" or tell people to "ask Jesus into your heart" to make this commitment. But as popular as these methods are, they are recent inventions, not found in any of the conversions recorded in the book of Acts—or in the rest of the Bible for that matter! They have really only been practiced by Christians during the last one hundred years.[147]

According to the Bible, the decision to become a Christian should be expressed in water baptism as the concrete means given by God. In this sense, we must reclaim the teaching that baptism—as an expression of faith in Jesus—is "for the remission of sins," as both the Bible (Acts 2:38) and the earliest Christian statements of faith, like the Nicene Creed, teach.[148]

I believe that God looks at the heart and often saves people who do not know about this *normative way*. But why live in the realm of exceptions to the norm? Why not just follow the Bible? It's way better to rely on the teachings of the Word of God than on human inventions.

People responded to the gospel and were baptized immediately in the Bible. They were baptized right away on the day of Pentecost, after hearing about Christ's salvation for the first time in a big crowd (Acts 2:38-42). An Ethiopian man did it immediately after understanding the teaching of Scripture, even in the midst of a long trip through the wilderness (Acts 8:36-40). A jailer even temporarily took his prisoners out of the jail in the middle of the night (Paul and Silas), so that he and his family could be immediately baptized (Acts 16:31-33). We should have that same sense of urgency today.

Water baptism seals and holistically solidifies our commitment to trust and follow Jesus—and thus become a Christian. It is the believer's spiritual wedding ceremony commitment to Christ. In the Bible, this was the special time in which the miracle of salvation typically occurred. We seek to restore and follow this normative practice in our day.

9. If you haven't been baptized, what is holding you back? If you have been baptized, how can you help others to follow this teaching?

Commitment

Remember the Gospel

The favorite word used to describe what Jesus provides for us, as we saw in previous chapters, is *gospel*, the Good News about Jesus. It is good news because it means that because of Jesus and his resurrection, everything has changed.[149] Before long, he will come back to fully consummate and establish his kingdom. Before he comes back, we want to respond to the gospel and live life in God's best way, in his initiated kingdom, while here on earth.

There are many short definitions of the gospel today. As mentioned earlier, my friend Bill Hull describes the "gospel elevator speech."[150] By that he means a brief description of the gospel, the kind of description that you could give to someone as you ride up on an elevator with them. Here is an example of a short gospel elevator speech:

> **Make the decision to trust and follow Jesus the Messiah, and he will take you into his kingdom and care for you both in this world and in the world to come.**

When you are ready to make the decision to trust and follow Jesus because you believe this gospel, for this world and the one to come, you are ready to become a Christian and a disciple.

The First Commitments Ever Made

We want to go back to the setting of Acts 2, where the Christian faith was publicly explained for the first time after Jesus' resurrection. The Apostle Peter is speaking to thousands of Israelites who are gathered in Jerusalem for a special feast called Pentecost.

Let's picture Peter as he tells them that Jesus is the promised Messiah. He tells this Jewish crowd that it was they themselves who cooperated with the Romans to put God's

Messiah to death, but that God raised him from the dead. Peter tells them that Jesus Christ is now exalted at the right hand of God in heaven, and he is pouring out the Holy Spirit as he promised long ago. Peter goes on to explain how they can respond and place their faith in God's Messiah.

> "Therefore let all Israel be assured of this: God has made this Jesus, whom you crucified, both Lord and Messiah." When the people heard this, they were cut to the heart and said to Peter and the other apostles, "Brothers, what shall we do?" Peter replied, "Repent and be baptized, every one of you, in the name of Jesus Christ for the forgiveness of your sins. And you will receive the gift of the Holy Spirit. The promise is for you and your children and for all who are far off—for all whom the Lord our God will call." With many other words he warned them; and he pleaded with them, "Save yourselves from this corrupt generation." Those who accepted his message were baptized, and about three thousand were added to their number that day (Acts 2:36-41).

We can learn several important facts from this account.

First, the people were to turn from sinful living ("repent") and be baptized in water to express their faith in Jesus Christ ("be baptized . . . in the name of Jesus Christ"). If they did this, Peter promised that their sins would be forgiven, and they would receive the Holy Spirit (2:38). To repent, as we will see below, is to change your mind about how you have been living and turn your life over to God.

Second, this response was given as a pattern for all people to the end of time. The promise of forgiveness of sins and the gift of the Holy Spirit was for those who heard Peter's appeal that day, for their children, and for those far off (in time, background, or proximity). In short, the promise is open to any person willing to turn from their sins and place faith in Jesus Christ (2:39).

Third, those who responded did so immediately. Three thousand people were baptized and, together with the apostles, they became the first Christians (2:40-41). As we will see, this response became a general pattern followed throughout the New Testament. If you want to study this material in greater depth, please read the book that I co-wrote with David Young and Tony Twist titled, *Baptism: What the Bible Teaches* (Renew, 2019).

There can be some confusion about making the commitment to trust and follow Christ in this way today, so let us embark on a five-part exposition of the commitment. We will consider, in order, the biblical teaching on faith, confession, repentance, discipleship, and baptism. By the end of this chapter, we should have a clear picture of the holistic response God has graciously given to us, and you, the reader, can make a decision about what it would mean for you to respond to this teaching today.

Faith

As we saw in previous chapters, at heart, faith is the sum total of our response to God. This faith has a central focus point—Jesus Christ and his death, burial, and resurrection (1 Corinthians 15:1-8). A Christian is someone who trusts and follows Jesus, meaning he or she believes in Jesus and that he died, was buried, and rose from the dead so that he or she can be right with God. The faith of a Christian allows him or her to trust in Jesus and his sacrifice to take away sin and give a right standing with God.

> We are made right with God by placing our faith in Jesus Christ. And this is true for everyone who believes, no matter who we are. For everyone has sinned; we all fall short of God's glorious standard. Yet God, in his grace, freely makes us right in his sight. He did this through Christ Jesus when he freed us from the penalty for our sins. For God presented Jesus as the sacrifice for sin. People are made right with God when they believe that Jesus sacrificed his life, shedding his blood. This sacrifice shows that God was being fair when he held back and did not punish those who sinned in times past, for he was looking ahead and including them in what he would do in this present time. God did this to demonstrate his righteousness, for he himself is fair and just, and he makes sinners right in his sight when they believe in Jesus (Romans 3:22-26, NLT).

Bible scholar K.C. Moser has given a good explanation of how a Christian relies on Jesus' work of atonement: "Faith or trust in the blood [of Jesus] is also a natural requirement of forgiveness . . . is the proper response of a soul toward a meritorious atonement."[51]

Faith is a total reliance, not just on the sacrifice of Christ, but on the person of Jesus Christ (John 3:16). The Christian entrusts their whole being to the care and leadership of Christ (Luke 9:23-27). A Christian trusts Jesus Christ and gives their life over to God, through him.

Faith's Holistic Response

Though faith is the singular response to God's actions in Jesus Christ, the commitment to place faith in Christ can be understood in four component parts: confession, repentance, covenant, and baptism. By his grace, God has provided this complete response so people can concretely express saving faith and experience a holistic conversion experience.

1. Confession

In its irreducible essence, faith is quite simple. It is the pledge in one's heart to trust and follow Jesus as Lord (King). The following passage shows the fundamental core of the conversion experience.

> If you declare with your mouth, "Jesus is Lord," and believe in your heart that God raised him from the dead, you will be saved. For it is with your heart that you believe and are justified, and it is with your mouth that you profess your faith and are saved. As Scripture says, "Anyone who believes in him will never be put to shame" (Romans 10:9-11).

The essence of Christianity is a simple faith, expressed in a brief confession. This confession was usually made in the water, just prior to baptism, as a verbal expression of the commitment to place one's faith in Jesus.[152]

2. Repentance

Repentance also joins confession as an integral expression of saving faith. The Greek word used in the New Testament for repentance (*metanoia*) literally means "to have another mind" or "a change of mind."[153] To truly place our faith in Jesus Christ, we must make the commitment to turn away from self-rule (where we live life our way) and away from what the Bible calls sin. In this way, repentance is a necessary part of faith and a requirement God makes for those who wish to receive his salvation. The Apostle Paul put it this way:

> In the past God overlooked such ignorance, *but now he commands all people everywhere to repent.* For he has set a day when he will judge the world with justice by the man he has appointed. He has given proof of this to everyone by raising him from the dead (Acts 17:30-31).

Repentance is a turning from self-rule and sin to God, as we recognize what God wants for us, how we have lived in the past, and how God wants us to live in the future. It is to turn away from what God says is sin by turning to and following Jesus Christ, God's remedy for sin.

Genuine repentance is recognized by a sense of sorrow about how we have lived as seen in the light of God's holiness. It is a determination that, with God's help, we will turn to God and change our ways. As the Apostle Paul said, "Godly sorrow brings repentance that leads to salvation" (2 Corinthians 7:10). Repentance is trusting what God says about sin, following God by turning away from sin, and with God's help, living apart from the control of sinful lifestyles.[154] Repentance does *not* mean that we will be perfect or without sin. It means that our lives take on a new direction. It is about direction, not perfection.

Repentance is a decision to be willing to die to the rule of the sinful self and sinful lifestyles and to become alive to righteousness (God's way of living). To use biblical language, in repentance one dies to sin and is raised to righteousness.

> But thanks be to God that, though you used to be slaves to sin, you have come to obey from your heart the pattern of teaching that has now claimed your allegiance. You have been set free from sin and have become slaves to righteousness (Romans 6:17-18).

Repentance, then, is the commitment to trust in and follow Jesus Christ and his way of living. This is often called the "Lordship of Christ" or "making Jesus your King." To be loyal to Jesus Christ means that a person renounces any other loyalty out of harmony with Christ and his way of life. Again, we are not saying that a person will become perfect in this new direction, but it is an expression of intention. In making the commitment to become a disciple, we are expressing the intention to live life God's way, as we rely on God's help.

True repentance, like true faith, is made evident in a person's life by their actions. The Bible teaches that external proof of internal repentance is necessary:

> First to those in Damascus, then to those in Jerusalem and in all Judea, and then to the Gentiles, *I preached that they should repent and turn to God and demonstrate their repentance by their deeds* (Acts 26:20).

The biblical teaching on repentance, like the biblical teaching on true faith, teaches us that mere mental assent that Jesus saves is not enough. When people turn to God, they must plan to concretely turn away from sinful behavior. There will be areas of growth that will take time and require God's help, but the new direction is clear.

John the Baptist gives us an explicit example of what repentance meant in practice for the people of Jesus' time. He was also very clear about the need to prove internal repentance by external deeds.

When the people from Jerusalem came out to him to be baptized, John warned them that they had better "produce fruit in keeping with repentance," or they would face certain punishment from God (Luke 3:7-9). The people wanted to know, then, exactly what they should do, so John told them:

> Tax collectors also came to be baptized. "Teacher," they asked, "what should we do?"
>
> "Don't collect any more than you are required to," he told them.
>
> Then some soldiers asked him, "And what should we do?"
>
> He replied, "Don't extort money and don't accuse people falsely—be content with your pay" (Luke 3:12-14).

John the Baptist taught that true repentance resulted in concrete actions. It should be this way today. When a person decides to make Jesus Savior and Lord, he or she should take to heart God's requirement to turn from sinful lifestyles. As John the Baptist explicitly told the people not to "extort money" or "accuse people falsely," so today, God requires that those who come to him give up sinful lifestyles.

One specific and detailed list of all the lifestyles from which we must turn when we become Christians is not given in the Bible. Some sections of the Bible like the Ten Commandments (Exodus 20) and the Sermon on the Mount (Matthew 5–7) provide specifics. Galatians 5:19-21 also provides a helpful summary of the sinful lifestyles we must renounce, even if we periodically stumble and fall:

> The acts of the flesh are obvious: sexual immorality, impurity and debauchery; idolatry and witchcraft; hatred, discord, jealousy, fits of rage, selfish ambition, dissensions, factions and envy; drunkenness, orgies, and the like. I warn you, as I did before, that those who live like this will not inherit the kingdom of God.

It is important to note that this is a list of sinful behaviors in which people "live." In turning from sin to God, it is impossible to be totally sinless (1 John 1:5-10), but with God's help, we must commit to turn from the lifestyle and regular practice of sin. The resolution that we will turn from our sinful ways is required. We need help to develop new habits and live the new lifestyle. Review the passage above again, and ask yourself this question: From what do I need to repent?

Please note that you do not have to make these changes on your own. You will make the decision only if you trust God to help you make the changes. Later on, we will see how God helps us through the Holy Spirit so that over time sinful habits have a decreasing power in our lives. But let's be clear: even the godliest Christian lives out their life struggling with, and at times, giving in to certain sins. This is why the Bible teaches that the blood of Christ continually cleanses those who follow him (1 John 2:1-2). Yet, according to the Bible, we must genuinely renounce and actively resist those things God says are sinful. In this way, repentance functions in the life of a believer as the "no" side of faith: we learn to continually say "no" to sin, but "yes" to Christ's leadership.

So in this way, repentance is an integral and required part of faith. As the Apostle Peter stated, "Repent, then, and turn to God, so that your sins may be wiped out, that times of refreshing may come from the Lord" (Acts 3:19).

3. Covenant

Conversion is about the future—the kind of person you want to become with God's help. A true conversion is also grounded in the concept of covenant. Covenants are a big deal in the Bible. A covenant is a special relationship where parties formally commit themselves to each other. It is not merely a transaction, but a deeply meaningful relationship commitment. The covenant offered to us is an agreement where God invites us, leads us, and freely binds himself to us. We respond, as his gracious Spirit leads, and commit ourselves to him. King Jesus calls to us to commit to him in a covenant where we will place our faith in him and commit to be his disciples (a process called discipleship).

In Luke 6:46-49, Jesus described what it means to place your faith in him. He described it as a commitment to his lordship, which means that he must be the leader, boss, and king of our lives. It is a commitment to discipleship.

Why do you call me, "Lord, Lord," and do not do what I say? As for everyone who comes to me and hears my words and puts them into practice, I will show you what they are like. They are like a man building a house, who dug down deep and laid the foundation on rock. When a flood came, the torrent struck that house but could not shake it, because it was well built. But the one who hears my words and does not put them into practice is like a man who built a house on the ground without a foundation. The moment the torrent struck that house, it collapsed and its destruction was complete.

In this way, the decision to commit our lives to Jesus by faith is a big deal. We are trusting God to help us in our commitment not only to listen to Jesus, but also to put his teachings into practice. If we do not have a faith willing to put his words into practice in our lives, we will face destruction. We want to be faithful to him; that is our commitment.

Picture a wedding ceremony, for it is a good analogy about entering into a covenant of placing your faith in Jesus. According to tradition, we pastors ask the man if he will "take this woman to be his wife, promising before God, his family, and friends that he will stay with her in sickness and in health, in prosperity and in adversity, so long as they both shall live." Then we turn and ask the woman the same thing about the man. In this pledge, the marriage ceremony becomes a covenant, an agreement between two parties, where they pledge themselves to each other. Again, it is not a mere transaction. It is two people entering into a deeply personal commitment to one another, with God and the congregation as witnesses. Covenants, such as wedding ceremonies, involve commitment, confession, and physical expression (e.g. exchanging rings).

Just like with a wedding ceremony, the commitment to place one's faith in Jesus is a deeply personal commitment. God is the initiator: he sent his Son for us and woos us by his Spirit. He promises forgiveness, his presence, and life in his kingdom. We respond with faith, which includes the commitment to follow Jesus for the rest of our lives as his disciples. As in a marriage, our covenant involves commitment, confession, and physical expression, namely, baptism.

4. Baptism

The fourth component in the biblical pattern of expressing saving faith brings everything together in one united and simple ceremony: water baptism. Baptism is an often neglected or misunderstood teaching in our day. So let us take a moment to highlight what the Bible teaches on this topic: *Water baptism plays the role of unifying faith, confession, repentance, and the call of discipleship together in a concrete moment of personal commitment.*

To gain a better understanding of biblical baptism, we will look at three related aspects of a biblical baptism.[155]

A. Baptism in the Bible was meant to express faith in Jesus and receive the forgiveness of sins.

Water baptism was the God-given vehicle or method by which people appealed to Jesus Christ by faith for salvation. Faith was the essential response, and baptism was the concrete method of expressing that faith in a holistic way. This biblical approach gives proper place to faith as the essential human response, while affirming baptism as the ceremonial aspect of the covenant-making process. To gain insight into the biblical understanding of baptism, it is helpful to review the following four important sections of the New Testament:

> When the people heard this, they were cut to the heart and said to Peter and the other apostles, "Brothers, what shall we do?" Peter replied, "Repent and be baptized, every one of you, in the name of Jesus Christ for the forgiveness of your sins. And you will receive the gift of the Holy Spirit" (Acts 2:37-38).

> Then he said: "The God of our fathers has chosen you to know his will and to see the Righteous One and to hear words from his mouth . . . . And now what are you waiting for? Get up, be baptized and wash your sins away, calling on his name" (Acts 22:14-16).

> God waited patiently in the days of Noah while the ark was being built. In it only a few people, eight in all, were saved through water, and this water symbolizes baptism that now saves you also—not the removal of dirt from the body but the pledge of a clear conscience toward God. It saves you by the resurrection of Jesus Christ, who has gone into heaven and is at God's right hand—with angels, authorities and powers in submission to him (1 Peter 3:20-22).

> So in Christ Jesus you are all children of God through faith, for all of you who were baptized into Christ have clothed yourselves with Christ. There is neither Jew nor Gentile, neither slave nor free, nor is there male and female, for you are all one in Christ Jesus (Galatians 3:26-28).

Notice that each of these passages relates baptism to a personal commitment. In Acts 2:38, Peter told the people to be baptized "in the name of Jesus Christ for the forgiveness of your sins."[156] The phrase "in the name of Jesus Christ" in this passage is a commitment of trust in Jesus Christ for the forgiveness of sins. I. Howard Marshall tells us how we should understand this passage:

> However precisely the phrase be understood, it conveys the thought that the person being baptized enters into allegiance to Jesus . . . . Thus Christian baptism was an expression of faith and commitment to Jesus as Lord.[157]

We see a similar point made in Acts 22:16. When Ananias finished telling Paul about Jesus and God's special mission for him, Paul was told to respond by arising and being baptized to wash away his sins. His baptism was the prescribed way to call upon Jesus' name for forgiveness. Baptism in this passage was a formal commitment or appeal to the saving merit of Jesus Christ.[158]

Galatians 3:26-27 explicitly states that baptism was a formal commitment to clothe oneself with Christ. This is also the meaning of baptism in the Great Commission. Jesus told the apostles to make disciples (followers) by baptizing them and teaching them to obey his commandments (Matthew 28:19-20).

These passages show that, for the early Christians, baptism was the God-given method for expressing one's covenant commitment to trust and follow Jesus Christ. A close look at 1 Peter 3:21 brings clarity to this point. Peter was encouraging Christians to be faithful to God, even though they were few in number. He reminded them of Noah, for he, too, was one of only a few who followed God in his time. Peter said Noah was saved through the waters of the great flood. The water through which Noah was saved served as a foreshadowing of Christian baptism. In the first century, the waters of baptism separated the few who were saved from the many who were unsaved.

> This water symbolizes *baptism that now saves you also*—not the removal of dirt from the body but the pledge of a clear conscience toward God. *It saves you by the resurrection of Jesus Christ* who has gone into heaven and is at God's right hand— with angels, authorities and powers in submission to him (1 Peter 3:21-22).

This passage shows that the real meaning of baptism is found not in the act itself, but in the appeal to the resurrection and power of Jesus Christ. Baptism, Peter says, points to the risen Lord, who has angels, authorities, and powers in submission to him. The water of baptism, or the act of baptism, has no merit in itself; it is simply the God-ordained method of appealing to the saving work of Jesus Christ for salvation.

It is important to clarify this point because without it some have wrongly concluded that the saving merit of baptism is found in the act itself. In the book *Hard Sayings of the Bible*, the writers nicely summarize how this matter was understood in biblical times:

> The normal point of salvation for Christians in the early church was baptism. Even here it is not the ritual itself or the water that saves, but the commitment that one makes to Jesus as Lord . . . . As in Paul, salvation is a relationship.

Baptism in Christianity, just as a wedding in marriage, is simply the way of entering into that relationship.[159]

God provides salvation through Jesus Christ, and baptism has its meaning *but only* as the God-given means by which we appeal to what God freely provides through Jesus. Galatians 3:26-27 smoothly relates the two: "So in Christ Jesus you are all children of God through faith, for all of you who were baptized into Christ have clothed yourselves with Christ."

Baptism, not as a work or thing of merit, but as the God-ordained mode of concretely appealing to Jesus and surrendering to him, is the biblical path. *In sum, baptism is the God-given form of the appeal for salvation and expression of personal faith in Jesus. Baptism is the form; faith is the substance.*

B. Baptism in the Bible expressed a personal commitment and was not for infants.

There are many different ideas about when a person is ready for baptism. Some think that infants can be baptized while others do not. We find in the Bible principles to guide us on this question.

First, as we have just seen, people had to believe in Jesus to be baptized. The biblical pattern was to receive the message (Acts 2:41) and believe in Jesus (Acts 8:12-13; 18:8) before being baptized. The Apostle Peter described baptism as the point at which a person was saved because at that time he or she *pledged a good conscience to God* (1 Peter 3:21; Acts 22:16). In this way, the Bible indicates that only those capable of personally believing in Jesus, pledging a clear conscience, and calling on his name were baptized.

Second, as noted above, baptism must express repentance. On the day of Pentecost, Peter told at least three thousand people that they were to "repent and be baptized" (Acts 2:38). The promise of the gift of the Holy Spirit and the forgiveness of sins was for those who could both repent and be baptized. Thus, to be baptized, we must come to terms with the fact that our ways have been sinful and that we have broken both God's laws and God's heart.

Third, baptism is a pledge of oneself to discipleship, to live the new life in Jesus. Romans 6:4-11 puts it succinctly:

We were therefore buried with him through baptism into death in order that, just as Christ was raised from the dead through the glory of the Father, we too may live a new life . . . . In the same way, count yourselves dead to sin but alive to God in Christ Jesus.

The pledge to live life as a disciple of Jesus is not something that an infant or small child can do; it can only be done by someone old enough to understand the decision, even if it is an elementary understanding.

It is true that, in the Old Testament, infants were automatically added to the covenant community when their parents had them circumcised. *But the New Covenant is different in this regard: it is only open to those who make the personal decision to trust and follow Jesus Christ.* The difference is that Christianity is not something you are born into, like an ethnic or national religion. Yes, Christian parents are to dedicate their children to God, pray for them, and raise them as followers of Christ. But in the final analysis, the Bible teaches that a person enters into a saving relationship with God *only by their personal faith.*[160] Notice how the Apostle Paul contrasted the two systems:

> In him you were also circumcised with a circumcision not performed by human hands. Your whole self ruled by the flesh was put off when you were circumcised by Christ, having been buried with him in baptism, in which you were also raised with him *through your faith in the working of God*, who raised him from the dead. When you were dead in your sins and in the uncircumcision of your flesh, God made you alive with Christ. He forgave us all our sins (Colossians 2:11-13).

Paul pointed out that baptism was like circumcision, in that through it people were brought into covenant relationship with God. But unlike circumcision, the one being baptized expressed "faith in the power of God." Baptism was an expression and a commitment of personal faith. In this sense, it was not something that parents could do for their children.

This is why the Bible never mentions infants being baptized, only people able to make the decision for themselves. And this is why infant baptism did not become a common practice until hundreds of years after the Bible was written.[161] If we are to follow the Bible, the only people who are eligible for baptism are those who are old enough to make the personal decision to turn away from their sins and trust in Jesus Christ.

There is a cluster of five truths that will direct us away from infant baptism:

i. There are *no passages* of Scripture that *clearly teach* infant baptism in the New Testament.

ii. There are *no clear examples* in the New Testament of infant baptism; all the clear and unambiguous examples are of believers being baptized. "Households" that were baptized in the Bible (Acts 11:14) included one's "relatives and close friends" (Acts 10:24-27). Infant baptism must be read into the text.

iii. The *correlation with circumcision in the New Testament is not infant baptism*, but the indwelling Holy Spirit (Romans 2:29), given when a person believes in Christ (Ephesians 1:13-14).

iv. *Believer's baptism (meaning that those who personally believe are baptized) was the practice of the church immediately after the Bible was written.* The first clear instance of infant baptism comes over one hundred years after Scripture was complete (Tertullian in 207 CE) and even then, infant baptism did not become a common practice until hundreds of years after the Bible was written. It wasn't until the time of Augustine in the early 400s that infant baptism became a common practice.

v. *Everybody agrees that believer's baptism is biblical.* But those who practice infant baptism follow something that must be read into the New Testament. In the process, something that is (at best) "an inference" becomes a substitute and replacement for what the Bible clearly teaches.

C. Baptism in the Bible was by immersion, which symbolized burial and resurrection.

The New Testament was written in the Greek language. The Greek word used in the New Testament for baptism is *baptizein*, and the verb is *baptizo*. The word means "to dip, plunge, or to immerse."[162] If God had wanted us to follow a different method of baptism, then he would have used other words to describe this act. If he had meant to say "pour," he could have used *ekcheo*, which means, "to pour out." If he wanted to say "sprinkle," he would have used *rantizo*, which means, "to sprinkle."

Immersion is the biblical method of baptism, because without exception, the Greek word for immersion (*baptizein*) is the word used when discussing this act.[163] Stated differently, if we follow the New Testament, we can know that when it speaks of baptism it means immersion because that is what the word for baptism meant in Greek.[164] Those who hold to a different position are basing it on human tradition and church history, not the Bible.

Even without knowing that the word for baptism in the original Greek was *baptizien*, one can still deduce what baptism is by the description of baptism presented in the New Testament. One of the clearest examples of this is found in Romans 6. The Apostle Paul wanted to remind these early Christians of the need for holy living. In order to remind them of God's grace and their original commitment, Paul recalled for them the time when they were baptized. He described baptism as a drama that pictured three distinct acts. The first act was a death. When a person went into the water, he or she pledged to identify with Christ's death (Romans 6:3). The second act was a burial. In this burial in water, a person re-enacted the burial of Christ (6:4). The third act was a resurrection. In coming out of the water, a person was raised to live a new kind of life (6:4-5). Whenever a person was baptized, there was a re-enactment of the death, burial, and resurrection of Jesus. No other action in water communicates this rich biblical principle except immersion.

> Or don't you know that all of us who were baptized into Christ Jesus were baptized into his death? We were therefore buried with him through baptism into death in order that, just as Christ was raised from the dead through the glory of the Father, we too may live a new life. For if we have been united with him in a death like his, we will certainly also be united with him a resurrection like his (Romans 6:3-5).

Baptism, as re-enactment of the death, burial, and resurrection of Christ, must have been immersion. For the baptism by which we commit ourselves to Christ is a pattern for the rest of our lives: we are constantly dying to self and raising Christ up (Romans 6:11).[165]

These passages show that the meaning of the commitment to follow Christ cannot be separated from the method used to make the commitment. Stated another way, the meaning is tied to the method. Full immersion in water is a re-enactment of the death, burial, and resurrection of Christ, as well as a picture of the entire Christian life: the constant dying to self and rising with Christ.

In sum, baptism by immersion was the concrete method by which people expressed faith in Christ and became Christians in the Bible. This is God's best and what we should seek as our normative practice as individuals and as a church today.

In Our Day

In our day, many confess their faith in Christ and turn from their sins without understanding or following biblical baptism. The sinner's prayer and asking Jesus into one's heart are modern substitutes that try to get at the heart or core element of our response to God's grace through making a confession as the Bible teaches (Romans 10:9-10). Faith is the key. And yes, we *can* find it in the Bible where God granted the indwelling Spirit (and salvation) apart from biblical baptism (Acts 15:7-9; 10:44-48).[166] God is able to save, as he sees fit, without baptism. But it is not what the Bible teaches as *the normative pattern.*

If we are seeking to follow the Bible, then we will insist that baptism is the method by which we make the commitment to turn from sin and place our faith in Christ. Baptism is given by God in the Bible as the prescribed way to express repentance, faith in Jesus, and a covenant commitment to the path of discipleship.

As common as the "sinner's prayer" and "asking Jesus into your heart" are, they are modern inventions, only about a hundred years old.[167] This method is not found in any of the conversions recorded in the book of Acts or in the rest of the Bible. According to the Bible, the decision to become a Christian should be expressed in water baptism as the concrete means given by God for making the commitment to trust and follow Christ.

The conversion narratives in Acts are replete with references to baptism when we would expect to find the sinner's prayer.[168] Men and women, Jews and Gentiles, hear the gospel, believe it, and are baptized.

Whenever a person questions the method given of placing one's faith in Jesus, according to the Bible, we should ask them to carefully read through the book of Acts. What does it show us? Do you find a prayer as the method of conversion or is it baptism?

Here are a few examples:

- "When the people heard this . . . those who accepted his message were baptized" (Acts 2:37, 41).
- "They believed Philip . . . they were baptized, both men and women" (Acts 8:11-12).
- "Simon himself believed and was baptized" (Acts 8:13).
- "Philip . . . told him the good news about Jesus . . . . They came to some water and the eunuch said, 'Look here is water. What can stand in the way of my being baptized?'"
- "Lydia . . . a worshiper of God. The Lord opened her heart to respond to Paul's message. When she and the members of her household were baptized . . ." (Acts 16:14-15).
- "They spoke the word of the Lord to him and to all the others in his house . . . . Then immediately he and all his household were baptized" (Acts 16:32-33).
- "Many of the Corinthians who heard him believed and were baptized" (Acts 18:8).
- "On hearing this, they were baptized in the name of the Lord Jesus" (Acts 19:5).

These texts call attention to the frequency with which baptism immediately follows receiving the word or believing the gospel. The following chart highlights the same truth:

TEXT	HEARD	BELIEVED	REPENTED	IMMERSED	HOLY SPIRIT	SAVED
Pentecost Acts 2:14-41	Heard 2:37	Believed 2:37	Repented 2:38	Immersed 2:41	At Immersion 2:38	Remission of Sins 2:38
Samaria Acts 8:5-13	Heard 8:12	Believed 8:13		Immersed 8:12-13	After Immersion 8:15-17	
Eunuch Acts 8:35-39	Heard 8:35	Believed 8:36		Immersed 8:38-39		Rejoicing 8:39
Saul Acts 9:1-18; 22:1-16; 26:9-18	Heard 9:4-6	Believed 22:10	Repented 9:9	Immersed 9:18	At Immersion 9:17-18	Washed Away Sins 22:16
Cornelius Acts 10:34-48 11:4-18; 15:7-11	Heard 10:44; 11:14	Believed 10:43	Repented 11:18	Immersed 10:48	Before Immersion 10:46-47	Purified Hearts 15:9
Lydia Acts 16:13-15	Heard 16:14	Believed 16:14		Immersed 16:15		
Jailor Acts 16:30-34	Heard 16:32	Believed 16:31	Repented 16:33	Immersed 16:33		Rejoiced 16:34
Corinthians Acts 18:8	Heard 18:8	Believed 18:8		Immersed 18:8		
Ephesian Disciples Acts 19:1-7	Heard 19:2	Believed 19:2		Immersed 19:5	After Immersion 19:6	

When we ask people to just read through the book of Acts and ask themselves, *What role did baptism play in conversions?* What do they find?

No one can find the sinner's prayer, and people see the role of baptism much more clearly when they complete this exercise.

This was also the viewpoint of the early church in the period immediately after the writing of the New Testament. Consider the following words of the earliest Church Fathers (the first leaders after the New Testament):

> Blessed are those who placed their hope in his cross and descended into water . . . we descend into the water full of sins and uncleanliness, and we ascend

bearing reverence in our heart and having hope in Jesus in our spirit (*Epistle of Barnabas* 11.1, 8, 11).

Then they are led by us to where there is water, and in the manner of the new birth by which we ourselves were born again they are born again. For at that time they obtain for themselves the washing in water in the name of God the Master of all and Father, and of our Savior Jesus Christ and of the Holy Spirit. For Christ said, "Unless you are born again, you cannot enter the kingdom of heaven" (Justin's *Apology* 1.6).

Now this is what faith does for us, as the elders, the disciples of the apostles, have handed down to us. First of all, it admonishes us to remember that we have received baptism for the remission of sins in the name of God the Father, and in the name of Jesus Christ, the Son of God, who became incarnate and died and was raised, and in the Holy Spirit of God; and that this baptism is the seal of eternal life and is rebirth into God (Irenaeus's *Proof of the Apostolic Preaching* 3).

These leaders typify the early Christian consensus.[169] They viewed baptism as the instrumental means given by God to place one's faith in Christ and accept him. This is the reason why the Nicene Creed of 381 CE clearly states that the doctrinal position of the early church held baptism as being "for the remission of sins."[170]

I believe in one God the Father Almighty; Maker of heaven and earth, and of all the things visible and invisible . . . I acknowledge one Baptism for the remission of sins; and I look for the resurrection of the dead and the life of the world to come. Amen.

This immediate practice of baptism, in contradistinction to what many churches do today, shows us what the first Christians really believed. People would not have felt this urgency for baptism unless it was God's normative way to express saving faith to become a Christian.

As a wedding ceremony makes a marriage concrete, so water baptism seals and holistically solidifies our commitment to trust and follow Jesus and become Christians. In the Bible, this was the special time in which the miracle of salvation typically occurred. In this sense, we must reclaim the teaching that baptism, as an expression of faith in Jesus, is "for the remission of sins," as both the Bible (Acts 2:38) and the earliest Christian statements of faith, like the Nicene Creed, affirm.[171]

We like to say it this way—baptism is the normative time, in the Bible, when human faith meets God's grace. This norm and this biblical pattern and practice should be restored to its rightful place and followed in our day. By this, God will be glorified and we will be blessed.

Summary

In conclusion, we have seen that, according to the Bible, a person making the commitment to place personal faith in Christ should do so through the holistic response of confession, repentance, and baptism. This is God's best as revealed in Scripture. There are five points that serve as a summary of the teaching found in this chapter.

1. Conversion is the decision to become a disciple of Jesus, someone who is willing to trust and follow him in all things.
2. The central focus of our faith is the gospel of Jesus Christ—the Good News—that by Jesus and his death, burial, and resurrection, God saves us from our sins.
3. We are to confess out loud what we believe about Jesus as part of our conversion experience. We believe that God raised Jesus from the dead, so with our mouths we declare that "Jesus is Lord."
4. Repentance is an expression of our faith that occurs when we change our mind about sin and turn from it because we now trust and follow Jesus. Genuine repentance should show itself in changed actions and behavior.
5. Water baptism brings everything together and plays the central role of expressing faith through confession, repentance, and a covenant commitment that leads to a life of discipleship. Baptism is *the normative method* given by God to express faith, receive God's promises, and fully enter into the journey of trusting and following Jesus Christ.

Is there anything that stands out to you from this section that you would like to note and discuss?

_____

_____

_____

_____

_____

CHAPTER 8

Disciple Making

Key Theme: We live as disciples (followers of Jesus) by relying on God's Spirit and participating in the local church.

We were created for a relationship with God, and commitment to be disciples of Jesus is the form or shape by which we pursue that goal. Stated differently, we were created to have a relationship with God the Father, *where we live by faith as disciples of his Son, Jesus Christ, in the power of his Spirit.*

A disciple is simply "a follower," "a student," or better, "an apprentice."[172] A Christian is "an apprentice" of Jesus Christ who is *learning from him* how to develop a deep and meaningful relationship with God. This was the original mandate that Jesus gave to his apostles.

> Matthew 28:19-20 - Therefore go and make disciples of all nations, baptizing them in the name of the Father and of the Son and of the Holy Spirit, and teaching them to obey everything I have commanded you. And surely I am with you always, to the very end of the age.

The goal of Jesus' first disciples was to "make disciples" of all nations. Jesus' call was at the same time an invitation to salvation and a summons to imitation and service.[173]

A person simply cannot be a Christian without being a disciple.[174] It would be like trying to be a human without breathing. A Christian is spiritually dead if they are not (on some level) a follower of Jesus. This truth is described in various ways (not always by using the term "disciple"). It is a major, fundamental, and underlying theme of the entire New Testament.[175] God has saved us through faith in Jesus Christ (Romans 3:22-25), and now God is transforming us into the image of Jesus Christ (2 Corinthians 3:16-17). God has predetermined that all things in our lives will work toward

Chapter 8 | Disciple Making   **181**

this end. The Apostle Paul stated it succinctly: "For those God foreknew he also predestined to be conformed to the likeness of his Son" (Romans 8:29).

The writer C.S. Lewis also put it succinctly:

> It is easy to think that the Church has a lot of different objects—education, building, missions, holding services . . . Church exists for nothing else but to draw men into Christ, to make them little Christs. If they are not doing that, all the cathedrals, clergy, missions, sermons, even the Bible itself, are simply a waste of time. God became Man for no other purpose.[176]

Dietrich Bonhoeffer was just as clear in his description:

> "Discipleship means adherence to Christ and, because Christ is the object of that adherence, it must take the form of discipleship."[177]

If we are to truly live as faithful disciples, we need to give and receive training, help, encouragement, and support so that we can learn how to become more and more like Jesus Christ. That is how the disciples of Jesus changed, and in turn, changed the world.

What a high calling it is to be a disciple of Jesus! You might say, "I know my weaknesses, and I am sure to stumble and fall. I want to live this way, but I do not have the ability."

"Yes," God answers, "you do not have the ability, but I will help you as I give to you my people, my power, and my Spirit."

So we can say with confidence, "God is my helper and he will enable me to truly follow Jesus. I will not do it perfectly, and I will often stumble and fall, but by God's grace working in me, I will make it."

1. In Acts 2, after the people had repented of their sins and been baptized, they gathered together as a church. Look at the following description of that church:

> Acts 2:42-47 - They devoted themselves to the apostles' teaching and to fellowship, to the breaking of bread and to prayer. Everyone was filled with awe at the many wonders and signs performed by the apostles. All the believers were together and had everything in common. They sold property and possessions to give to anyone who had need. Every day they continued to meet together in the temple courts. They broke bread in their homes and ate together with glad and sincere hearts, praising God and enjoying the favor of all the people. And the Lord added to their number daily those who were being saved.

How would you describe the early church and the people in it? How does this differ from your church experience?

_____

_____

_____

2. If we are willing, God helps us to live as disciples of Jesus through his Holy Spirit, who lives within a true Christian.

> Ephesians 3:14-17 - For this reason I kneel before the Father, from whom every family in heaven and on earth derives its name. I pray that out of his glorious riches he may strengthen you with power through his Spirit in your inner being, so that Christ may dwell in your hearts through faith.

How will God strengthen you with power through his Spirit?

_____

_____

_____

3. Prayer is vital for us because that is how we commune with God. Most of us need help to effectively pray. The Lord's prayer—used as a prayer outline—is a very effective prayer model. I have used it with great benefit daily for more than twenty-five years.

It is taken from Matthew 6:9-13 as a model for us to use when praying.

Our Father in heaven, hallowed be your name,

God, you are holy, separate from us, and morally pure. Let us take a few moments to pray about making you and your name pure in our minds and lives.

Your kingdom come, your will be done, on earth as it is in heaven.

God, we look forward to Jesus' return when your kingdom will be fully established. Let us take a few moments and place our hope on the merging of heaven and earth in the new heavens and new earth that you are bringing to us.

Give us today our daily bread.

We trust you for today. You teach us that today has enough trouble in it already and that today is enough for us to focus on. Provide for our basic needs today. Let us take a few moments to express them to you now.

Forgive us our debts,

God, we are sinful people, even though we try not to sin. As we reflect for a few moments, please forgive the following sins . . .

As we also have forgiven our debtors.

God, you teach us that we must forgive as we have been forgiven. We now reflect on those we need to forgive, and we forgive them.

And lead us not into temptation but deliver us from the evil one.

As we take a few moments to think about upcoming struggles, help us Lord! Guide us away from things that will tempt us. Protect us from Satan in the upcoming challenges.

Prayer draws us closer to God—what hinders you in your prayers and in what way could this model help you?

_____

_____

_____

4. God gives us church leaders to help us "grow up" and "mature." The Apostle Paul described his ministry as a leader in God's church in this light:

> Colossians 1:28-29 - We proclaim him, admonishing and teaching everyone with all wisdom, so that we may present everyone perfect in Christ. To this end I labor, struggling with all his energy, which so powerfully works in me.

2 Corinthians 3:3 - You show that you are a letter from Christ, the result of our ministry, written not with ink but with the Spirit of the living God, not on tablets of stone but on tablets of human hearts.

Galatians 4:19-20 - My dear children, for whom I am again in the pains of childbirth until Christ is formed in you, how I wish I could be with you now and change my tone, because I am perplexed about you!

How can church leaders help you to more fully mature in trusting and following Jesus?

_____

_____

_____

5. Church is essential for faithful disciples, as the Bible tells us, because Christians need to spur one another on to be and to do what Jesus wants us to do.

Hebrews 3:12-14 - See to it, brothers and sisters, that none of you has a sinful, unbelieving heart that turns away from the living God. But encourage one another daily, as long as it is called "Today," so that none of you may be hardened by sin's deceitfulness. We have come to share in Christ, if indeed we hold our original conviction firmly to the very end.

Hebrews 10:23-25 - And let us consider how we may spur one another on toward love and good deeds. Let us not give up meeting together, as some are in the habit of doing, but let us encourage one another—and all the more as you see the Day approaching.

Do you have negative experiences that make it difficult to be committed to your local church? If so, how can you heal enough to get involved?

_____

_____

_____

6. Jesus' method of discipleship was grounded in the environment of "agape love," also described as "Jesus-like love." This kind of love is a love that acts according to what is best for the other person. Jesus loved people this way and he commands us to show this same kind of love for one another. He describes it for us in John 13:34-35:

> A new command I give you: Love one another. As I have loved you, so you must love one another. By this everyone will know that you are my disciples, if you love one another.

Is it easy for you to give and receive this kind of love? Why is it so important in the local church?

_____

_____

_____

7. As Christians, God has given us all responsibilities to serve others. We do this in different ways, but especially in the local church. A simple passage teaching this concept is Romans 12. Notice what Paul says here. He says that each of us—regular, everyday Christians—is part of the body of Christ (the church), and we are members of each other. We belong to one another.

> Romans 12:4-8 - For just as each of us has one body with many members, and these members do not all have the same function, so in Christ we, though many, form one body, and each member belongs to all the others. We have different gifts, according to the grace given to each of us. If your gift is prophesying, then prophesy in accordance with your faith; if it is serving, then serve; if it is teaching, then teach; if it is to encourage, then give encouragement; if it is giving, then give generously; if it is to lead, do it diligently; if it is to show mercy, do it cheerfully.

Why is it important to use one's gifts to serve others, especially in the church?

_____

_____

_____

8. In addition to giving our time and efforts, the Bible teaches us that we should support the local church with our finances. The Bible often points to a standard of 10 percent as a good goal but not a law. The more important focus is to give generously, from the heart, not reluctantly, as one giving back to God.

> 2 Corinthians 9:6-8 - Remember this: Whoever sows sparingly will also reap sparingly, and whoever sows generously will also reap generously. Each of you should give what you have decided in your heart to give, not reluctantly or under compulsion, for God loves a cheerful giver. And God is able to bless you abundantly, so that in all things at all times, having all that you need, you will abound in every good work.

Giving cheerfully is important to God. Why do you think this is, and why is it especially important in our finances?

_____

_____

_____

As we end this study, what is the next step for you on your journey with God, and are you willing to commit to doing it with us now?

_____

_____

_____

Disciple Making

It is easy to fall into error when it comes to discipleship. On one extreme, some Christians make the mistake of thinking God will change them and make them into fully devoted followers of Jesus strictly by his mercy and grace. "No human effort can accomplish this," they say, "it is strictly a work of Grace." But this is an unbiblical and unhealthy assumption, as even a quick review of passages such as 2 Peter 1:3-11 make clear. God made us so we could freely have a relationship with him. Robots can be programmed to respond, but God made humans with free will to be able to freely relate to him and walk with him.[178] On the other hand, there are those who make the mistake of thinking that change is all by human effort. However, true spiritual transformation involves God working in us and through us (Philippians 2:12-13). God's grace and our free will work together, as a dance where one partner leads the other.

Richard Foster helps us visualize the biblical path in his book, *Celebration of Discipline*:[179]

> Picture a long, narrow ridge with a sheer drop off on either side. The chasm to the right is the way of moral bankruptcy through human strivings for righteousness. Historically this has been called the heresy of moralism. The chasm to the left is moral bankruptcy through the absence of human strivings. This has been called the heresy of antinomianism. On the ridge there is a path, the Disciplines of the spiritual life. This path leads to the inner transformation and healing for which we seek. We must never veer off to the right or the left, but stay on the path . . . . As we travel on this path, the blessing of God will come upon us and reconstruct us into the image of Jesus Christ.

Our responsive faith (expressed in our efforts) and the empowering work of God's Spirit combine to produce the character of Jesus in our lives. This change in character, in which we become more and more like Jesus, is often called "spiritual formation." Dallas Willard describes it this way: "Spiritual formation for the Christian basically refers to the Spirit-driven process of forming the inner world of the human self in such a way that it becomes like the inner being of Christ himself."[180] When our inner world has been formed in such a way, our outer actions will be more and more like those of Christ.

We Meet in Church to Become More Like Jesus

Spiritual formation is the path of discipleship. To lead us down this path, God provides the local church. Many people think of church as an event. They think of it as something you must go to each week to please God—that you go to church, worship, hear a message, and then leave. Because they think of it as a required event, they like those churches that create the best events. They look for inspiration, excellent music, and an encouraging sermon. Some of us are so busy that we also put a premium on a short church service. Like a restaurant that promises we can get in, have a great meal, and get out quickly, some of us want a church that can do the same. I recently heard of a church in Florida that has a billboard advertisement. They promise you "an inspirational service in forty-seven minutes or less." This can be very appealing to busy people: we can do the "God thing," feel better, and then get on to seemingly more important things.

Now, please understand me: I personally believe churches need to make good use of people's time. I also believe it is important to provide inspiration, excellent music, and a good sermon. I spend a significant part of every week working very hard to help create such a church service. But I also believe that concepts such as I just described miss the biblical purpose of church.

A biblically functioning church knows that its underlying purpose is to help people place their faith in Jesus Christ and then help them learn to walk so closely with God so that every day they become more like him. We were made for a Christ-centered relationship with God and people, and the purpose of church is to help us to be disciples of Jesus in that quest.

The average person measures a church's effectiveness by the not-so-holy trinity of *bodies, bucks,* and *buildings*.[181] How many people showed up? How much money did they give? And how big and beautiful are the church's buildings? These are the wrong questions! By this criterion, much of American Christianity appears healthy, but in reality, is not. If you demand little and put on a good show, you can always get a crowd. Large crowds often only demonstrate that there are talented and creative people leading the show.

Here are some better questions: How many people have come to know Christ as Savior in this church? How honest and committed to being like Christ are these people? Will they truly accept me and help me to learn to live for Christ? What kind of marriages do they have? What kind of families do they lead? Are they honest in business? Are they making a difference in their homes, neighborhoods, workplaces, and community? In short, are people really learning to trust and become like Jesus Christ in this place?

When we experience this shift, we come to expect different things from church than most people. When a church is full of people who want to grow and closely follow Jesus Christ, they look at their church and leaders in a very different light.[182] We need leaders who will teach us and mentor us in the ways of Jesus. We know that we must get help to be faithful disciples, and simply do not know how to live that way by ourselves. Disciples are made, not born.

To the extent that we are honest, each of us knows that we must learn how to "grow up" and "mature" (Ephesians 4:11-16). We need people who will show us God's way, help us in it, and if necessary, get us back on track (2 Timothy 3:14-4:4; Galatians 6:1-2). The Apostle Paul described his ministry, as a leader in God's church, in this light:

> He is the one we proclaim, admonishing and teaching everyone with all wisdom, so that we may present everyone fully mature in Christ. To this end I strenuously contend with all the energy Christ so powerfully works in me (Colossians 1:28-29).

> You show that you are a letter from Christ, the result of our ministry, written not with ink but with the Spirit of the living God, not on tablets of stone but on tablets of human hearts (2 Corinthians 3:3).

> My dear children, for whom I am again in the pains of childbirth until Christ is formed in you, how I wish I could be with you now and change my tone, because I am perplexed about you (Galatians 4:19-20)!

If maturity in Christ is our goal as a church, the questions we ask will change. What kinds of lives do these teachers live (Matthew 7:15-22)? Are the elders in this church men of character and good family men (1 Timothy 3:5; Titus 1:5-9)? What will my life look like if I follow them and imitate their lives (1 Corinthians 4:16)? Can I be honest with them, and will they help me to be the kind of person God wants me to be?

In the end, there are really only two fundamental questions to ask about a church. What should it be doing? And how successful is it at that? And the two questions that every church must ask itself are these: Are people coming to know Christ in this church? And are they developing a vital relationship with God so that they are slowly, but surely, becoming Christ-like people?

Find Discipling Relationships

Relationships are the primary means of discipleship in the Bible and in real life.[183] The concept of the isolated individual, studying the Bible by himself, learning to pray on his own, and developing a Christ-like life through personal effort is not the biblical ideal, nor is it effective. Jesus came into this world and engaged in relationships. His primary method of instruction combined teaching and modeling, in the context of relationships. Those who came after him attached themselves to him and "imitated him." They, too, developed relationships. In the midst of those relationships, they taught and demonstrated for others the path of relational discipleship.

After Jesus left the world, those who learned from his teachings and example carried his ministry on by developing relationships and teaching and modeling it for others. They then taught those who came after them to "imitate them as they imitated Christ" (see 1 Thessalonians 1:6; 1 Corinthians 4:16; Hebrews 13:7). God's method is to first send a person to develop relationships with people, and then that person points them back to God's revelation (usually in Scripture). Throughout the Bible, relationships are God's primary means of helping people learn to follow him.

That is why church is first and foremost about relationships. A church must be a place where Christians help each other learn, practice, and receive encouragement in the ways of Jesus. Encouragement in Christ and his ways is the heart of what should happen in a biblically functioning church. Church is essential, the Bible tells us, because Christians need to spur one another on to be and do what Jesus wants for us.

> See to it, brothers and sisters, that none of you has a sinful, unbelieving heart that turns away from the living God. But encourage one another daily, as long as it is called "Today," so that none of you may be hardened by sin's deceitfulness. We have come to share in Christ, if indeed we hold our original conviction firmly to the very end (Hebrews 3:12-14).

And let us consider how we may spur one another on toward love and good deeds. Let us not give up meeting together, as some are in the habit of doing, but let us encourage one another—and all the more as you see the Day approaching (Hebrews 10:23-25).

Every Christian needs to give and receive this kind of encouragement. In a biblically functioning church, we will study the Bible, break bread (the Lord's Supper), pray, worship, give money, sing, serve, and do all kinds of things. But we must remember that encouraging one another to trust and follow Jesus Christ is our primary aim. And this, more than anything else, is why a Christian must be involved in church.[184]

Few, if any, can make it without others. We must huddle together and help each other make it. Studies have proven this in both the animal and human kingdom. For example, studies have been done of the rate at which mice are killed by amphetamine (who would do such studies?!). They determined how much it takes to kill one isolated mouse. They then found that it takes *twenty times* that amount to kill a mouse if he is together with other mice in a group. But note this too: experiments have also found that if a mouse is given no amphetamine at all, it will still die within ten minutes if it is placed in the middle of a group of mice who are dying from the drug.[185]

Relationships are fundamental! This is why Jesus was so insistent that we learn to love each other in relationship.

Jesus-Like Love Is the Focus

Jesus' method of discipleship was grounded in the environment of "*agape* love," which we could describe as "Jesus-like love." This is a love that acts according to what is best for the other person. Jesus loved people this way and he commands us to show this same love for one another. Jesus described it for us in John 13:34-35:

"A new command I give you: Love one another. As I have loved you, so you must love one another. By this everyone will know that you are my disciples, if you love one another."

The last statement tells us that the chief hallmark of discipleship is Jesus-like love. It is the most important trait by which a true disciple is known.

Later in the Bible, the Apostle John describes something similar when he writes, "This is how we know what love is: Jesus Christ laid down his life for us. And we ought to lay down our lives for our brothers and sisters" (1 John 3:16). Clarity on this point is important because there are other good things in the Bible that might appear to be equally important. Yet, *agape* love is the most important.

For example, some people talk a great deal about the Holy Spirit. There are people who claim that experiences of the Holy Spirit are most important. But under inspiration, the Apostle Paul tells us, "If I speak in the tongues of men or of angels, *but do not have love*, I am only a resounding gong or a clanging cymbal" (1 Corinthians 13:1).

Some might reply that truth, orthodoxy, correct belief, loyalty to the doctrines of Scripture, and the Reformation confessions are most important. Yes, biblical doctrine is vital. We must fight the good fight of the faith. But Paul goes on and says, "If I have the gift of prophecy and can fathom all mysteries and all knowledge . . . but do not have love, I am nothing" (1 Corinthians 13:2).

Others can reply that faith is the key. But Paul says, "If I have a faith that can move mountains, but do not have love, I am nothing" (1 Corinthians 13:2). *Agape* love is the most important reflection of Christ-likeness and discipleship within the church.

Still others focus on service. Those with the gift of mercy or those drawn to social justice and serving the poor will say, "Well, the authentic mark of a true believer is in the realm of service, especially in service to the poor and the needy." Yet service does not necessarily spring from loving others. Service can spring from various kinds of motives. Love is more important: "If I give all I possess to the poor and give over my body to hardship that I may boast, but do not have love, I gain nothing" (1 Corinthians 13:3).

The most important sign of authentic discipleship, the most important attribute of the Christian life, is *agape* love.

- It is *not* a worship experience.
- It is *not* experiences of the Holy Spirit.
- It is *not* correct doctrine.
- It is *not* faith.
- It is *not* service to the poor and needy.

Agape love is the environment and foundation that God wants for the church. It is the first and most important aspect of the Holy Spirit's fruit in our lives (Galatians 5:22).

The Apostle Paul describes Jesus-like love in the following passage:

> Love is patient, love is kind. It does not envy, it does not boast, it is not proud.
> It does not dishonor others, it is not self-seeking, it is not easily angered, it keeps

no record of wrongs. Love does not delight in evil but rejoices with the truth. It always protects, always trusts, always hopes, always perseveres. Love never fails (1 Corinthians 13:4-8).

Paul describes our priority in Galatians 6:10: "Therefore, as we have opportunity, let us do good to all people, especially to those who belong to the family of believers." We must actively and devotedly love those who are within the family of believers. There is no more heart-piercing passage in this regard than the parable Jesus told in Matthew 25:31-46. In this passage, Jesus tells us that, in the end, we will be judged based on how well our faith led us to love our brothers and sisters in Christ.

> Then the King will say to those on his right, "Come, you who are blessed by my Father; take your inheritance, the kingdom prepared for you since the creation of the world. For I was hungry and you gave me something to eat, I was thirsty and you gave me something to drink, I was a stranger and you invited me in, I needed clothes and you clothed me, I was sick and you looked after me, I was in prison and you came to visit me" (vv. 34-36).

Jesus describes those who are saved as those who fed the hungry, showed hospitality to the stranger, clothed the naked, took care of the sick, and visited those in prison. The key point, often overlooked, is that Jesus is talking about how Christians took care of other Christians. Jesus says it this way: "Whatever you did for one of the least of these brothers and sisters of mine, you did for me" (Matthew 25:40). Brothers and sisters in this passage (and throughout Matthew) refer to other Christians. This passage was written to describe how true disciples will love and take care of each other and that it should be an important priority for us.

Serve God

As Christians, God has given us all responsibilities in the local church. A simple passage teaching this concept is Romans 12:4-8. Notice what Paul says here. He tells us that each of us—regular, everyday Christians—are a part of the body of Christ, and we are members of each other:

> For just as each of us has one body with many members, and these members do not all have the same function, so in Christ we, though many, form one body,

and each member belongs to all the others. We have different gifts, according to the grace given to each of us. If your gift is prophesying, then prophesy in accordance with your faith; if it is serving, then serve; if it is teaching, then teach; if it is to encourage, then give encouragement; if it is giving, then give generously; if it is to lead, do it diligently; if it is to show mercy, do it cheerfully.

Each Christian belongs to the other Christians in the local church. As a part of the body, we all have gifts and abilities, and God teaches us we must use them in his church:

As each has received a gift, use it to serve one another, as good stewards of God's varied grace: whoever speaks, as one who speaks oracles of God; whoever serves, as one who serves by the strength that God supplies—in order that in everything God may be glorified through Jesus Christ (1 Peter 4:10-11, ESV).

How can we do this if we are not actively involved in the church? The only way we can fulfill these teachings is when we are functioning as a part of the church body (see also 1 Corinthians 12:13-29; Ephesians 4:11-16).

The Leadership Structure of the Local Church

Ephesians 2 briefly describes the leadership structure of the church, with Christ as its foundation:

Consequently, you are . . . fellow citizens with God's people and also members of his household, built on the foundation of the apostles and prophets, with Christ Jesus himself as the chief cornerstone (Ephesians 2:19-20).

Here the Bible teaches that Jesus Christ is the most important part of the church and that everything else draws its meaning from him. He is both the chief cornerstone and the head of the church (Ephesians 1:20-22). The foundation of the church is also built on the apostles and prophets. The reference to apostles and prophets in this context is a reference to unique and foundational roles in the early church, which probably do not exist in the same way today.[186] These roles and the people who fulfilled them had a foundational work, and when it was done, the church had her footing and they were no longer required. We now have a record of those foundations in the Bible.

The local churches described in the Bible had a common structure, designed to be a lasting format, put in place so that churches could carry on without the apostles (1 Timothy 3:14-16).[187] The enduring local leadership structure focused on three roles:

1. *Elders/Pastors* – After churches have been established, the most important leadership for the long-term health and maturity of the church is for the church to be led by wise, tried-and-true Christian men called "elders" or "pastors" or "bishops." These three terms all refer to the same men and are used synonymously in the Bible (1 Timothy 3:1-7; Titus 1:5-9; 1 Peter 5:1-4).[188] These men are given the responsibility of "watching over," "protecting," "guiding," "leading," "teaching," and "equipping" the church.

2. *Teachers* – Evangelists and elders usually function as the main teachers in the local church, but in addition to these men, there are others who are also gifted in teaching who build up and strengthen the local church (1 Corinthians 12:28; James 3:1).

3. *Deacons* – There are often various service and administrative works in a local congregation which require the efforts of competent and committed Christians. Deacons are not mentioned in Ephesians 4, along with evangelists, elders, and teachers, because their work is not so much equipping the church for ministry as it is doing or coordinating the various works of ministry. Although there is some dispute, it is likely that both men and women served as deacons in biblical times (1 Timothy 3:8-12; Acts 6:1-8; Romans 16:2).[189]

These three roles form the leadership structure in the local church, according to the Bible. In this way, the local church matures and grows through the influence of people who have godly character, wisdom, and passion. These people, when appointed and functioning in a biblical manner, equip the church for a strong and lasting community life.

Personal Spiritual Habits

When we become Christians, we do not automatically change. We have many thoughts, habits, and behaviors that do not please God, but are a part of our character. In C.S. Lewis's *Screwtape Letters*, the main demon teaches his apprentice demon how new Christians will often fail because of their frustration when their lives do not seem to change. Even though someone has become a Christian, this evil guide boasts, "There is no need to despair; hundreds of these adult converts have been reclaimed after a brief sojourn in the enemy's camp (the church) and are now with us. All the habits of the patient, both mental and bodily, are still in our favor."[190] Even after years of being a Christian, many of us have habits and behavioral patterns that are not godly.

We need help if our habits are going to change. In 2 Peter 1, we see how God gives us everything needed for life and godliness, but at the same time, how we must respond with sustained effort and work:

> For this very reason, make every effort to add to your faith goodness; and to goodness, knowledge; and to knowledge, self-control; and to self-control, perseverance; and to perseverance, godliness; and to godliness, mutual affection; and to mutual affection, love. For if you possess these qualities in increasing measure, they will keep you from being ineffective and unproductive in your knowledge of our Lord Jesus Christ . . . . For if you do these things, you will never stumble, and you will receive a rich welcome into the eternal kingdom of our Lord and Savior Jesus Christ (2 Peter 1:5-11).

Behind this teaching, and throughout the entire Bible, is the assumption that such a life requires the development of special habits.[191] These habits are often called spiritual disciplines. Jesus used them, Paul used them, as well as Moses, Elijah, Daniel, and all the men and women God has mightily used in history. At a basic level, every person attending church is engaged in an important spiritual habit or discipline because during a church service, you will study, pray, sing songs of praise, etc.

1. Read Your Bible Daily

Reading your Bible is a specific way of listening to God. Because listening is different from merely reading, we use the word *reading* carefully. There are many ways to read words on a page. When we read God's Word with the goal of listening to God, we allow it to affect our lives in all sorts of ways.

One way Christians over the centuries have developed the skill of listening to God's voice is by meditating on Scripture as they read it. Dietrich Bonhoeffer instituted a practice of Scripture meditation among his students in the Confessional Church Seminary he helped found during Hitler's regime.[192] Even when they were eventually scattered across the country, Bonhoeffer, his students, and his friends would meditate on one passage from the Bible for thirty minutes every morning. They all chose the same reading schedule so they could think about the same passage every day. Each person would pick one word, one phrase, or one sentence and, during a time of silence, would focus their thoughts on that particular message from God.

What was unique was that those meditating received Scripture as God's personal message to them. It was as if Jesus spoke it directly to them, and it was as applicable now as it was then. This discipline, also practiced in a similar way by C. S. Lewis, was a constant source of strength and encouragement to Christians resisting the force of Nazism over Christianity. One of our goals as Christians is to be men and women who meditate on God's Word all day, even into the night.

The writer of Psalms put it well:

> Blessed is the one who does not walk in step with the wicked or stand in the way that sinners take or sit in the company of mockers, but whose delight is in the law of the Lord, and who meditates on his law day and night (Psalm 1:1-2).

We've found that one of the most important disciplines for Christians to learn is to read the Word for themselves. In working with Cally Parkinson of the Willow Creek Association on the results of the REVEAL Study, I asked her what they learned about the role of personal Bible study and how it impacts a person's growth. She summed up for me what they learned after surveying more than 250,000 Christians and 1,500 churches. She said, "The single most important thing a church can do to help people to grow is to help them to engage with God in the Bible on a daily basis."[193] For this reason, among many others, we feel that we cannot overstate the importance of developing a habit of reading the Bible every day and listening for God to speak to you as you read.

2. Pray Daily and Use a Model

Prayer is one of the few practices Jesus took for granted among his disciples. In the Sermon on the Mount, he said to them, "When you pray . . . ." He assumed they were praying people and that they just needed direction on how to pray.

In the Sermon on the Mount, Jesus focuses on praying by oneself, not for show, though prayer is appropriate in more public contexts as well. Jesus told his disciples, "When you pray, do not be like the hypocrites . . . . But when you pray, go into your room, close the door and pray to your Father, who is unseen. Then your Father, who sees what is done in secret, will reward you" (Matthew 6:5-6).

The goal is not to compartmentalize your life into separate categories: prayer time and the rest of life. The goal is that your focused times of prayer will spill into your everyday events and that you'll even pray spontaneously! As Paul said, "In every situation, by prayer and petition, with thanksgiving, present your requests to God" (Philippians 4:6).

Here is a common prayer plan:

Find a *regular time each day* (10–30 minutes).

Most people find it is easiest to find time to pray in the morning. Others find time during the day or at night. The key thing is to find a regular, daily time to pray.

Find a *regular place* (quiet, secluded, no interruptions).

It may surprise you, but most of us also need a set private place to pray. Find a place where you can pray without interruption. It will be best if there are no distractions from things like television, music, etc.

Read your *Bible* first.

You will find it much easier to pray if you first read the Bible. For some reason, most of us find that if we read the Bible, it attunes our hearts and minds. We read, and then it helps us to pray.

If you have no specific plan, I recommend that you begin by reading one chapter of the Bible. I also recommend you start with Matthew. If you read one chapter a day, you will be able to read the whole New Testament in one year in just four minutes a day. The following prayer model is referred to earlier in this book, but here it is again in a slightly different format.

Pray by following a model (like the Lord's Prayer).

Most of us need a guide to pray effectively. I have found that the Lord's Prayer—used as a prayer outline—is a very effective prayer model. I have used it with great benefit daily for over twenty years. It is taken from Matthew 6:9-13.

I. "*Our Father in heaven, hallowed be your name,*

I pray that God would be held holy in my life . . .

II. *Your kingdom come, your will be done, on earth as it is in heaven.*

I pray that God's will would be done, and I ask for help focusing on the future consummation of his kingdom, when heaven and earth become one.

III. *Give us today our daily bread.*

I pray over my needs coming up in the next 24 hours.

IV. And forgive us our debts,

I describe my sins of thought, word, and deed, and I ask God to forgive them.

V. As we also have forgiven our debtors.

With God, I review those who have hurt or attacked me, and pledge or renew my forgiveness of them.

VI. And lead us not into temptation, but deliver us from the evil one.

I pray for spiritual protection from Satan and for spiritual strength.

3. Practice Financial Giving

Jesus assumes his disciples will practice giving, including giving to the poor. "When you give to the needy, do not let your left hand know what your right hand is doing, so that your giving may be in secret. Then your Father, who sees what is done in secret, will reward you" (Matthew 6:3-4).

God's church (and its mission) and God's ministers need financial support. The Bible teaches that we are to support those who minister the Word to us and spiritually guide us (1 Corinthians 9:13-14; Galatians 6:6; 1 Timothy 5:17-18). Churches require offices, supplies, support staff, buildings, and money to support the ministry of the church and to help members in need. More money given to the church will result in better programs and care for the members and a greater impact on the lost world. Under normal circumstances, the local church needs as much support from each member as possible, to minister to as many as possible. The need is even more pronounced in new and developing churches.

In 1 Corinthians 9:13-14, the Apostle Paul teaches that the principle of financial support for the temple/priesthood in the Old Testament now applies to the ministry of the New Testament church. At the same time, the leaders of the church must give an account for all the money entrusted to them. Churches ought to regularly publish a general budget for all to see. Beyond the general budget, members are to have access, upon request, to all spending records, including the salaries of each minister and expenditures in specific ministries. The leaders ought to regularly review the church's financial matters.

There are also Old Testament principles that should lead disciples of Jesus to financially support the local church, since there is a correlation from the Old Testament priesthood (men who received Israel's tithes) to leaders in the local church. This principle leads many to recommend that tithing should go to the local church. Many groups solicit donations from people only after they have given their tithes to the local church. Certainly, our first priority in giving should be to those who teach us the Word and spiritually guide us in the local church (1 Corinthians 9:7-14; Galatians 6:6; 1 Timothy 5:17-18).

As you work through these principles, we recommend that you get help from someone who can disciple you in what to do with your money. If you can do so, it is a good thing to learn to tithe. We have learned that tithing is a *helpful heart-training tool*. It enables us to trust God and follow Jesus in a sacrificial way that avoids the extremes of unhealthy guilt ("I never give enough!") and selfishness ("I don't need to give anything!"). Stated differently, it gives us a concrete, doable, and sacrificial benchmark.

Tithing is concrete; it helps us feel that we are truly giving back to God by an objective standard that was followed in the Bible and throughout the centuries (even when Christians had a lot less money than we do today). By tithing, people have a concrete standard that leads them to give sacrificially and joyfully and then freely enjoy and utilize God's money for themselves and their families, as God intends, without the extremes of anxious guilt or stinginess.

After all that God has done for us in Christ, can we willingly and joyfully give back to him? Do we want to follow Jesus and sacrifice for others as he did? Do we know the joy of participating in the sacrifices of Christ and fixing our eyes on heaven? Martin Luther summarized giving and the entire Christian life well when he said, "The cross puts everything to the test!"[194] Can we say that we have discovered the joy of making the decision to deny ourselves, pick up the cross, and sacrificially give so that our finances help lead people to Christ and change lives? Can we sacrificially support the cause for which Jesus gave his life?

Is there anything that stands out to you from this section that you would like to note and discuss?

_____

_____

_____

_____

_____

ENDNOTES

1. Bobby Harrington and Jason Henderson, *Conviction and Civility: Thinking and Communicating Clearly about What the Bible Teaches* (Nashville: Renew, 2019). You can find it on Amazon.com and also check out the discussions at Renew.org.

2. Albert Mohler, president of Southern Theological Seminary, arrived at a similar proposal to the one I advocate here, which I adopted in the late 1990s. See Albert Mohler, "A Call for Theological Triage and Christian Maturity," May 20, 2004, http://www.albertmohler.com/2004/05/20/a-call-for-theological-triage-and-christian-maturity-2/, accessed February 2020.

3. Parts of this statement are drawn from and adapted from "The Gospel of Jesus Christ: An Evangelical Celebration," (1999), Committee on Evangelical Unity in the Gospel, P.O. Box 5551, Glendale Heights, IL, 60139-5551, which was first published in *Christianity Today* (August 1999).

4. See Matthew Bates, *Gospel Allegiance* (Ada: Brazos Press, 2019).

5. John P. Koster, *The Atheist Syndrome* (Brentwood: Wolgemuth & Hyatt, 1989).

6. The best websites on these questions, in my opinion, are reasons.org and reasonablefaith.org. Two books that are good starting points are Hugh Ross, *Navigating Genesis: A Scientist's Journey through Genesis 1–11* (Reasons to Believe Press, 2014) and Francis Collins, *The Language of God: A Scientist Presents Evidence for Belief* (Free Press, 2006).

7. Michael D. Lemonick, "Cosmic Fingerprint," *Time* (Feb. 24, 2003): 45.

8. Stephen Hawking, *The Nature of Time and Space* (Princeton Univ. Press, 1996), 20.

9. William Lane Craig, "Why I Believe God Exists," in *Why I Am a Christian* (Grand Rapids: Baker, 2001), 63.

10. Ibid., and J.P. Moreland, *Scaling the Secular City* (Grand Rapids, MI: Baker Books, 1987).

11. John M. Hayes, "The Earliest Memories of Life on Earth," *Nature* 384 (1996): 21-22. See also S. J. Mojzsis, et. al., "Evidence for Life on Earth before 3,800 Million Years Ago," *Nature* 384 (1996), 55-59; J. William Schopf, "Microfossils of the Early Archean Apex Chert: New Evidence of the Antiquity of Life," *Science* 260 (1993), 640-46.

12. H. Morowitz, "Biological Self-Replicating Systems," in *Progress in Theoretical Biology*, Ed. F. Snell (New York: Academic Press, 1967), 35.

13. Fred Hoyle, *The Intelligent Universe* (Michael Joseph, 1983).

14. This statement is summarized in Lee Strobel, *The Case For Faith* (Grand Rapids: Zondervan, 2000).

15. Quoted in Lee Strobel, *The Case For Faith* (Grand Rapids: Zondervan, 2000), 110.

16. Francis Crick, *Life Itself: Its Origin and Nature* (New York: Simon and Schuster, 1981), 88 states it well: "An honest man, armed with all the knowledge available to us now, could only state that in some sense, the origin of life appears at the moment to be almost a miracle, so many are the conditions which would have been satisfied to get it going."

17. See Hugh Ross, Kenneth Samples, and Mark Clark, *Lights in The Sky and Little Green Men* (Colorado Springs: NavPress, 2002), 39. See also www.Reasons.org for Hugh Ross's most recent updates on the statistical probabilities involved.

18. See Stephen Meyer, *Darwin's Doubt: The Explosive Origin of Animal Life and the Case for Intelligent Design*, rev. ed. (HarperOne, 2014).

19. John Barrow and Frank Tipler, *The Anthropic Cosmological Principle* (Oxford: Clarendon Press, 1986).

20. Hugh Ross, *The Creator and the Cosmos*, rev. ed. (Colorado Springs: NavPress, 2001).

21. Hugh Ross, Kenneth Samples, and Mark Clark, *Lights in The Sky and Little Green Men* (Colorado Springs: NavPress, 2002), 39. See also www.Reasons.org for Hugh Ross's most recent updates on the statistical probabilities involved.

22. Stephen Meyer, *Signature in the Cell: DNA and the Evidence for Intelligent Design*, reprint ed. (HarperOne, 2010).

23. William Bembski and James M. Kushiner, *Signs of Intelligence* (Ada: Brazos Press, 2001).

24. Hugh Ross, "The Cambrian Explosion and Evolutionists' Responses," July 27, 2016, https://reasons.org/explore/blogs/todays-new-reason-to-believe/read/todays-new-reason-to-believe/2016/07/28/the-cambrian-explosion-and-evolutionists-responses, accessed February 9, 2020.

25. Philip Johnson, *Darwin on Trial* (Downers Grove: InterVarsity Press, 1993).

26. Almost everyone has heard that the Bible says that God created the universe and everything in it, including human life, in six days. Many people, however, do not know the six days have been understood as six "ages" or six "epochs" by biblical scholars (in both ancient and modern times). If we take the Hebrew word for day ("Yom") as the preferred meaning in this context, then we will see a strong correlation between the "day-ages" of Genesis and the facts of science and the fossil record. We find that the formation work on planet earth during the first "day-

age" will match with the fact that earth—as we now know it—was formed four and one half billion years ago. We will also find that the creation of simple life forms on the third day-age correspond with the appearance of such forms on earth 3.86 billion years ago. Not only do we find a correlation between the facts of science and the Bible, we also find that the information in Genesis is the key to explaining what science *cannot explain*—namely, how life could have started in the first place. Please note that my view is *not* theistic evolution. The "Day-Age" view holds to the inerrancy of Scripture, the special creation of Adam and Eve, and all that the Bible affirms. It is the view of several early Church Fathers (like Augustine) who lived centuries before the theory of evolution was proposed. See Hugh Ross, *Creation and Time* (Colorado Springs: NavPress, 1994) and see the weekly scientific updates at the very useful website created by the *Reasons to Believe* organization at www.reasons.org.

27. Hugh Ross, *The Genesis Question* (Colorado Springs: NavPress, 1998).

28. Ed Larson and Larry Witham, "Scientists are Still Keeping the Faith," *Nature* 386 (1997): 436-37.

29. The following storyline is taken from the book written by myself and Josh Patrick, *The Disciple Maker's Handbook* (Grand Rapids: Zondervan, 2017).

30. Bill Hull describes the importance of this broader paradigm in *Christlike: The Pursuit of Uncomplicated Obedience* (Colorado Springs: NavPress, 2010), 44.

31. Lawrence Mykytiuk, "Did Jesus Exist? Searching for Evidence Beyond the Bible," *Biblical Archaeology Review* (January/February 2015): 45-51, 76.

32. N.T. Wright, *Simply Good News: Why the Gospel Is News and What Makes It Good* (Harper One, 2015), 58-59.

33. William Lane Craig may be the foremost expect of the evidence for the resurrection of Jesus. See his summary article at https://www.reasonablefaith.org/writings/popular-writings/jesus-of-nazareth/the-resurrection-of-jesus/, accessed February 21, 2020. See also a review on two of the most important books on this topic: http://christianapologeticstraining.com/2-must-read-books-on-the-resurrection-of-jesus, accessed November 28, 2016.

34. I recommend the following to those who want even more background information: *New Encyclopedia of Archaeological Excavations in the Holy Land* (5 vols.), ed. by Ephraim Stern (Jerusalem: Carta, 1993, and Washington: Israel Exploration Society/Biblical Archaeology Society, 2008).

35. For more information, see Peter Walker, *In the Steps of Jesus* (Grand Rapids: Zondervan, 2006).

36. James W. Fleming, *Turning Points in the Life of Jesus* (Biblical Resources, LaGrange, GA: 1999).

37. Thomas Friedman, *From Beirut to Jerusalem*, Revised Edition (New York: Picador, 2012), 429.

38. Joey Corbett, ed., *Ten Top Archaeological Discoveries* (Washington: Biblical Archaeological Society, 2011), 68-85.

39. See R. Steven Notley, *In the Master's Steps: The Gospels in the Land* (Carta Jerusalem, 2014).

40. Read one of the first reports on the discovery by Michael Specter, "Tomb May Hold the Bones of Priest Who Judged Jesus," *New York Times*, August 16, 1992, https://www.nytimes.com/1992/08/14/world/tomb-may-hold-the-bones-of-priest-who-judged-jesus.html.

41. Tom Powers, "Treasures in the Storeroom: Family Tomb of Simon of Cyrene," *Biblical Archaeology Review* (July–August, 2003), 46-51, 69.

42. Tom Powers, "A Second Look at the 'Alexander Son of Simon' Ossuary: Did It Hold Father and Son?" *Biblical Archaeology Society*, September 26, 2006, https://israelpalestineguide.files.wordpress.com/2010/06/alexander-simon-ossuary-a-second-look-from-bar.pdf.

43. Joseph Zias and Eliezer Sekeles, "The Crucified Man from Giv'at ha-Mitvar: A Reappraisal," *Israel Exploration Journal*, vol. 35 (1985), 22-27.

44. The author took the picture at Explorations in Antiquity in April 2015. See http://www.explorationsinantiquity.com.

45. Again, see William Lane Craig, "The Resurrection of Jesus," *Reasonable Faith*, https://www.reasonablefaith.org/writings/popular-writings/jesus-of-nazareth/the-resurrection-of-jesus/.

46. Craig Evans, *Jesus and His World: The Archaeological Evidence* (Louisville: Westminster John Knox Press, 2012), 9.

47. Josephus, *Ag. Ap.* 2.204; see Craig Evans, *Jesus and the Remains of the Day* (Peabody: Hendrickson Publishing, 2015), 70.

48. See Craig Evans, *Jesus and the Remains of the Day* (Peabody: Hendrickson Publishing, 2015), and Ann Spangler and Lois Tverberg, *Sitting at the Feet of Rabbi Jesus: How the Jewishness of Jesus Can Transform Your Faith* (Grand Rapids: Zondervan, 2009), 24.

49. Craig Blomberg, "The Historical Reliability of the Gospels," *North American Mission Board*, March 30, 2016, https://www.namb.net/apologetics-blog/the-historical-reliability-of-the-gospels-1/, accessed February 21, 2020.

50. Craig Blomberg, *Can We Still Believe the Bible? An Evangelical Engagement with Contemporary Questions* (Ada: Brazos Press, 2014). See also Michael Kruger, *The Question of Canon* (Downers Grove: InterVarsity Press, 2013), Michael Kruger, *The Canon Revisited: Establishing the Origins and Authority of the New Testament Books* (Wheaton: Crossway, 2012).

51. See Kenneth Kitchen, *On the Reliability of the Old Testament* (Grand Rapids: Wm. B. Eerdmans, 2006), James K. Hoffmeier, *Israel in Egypt: The Evidence for the Authenticity of the*

Exodus Tradition (New York: Oxford University Press, 1999), and Anso Rainer and Steven Notley, *The Sacred Bridge* (Jerusalem: Carta, 2005).

52. Walter C. Kaiser, *The Old Testament Documents: Are They Reliable* (Downers Grove: IVP Academic, 2001) covers the state of the evidence and makes a positive case.

53. For an in-depth study on this topic, see John Wenham, *Christ and the Bible*, 3rd ed. (Portland: Wipf & Stock, 2009).

54. Clark H. Pinnock, *The Scripture Principle* (New York: Harper and Row, 1984), 48.

55. Robert Earl Woodrow, "The Nature of Biblical Authority and The Restoration Movement" (M.A. Thesis, Abilene Christian University, 1983), 196. See also John Bright, *The Authority of the Old Testament* (Grand Rapids: Baker Book House, 1975).

56. For the question of the Christian and the Sabbath, consult D. A. Carson, ed., *From Sabbath To Lord's Day* (Grand Rapids: Zondervan Publishing House, 1982).

57. For more detailed information about what follows, consult the seminal works of F. F. Bruce, *The Canon of Scripture* (Downers Grove: InterVarsity Press, 1988), and Bruce M. Metzger, *The Canon of the New Testament* (Oxford: Oxford University Press, 1987).

58. F. F. Bruce, *The Canon of Scripture*, 17.

59. Ibid., quoting R.P.C. Hanson, *Origen's Doctrine of Tradition* (London: S.P.C.K., 1954).

60. See Carson and Moo, *An Introduction to the New Testament* (Grand Rapids: Zondervan, 2005) and Donald Guthrie, *Introduction to the New Testament* (Downers Grove: InterVarsity Press, 1979).

61. Clark Pinnock, *The Scripture Principle* (Vancouver: Regent College Publishing, 1984), 52.

62. See Bruce M. Metzger, *The Canon of the New Testament* (Oxford: Oxford University Press, 1987).

63. This is a distinctive and important fact that is in contradistinction to the claims of the Roman Catholic Church. This point was definitively stated by Oscar Cullmann in the advanced debates leading up to Vatican II; see, "The Tradition," in *The Early Church* (London: SCM Press, 1956).

64. Ibid., 91.

65. Pinnock, *The Scripture Principle*, 81-82.

66. Again, the canon of the church was not delivered to the church by some ecclesiastical authority. On the contrary, as the canon was refined in the early centuries, the councils that were held simply recognized the practices and the beliefs of early Christians who had accepted these works from earlier times. The timeless words of F. F. Bruce put the matter plainly in his book, *The New Testament Documents* (Grand Rapids: Wm. B. Eerdmans, 1981), 27: "The New Testament books did not become authoritative for the church because they were formally

included in a canonical list; on the contrary, the church included them as divinely inspired, recognizing their innate worth and generally apostolic authority, direct or indirect . . . . What these councils did was not to impose something new upon the Christian communities but to codify what was already the general practice of those communities."

67. For the dating of these books, see R. K. Harrison, *Introduction to The Old Testament* (Grand Rapids: Wm. B. Eerdmans, 1969). Also, much that follows comes from Harrison's work.

68. See John F. Wenham, *Christ and The Bible* (Downers Grove: InterVarsity Press, 1973).

69. The Rylands Papyrus 458, is dated at 150 BCE; the Qumran papyrus, is dated in the first century CE; and, the Chester Beatty Papyri is dated at 150 CE There are other translations such as the Old Latin Version (200 CE), the Peshitta (2nd or 3rd century CE), and the Ethiopic Version (4th century CE), etc.

70. Harrison, *Introduction to The Old Testament*, 216.

71. Gleason L. Archer, Jr., *A Survey of Old Testament Introduction* (Chicago: Moody Bible Institute, 1974), has more information on the dates, composition, etc.

72. All of the Dead Sea Scrolls have not yet been thoroughly reviewed by scholars. Some of the manuscripts of the Old Testament may date as far back as 300+ BCE. See the more recent editions of *Biblical Archaeology Review* for the latest and most up-to-date information on the Dead Sea Scrolls.

73. In his book, *The Text of the Old Testament* (Grand Rapids: Wm. B. Eerdmans Pub. Co., 1979; Translated from *Der Test Des Alten Testaments*, 1973), 19. Ernest Wurthwein states the following about the care exercised in the transmission of the Hebrew Text from the time of Qumran onward: "From this time onward the transmission of the text was to be governed by strict regulations. No pains were spared in preventing errors from entering the sacred text, or in discovering and eliminating them if they should creep in . . . . This was the purpose of the scribe's meticulous work. They counted verses, words, and letters of the Law and other parts of the Scriptures as a procedural aid in preparing manuscripts and in checking their accuracy."

74. Gleason L. Archer, Jr., *A Survey of Old Testament Introduction* (Chicago: Moody Bible Institute, 1974), 66-67.

75. Harrison, *Introduction to The Old Testament*, 255.

76. Walter Kaiser, *The Old Testament Documents: Are They Reliable and Relevant?* (Grand Rapids: InterVarsity Press, 2001).

77. The New Testament text which we have today (as will be shown) is a reliable representation of the original text from the late first century. A handful of radical leftist scholars (The Jesus Seminar), often presenting themselves as "mainstream scholarship," have raised questions about the historical reliability of the events referred to by the writers of the New Testament

texts. These questions have been answered by other mainstream scholars. See Craig Blomberg, *The Historical Reliability of the Gospels* (Downers Grove: InterVarsity, 1987); Paul Barnett, *Jesus and the Logic of History* (Grand Rapids: Eerdmans, 1997); and Luke Timothy Johnson, *The Real Jesus* (San Francisco: Harper SanFrancisco, 1996). For an excellent popular survey, see Lee Strobel, *The Case for Christ* (Grand Rapids: Zondervan, 1998).

78. To the chagrin of the radicals, the Gnostic gospels, for example, were never accepted by the church and never will be accepted because they were written after the writings of the apostles, they never taught the apostolic faith of the apostles, and they were never widely accepted in the churches from the beginning. They have always been regarded as heretical. See the important works of Ben Witherington, *The Jesus Quest* (Downers Grove: InterVarsity Press, 1995), and Philip Jenkins, *Hidden Gospels: How the Search for Jesus Lost Its Way* (New York: Oxford University Press, 2001).

79. The standard textbook on this topic is Bruce M. Metzger's, *The Text of the New Testament* (Oxford: Oxford University Press, 1968).

80. See F. F. Bruce, *The Canon of Scripture* (Downers Grove: InterVarsity Press, 1988), and Bruce M. Metzger, *The Canon of the New Testament* (Oxford: Oxford University Press, 1987).

81. Ibid.

82. Quoted in Lee Strobel, *The Case for Christ* (Grand Rapids: Zondervan, 1998). F.F. Bruce, *The New Testament Documents: Are They Reliable*, 19-20 says something very similar to Metzger: "The margin of doubt left in the process of recovering the exact original wording is not so large as might be feared; it is in truth remarkably small. The variant readings about which any doubt remains among textual critics of the New Testament affect no material question of historic fact or of Christian faith and practice."

83. Pinnock, *The Scripture Principle*, 55.

84. I. Howard Marshall, *Biblical Inspiration* (Grand Rapids: Wm. B. Eerdmans Publishing Co., 1982), 53.

85. This is not to say that tradition and history are not important in correct interpretation. They are also very important matters. For an excellent contemporary statement of the nature of Scripture for Christians today, see Anthony N.S. Lane, "Sola Scriptura? Making Sense of a Post-Reformation Slogan," in *A Pathway into The Holy Scripture*, ed. Philip Satterthwaite and David Wright (Grand Rapids: William B. Eerdmans Publishing Co., 1994).

86. The Westminster Confession of Faith correctly states the principle with the following words: "The Scriptures manifest themselves to be the Word of God, by their majesty and purity, by the consent of all the parts, and the scope of the whole, which is to give all glory to God; by their light and power to convince and convert sinners, to comfort and build up believers unto

salvation: but the Spirit of God bearing witness by and with the Scriptures in the heart of man, is alone able fully to persuade it that they are the very Word of God."

87. Quoted in Michael Green, *Illustrations for Biblical Preaching* (Grand Rapids: Baker Book House, 1989), 30.

88. R.C. Sproul, *The Holiness of God* (Wheaton: Tyndale House Publishers, 1985), 53.

89. We cannot understand God or the Bible until we understand that God is holy! This is probably why when Jesus taught us a model prayer—the Lord's prayer—that prayer began with the petition for God's name to be held "holy." We pray, "Our Father in heaven, *hallowed* be your name" (Matthew 6:9). This prayer draws us to the heart of God: His name must be held up among us as "holy."

90. On the question of whether this is primarily a literal or a symbolic account of humankind's origin, see Clark H. Pinnock, "Climbing Out of a Swamp: The Evangelical Struggle to Understand the Creation Texts," *Interpretation* 63 (1989): 143-55; Bruce Waltke, "The First Seven Days: What is the Creation Account Trying to Tell Us?" *Christianity Today* (August 12, 1988): 42-46; and Henri Blocher, *In the Beginning: The Opening Chapters of Genesis* (Downers Grove: InterVarsity Press, 1984).

91. Francis Schaeffer did a masterful job showing the parameters for the creation-science debate almost forty years ago in his book, *No Final Conflict* (Downers Grove: InterVarsity, 1975). In addition to the works referred to above, see *The Genesis Debate*, ed. Ronald Youngblood (Grand Rapids; Baker Book House, 1990), and Hugh Ross's, *Navigating Genesis* (Colorado Springs: NavPress, 2014).

92. For more information, see Hugh Ross, "Four Views of the Biblical Creation Account," *Reasons*, August 8, 2000, https://www.reasons.org/explore/publications/rtb-101/read/rtb-101/2000/08/08/four-views-of-the-biblical-creation-account, Duane Garrett, *Rethinking Genesis* (Mentor, 2001), and the up-to-date information by Biologos, such as Mitchell Prins, "Why Should Christians Consider Evolutionary Creation?" *BioLogos*, https://biologos.org/common-questions/why-should-christians-consider-evolutionary-creation. The following is a longer summary.

The Appearance of Age – *The 24-Hour Day Interpretation* is often called the literal view or the 24-hour view. It is the natural, literal reading. It accepts the first chapter of Genesis as historical and chronological in character and takes the creation week as consisting of six 24-hour days, followed by a 24-hour Sabbath. Since Adam and Eve were created as mature adults, so the rest of creation came forth from its Maker as mature, appearing old. The Garden included full-grown trees and animals, which Adam named. Those holding this view believe this is the normal understanding of the creation account and that this has been the most commonly held understanding of this account both in Jewish and Christian history. In this view, the universe appears to be older than it is because it was created in a mature state.

The Re-created World – According to the *Creation & Re-Creation Interpretation*, the key interpretive issue is the translation of the beginning of Genesis 1:2. Genesis 1:1 describes the creation of the heaven and earth. Genesis 1:2 is then normally translated to read, "The earth was formless and empty." But it can also be translated to say, "The earth *became* formless and empty." Some Hebrew scholars say that Genesis 1:2 could be describing a re-creation of the world after some type of cosmic breakdown. Before the re-creation, some hypothesize there was the initial creation and eventual extinction of the dinosaurs and other life forms. According to this view, the re-creation of the world is a recent event, literally occurring in six twenty-four hours days not too many thousands of years ago. The fossil and cosmological evidence for an old universe could be compatible with this viewpoint.

Six Days to Reveal Creation – The *Genesis Creation Revelation Theory* says Genesis 1 and parts of Genesis 2 describe Moses' creation vision. Many proponents of this view argue that events were revealed to Moses during six consecutive days, and each day represents what was revealed, not what historically happened, in a 24-hour period. Duane Garrett argues that the seven creation days have a six plus one heptadic structure, which is found elsewhere in apocalyptic literature. In Revelation 6:1-8:1; 8:2-11:19; and 16:1-21, "The pattern is of six related events followed by a seventh": seven seals, seven trumpets, and seven bowls of wrath, with the seventh component of each series fundamentally different from the preceding six.

Six Days as a Symbolic Structure – The distinctive feature of the *Framework Interpretation View* is its understanding of the week as a creative metaphor for the ancient Israelites. The Hebrew week is a framework by which Moses described the creation of the world. According to this interpretation, Moses used the metaphor of the week to narrate God's acts of creation symbolically, but there is no need for a correspondence or concordance with the facts of creation (as in the "day-age" theory). The week is simply a symbol; it is figurative. It is a symbol for God's creative acts, described as happening through the figurative framework of a week. The purpose of the metaphor is to call Adam to imitate God in work, with the promise of entering his Sabbath rest (the seventh day). Creation events are grouped in two triads of days: Days 1-3 (creation's kingdoms) are paralleled by Days 4-6 (creation's kings). Adam is king of the earth; God is the King of Creation.

93. Hugh Ross, *Navigating Genesis: A Scientist's Journey through Genesis 1-11* (Covina: RTB Press, 2014).

94. Ibid.

95. See https://reasons.org/explore/blogs/todays-new-reason-to-believe/read/tnrtb/2006/07/11/creation-timeline, accessed February 29, 2020.

96. For a technical word study that demonstrates the intimacy language of the account, consult Jon Hauser, "Genesis 2–3: The Theme of Intimacy and Alienation," in *Art and Meaning: Rhetoric in Biblical Literature*, ed. David J. Clines, David. M. Gunn, and Alan. J. Hauser (Sheffield, England: JSOT Press, 1982), 20–36. On the question of the relationship between the creation account and the fossil evidence for evolution, etc., see Gleason Archer, *A Survey of Old Testament Introduction* (Chicago: Moody Press, 1974) for various Biblical viewpoints.

97. See John T. Willis, *Genesis*, The Living Word Commentary on the Old Testament (Austin: Sweet Publishing Company, 1979), 110.

98. See Gordon Wenham, *Genesis 1–15*, The Word Biblical Commentary Series (Waco: Word Publishing Company, 1989), 61.

99. See Bruce Vawter, *On Genesis: A New Reading* (Garden City, New York: Doubleday & Company, 1977), 74-75.

100. Quoted in Wenham, *Genesis*, 69.

101. Wenham has useful information on this point, *Genesis*, 64.

102. Ibid. I am indebted to Wenham for much of this material.

103. Richard Lovelace traces this theme out in more detail. See *The Dynamics of the Spiritual Life: An Evangelical Theology of Renewal*, expanded ed. (Downers Grove: IVP Academic, 2020).

104. R.C. Sproul, *The Holiness of God* (Wheaton: Tyndale House Publishers, 1985), 53.

105. When God first revealed himself to the nation of Israel, he started with Moses, their leader. At first Moses did not know God and he was by himself in a desert area. God caused a bush to be on fire, but it did not burn up. It got Moses' attention. So Moses drew closer and closer, looking at the bush, trying to figure out why it kept burning, without burning up. As Moses approached the bush, God spoke to him out loud.

"Do not come any closer," God said. "Take off your sandals, for the place where you are standing is holy ground." Then he said, "I am the God of your father, the God of Abraham, the God of Isaac and the God of Jacob" (Exodus 3:5-6).

God's command for Moses to take off his sandals sounds strange to us, but to the ancient people it didn't. Moses' shoes were a symbol of his stature; he was of the earth, and he was creaturely. Moses was standing on holy ground—in the presence of God—and Moses was unholy. The impact of this encounter on Moses was immediate and life-changing. The Bible says that Moses hid his face, because he was afraid to look at God (Exodus 3:6). Fear is the automatic and appropriate human response to God's holiness. This is why the Bible teaches that "the fear of the Lord is the beginning of knowledge" (Proverbs 1:7). God's holiness must be placed in the context of God's other qualities, especially with the reality that God is love. As much as God is love, God is holy. We are going to look at God's other qualities, especially his love, but we first must fully grasp his holiness. Most people do not understand this concept anymore.

God sought to help the nation of Israel appreciate his holiness by the institution of a special place of worship called the tabernacle (God's dwelling place), and in this tabernacle, they could only worship God if they sacrificed animals to take away their sins. The sacrifices for sin removed human sin and allowed them to connect with a holy God. God also established a special priesthood—men who represented God. To represent God's holiness, the priests had to meet specific qualifications, carefully follow ceremonial procedures, and wear special clothes, including a headband that summed it all up by saying, "HOLY TO THE LORD" (Exodus 28:36-37).

God's holiness was so important that he also required daily sacrifices from the people for their sins. God gave the priests clear instructions about how the required sacrifices were to be made. Nadab and Abihu, the first two priests, failed to treat God as holy. They disobeyed his specific ceremonial commandments.

Aaron's sons Nadab and Abihu took their censers, put fire in them and added incense; and they offered unauthorized fire before the LORD, contrary to his command. So fire came out from the presence of the LORD and consumed them, and they died before the LORD. Moses then said to Aaron, "This is what the LORD spoke of when he said: 'Among those who approach me I will be proved holy; in the sight of all the people I will be honored'" (Leviticus 10:1-3).

This rare and shocking account showed the Israelites that God was not to be treated lightly. God killed these priests to set an example, whereby the Israelites would never forget God's holiness. (I am glad to know that this is not God's common practice today!)

At the center of God's holy tabernacle was the "most holy place," the intimate dwelling of God, where only the high priest could go, once a year, and only after elaborate cleansing ceremonies and animal sacrifices for sin (Leviticus 16). It wasn't just the tabernacle and sacrificial system that communicated God's holiness. God also established a very strict judicial system which gave quick and severe punishment for those who violated his holiness. Once it was proved that a man or a woman was guilty of *willfully* committing certain severe sins, God commanded that they be stoned to death. To those of us living in the twenty-first century, this teaching seems exceptionally harsh. But behind this teaching, God was helping his people to "Be holy because I, the LORD your God, am holy" (Leviticus 19:2). It is frightening to see how widely accepted these sinful behaviors are today, especially in the light of God's holiness revealed in the Bible.

The Bible repeatedly teaches us to remember that God is holy. Let me state it in the strongest terms possible: we cannot understand God or the Bible until we understand that God is holy! This is probably why when Jesus taught to us a model prayer—the Lord's Prayer—that prayer begins with the petition for God's name to be held "holy." We pray, "Our Father in heaven, *hallowed* be your name" (Matthew 6:9). This prayer draws us to the heart of God: His name must be held up among us as "holy."

106. The garden of Eden was likely removed from the earth during Noah's flood, if not before. See Hugh Ross, *The Genesis Question* (Colorado Springs: NavPress, 1998).

107. See the more detailed explanation of this point by R. Alan Streett, *Heaven on Earth: Experiencing the Kingdom of God in the Here and Now* (Eugene: Harvest House Publishers, 2013).

108. Stephen R. Covey, *The 7 Habits of Highly Effective People: Powerful Lessons in Personal Change* (New York: Free Press, 2004), 95-144.

109. A.T. Robertson, *Word Pictures*, vol. 14 (Nashville: B & H Publishing, 1958), 525.

110. This line of thought is drawn from one of my former Bible College teachers, Jimmy Allen, *Survey of Romans*, rev. ed. (Searcy: Harding College Press, 1976), 31.

111. C.E.B. Cranfield, *Romans: A Shorter Commentary* (Grand Rapids, MI: Eerdmans, 1985), 211-12.

112. See Bill Hull, *Conversion and Discipleship: You Can't Have One Without the Other* (Grand Rapids: Zondervan, 2016).

113. The following material is taken from the book by Bobby Harrington, *How to Trust and Follow Jesus: A Study Guide* (Renew, 2017), 14.

114. We are grateful for several scholars whose work on the gospel has helped us. We especially commend the extensive work on the New Testament teaching on the gospel in Matthew Bates's book, which we were able to preview, *Gospel Allegiance* (Ada, MI: Brazos, 2019).

115. For an in-depth study on the New Testament meaning of faith, see Matthew Bates, *Salvation by Allegiance Alone: Rethinking Faith, Works, and the Gospel of Jesus the King* (Grand Rapids: Baker Academic, 2017).

116. For more on this definition of a disciple, see Discipleship.org, and Jim Putman and Bobby Harrington, *DiscipleShift* (Grand Rapids: Zondervan, 2013).

117. Parts of this statement are drawn from and adapted from "The Gospel of Jesus Christ: An Evangelical Celebration," (1999), Committee on Evangelical Unity in the Gospel, P.O. Box

5551, Glendale Heights, IL, 60139-5551, which was first published in *Christianity Today* (August 1999).

118. Ibid.

119. Matthew Bates devotes significant time to this correlation in his book, *Salvation by Allegiance Alone: Rethinking Faith, Works, and the Gospel of Jesus the King* (Grand Rapids: Baker Academic, 2017).

120. We're not saying God can't save those from these *Christian groups,* but when he does, it will be the result of people finding the true gospel—and in most cases, it will be in spite of what these groups teach about it.

121. Thomas Oden, *The Word of Life*, Systematic Theology: Volume Two (San Francisco: Harper Collins, 1989), 350.

122. See the book of Leviticus for full details.

123. This line of thought is drawn from one of my former Bible College teachers, Jimmy Allen, *Survey of Romans*, rev. ed. (Searcy: Harding College Press, 1976), 31.

124. C.E.B. Cranfield, *Romans: A Shorter Commentary* (Grand Rapids: Eerdmans, 1985), 211-12.

125. C.A. Dismore, *Atonement in Literature and Life* (1906), quoted in J.K. Mozley, *The Impassibility of God: Survey of Christian Thought* (Cambridge: Cambridge University Press, 1926), 148.

126. Peter Cotterell quoted in John Stott, *Evangelical Truth: A Personal Plea for Unity, Integrity, and Faithfulness* (Downers Grove: InterVarsity Press, 1999), 45-46.

127. A good book on the exclusivity of salvation through Christ is by Ronald Nash, *Is Jesus The Only Savior?* (Grand Rapids: Zondervan, 1994).

128. Robertson, *Word Pictures*, vol. 14, 525.

129. Philip Yancey, "What's So Amazing About Grace? Part 1," *Christianity Today*, October 6, 1997, https://www.christianitytoday.com/ct/1997/october6/7tb52a.html.

130. Scot McKnight, *Kingdom Conspiracy* (Ada: Brazos, 2014) for an in-depth presentation of what follows.

131. As late as 2010, up to 85 percent of Americans claimed to be Christian, though it had fallen to 76 percent by 2015. See George Barna, *Futurecast* (Carol Stream: Tyndale, 2011), Kindle location 124. See also the Navigators, *The State of Discipleship* (Tyndale, 2015).

132. Dallas Willard, *The Great Omission: Reclaiming Jesus's Essential Teachings on Discipleship* (New York: HarperOne, 2006), xv. Willard encourages us to think of disciples as "apprentices of Jesus."

133. Jim Putman and Bobby Harrington (with Robert Coleman), *DiscipleShift: Five Shifts to Help Your Church Make Disciples Who Make Disciples* (Grand Rapids: Zondervan, 2013).

134. Spiritual formation is a big topic, and we are grateful for writers such as Richard Foster, Dallas Willard, John Ortberg, and others who describe how the Holy Spirit brings change. In this book, we focus more on the relational components used by the Holy Spirit to develop Christlike people. If we had more space, we would use it to advocate spiritual practices and disciplines. We are grateful for those who teach us about these habits and commend them to our readers.

135. See A.T. Robertson, *Word Pictures in the New Testament* (Nashville, Broadman, 1930; reprint, New York: R.R. Smith, Inc., 1931), 4:525.

136. See David Platt, *Follow Me: A Call to Die. A Call to Live* (Carol Stream: Tyndale House, 2013) and Robert Picirilli, *Discipleship: The Expression of Saving Faith* (Nashville: Randall House, 2013).

137. John MacArthur, Jr., *The Gospel According to Jesus* (Grand Rapids: Zondervan Publishing House, 1988), 178.

138. See David Platt, *Follow Me: A Call to Die. A Call to Live* (Carol Stream: Tyndale House, 2013) and Robert Picirilli, *Discipleship: The Expression of Saving Faith* (Nashville: Randall House, 2013).

139. As late as 2010, up to 85 percent of Americans claimed to be Christian, though it had fallen to 76 percent by 2015. See George Barna, *Futurecast* (Carol Stream: Tyndale, 2011), Kindle location 124. See also the Navigators, *The State of Discipleship* (Carol Stream: Tyndale, 2015).

140. Ed Stetzer, "Barna: How Many Have a Biblical Worldview?," *Christianity Today*, March 9, 2009, http://www.christianitytoday.com/edstetzer/2009/march/barna-how-many-have-biblical-worldview.html. Accessed April 17, 2020.

141. See C.B. Cranfied, *Romans: A Shorter Commentary* (Grand Rapids, MI: Eerdmans, 1985), 257. In regard to Romans 10:9-10, he states, "It seems clear that 'Jesus is Lord' was already an established confession formula. It is probable that it was used in connection with baptism . . . ."

142. For more information see Walter Bauer, *A Greek-English Lexicon of the New Testament and Other Early Christian Literature.* 2nd. ed., rev. by William Arndt and F. Wilbur Gingrich (Chicago: University of Chicago Press, 1979).

143. The position on the meaning of baptism, which is sketched out here, is the earliest Christian understanding of baptism, reflected in the writing of Christians in the first centuries. See the Nicene Creed of 381 CE in *The Creeds of Christendom*, 3 Volumes, edited by Philip Schaff (Grand Rapids: Baker Book House, 1996). For a technical and scholarly support, Everett Ferguson: *Baptism in the Early Church: History, Theology, and Liturgy in the First Five Centuries* (Grand Rapids: Wm. B. Eerdmans Publishing Co., 2009). For information on the

historical heritage of this view see David Fletcher, ed., *Baptism and the Remission of Sins: An Historical Perspective* (Joplin: College Press, 1990).

144. *Baptism: What the Bible Teaches*, by Tony Twist, Bobby Harrington, and David Young (Renew, 2019) available on Renew.org or through Amazon.com.

145. A child's inherent standing before God (Matthew 19:13-15) and the sanctifying influence of the parent's faith (1 Corinthians 7:14) influence children until they reach the necessary level of spiritual development where they can make the personal decision to turn away from sin (even as a future life path) to faith in Christ.

146. For more information, see Walter Bauer, *A Greek-English Lexicon of the New Testament and Other Early Christian Literature.* 2nd ed., rev. by William Arndt and F. Wilbur Gingrich (Chicago: University of Chicago Press, 1979). Also, consult the comprehensive study of Thomas Conant, *The Meaning and Use of Baptizein* (Grand Rapids: Kregel Publications, 1977).

147. See Paul Chitwood, *The Sinner's Prayer: An Historic and Theological Analysis* (PhD Dissertation, Southern Baptist Theological Seminary, 2001).

148. The Nicene Creed of CE 381 states "I acknowledge one Baptism for the remission of sins." See *The Creeds of Christendom*, 3 Volumes, edited by Philip Schaff (Grand Rapids: Baker Book House, 1996).

149. See N.T. Wright, *Simply Good News: Why the Gospel Is News and What Makes It Good* (New York: HarperOne, 2015).

150. Bill Hull, *Conversion and Discipleship: You Can't Have One Without the Other* (Grand Rapids: Zondervan, 2016).

151. Ken C. Moser, *The Way of Salvation* (Delight: Gospel Light Publishing Co., 1933), 31, 33, and 41-42.

152. See C.E.B. Cranfied, *Romans: A Shorter Commentary* (Grand Rapids: Wm. B. Eerdmans Publishing, 1985), 257. In regard to Romans 10:9-10, he states, "It seems clear that 'Jesus is Lord' was already an established confession formula. It is probable that it was used in connection with baptism."

153. For more information, see Walter Bauer, *A Greek-English Lexicon of the New Testament and Other Early Christian Literature.* 2nd ed., rev. by William Arndt and F. Wilbur Gingrich (Chicago: University of Chicago Press, 1979).

154. K. C. Moser, *The Way of Salvation*, 63-64.

155. The position on the meaning of baptism, which is sketched out here, is the earliest Christian understanding of baptism, reflected in the writing of Christians in the first centuries. See the *Nicene Creed* of 381 CE in *The Creeds of Christendom*, 3 vols., ed. Philip Schaff (Grand

Rapids: Baker Book House, 1996). For a technical and scholarly support, see G.R. Beasley Murry, *Baptism in the New Testament* (Grand Rapids: Wm. B. Eerdmans Publishing Co., 1962), the standard English-written scholarly work on baptism in our day. For information on the historical heritage of this view, see David Fletcher, ed., *Baptism and the Remission of Sins: An Historical Perspective* (Joplin: College Press, 1990). Larry Stalley did extensive research for a Master's degree on baptism in the Post-Apostolic church; see Larry Stalley, *Baptism in the Early Post-Apostolic Church* (M. A. R. Guided Research, Harding University Graduate School, 1980). See also Jack P. Lewis, "Baptismal Practices of the Second and Third Century Church," *Restoration Quarterly*, vol. 26 (1983): 1-17; and Everett Ferguson, *The Early Christians Speak*, reprint (Abilene: ACU Press, 1994). On a popular level, consult Jack Cottrell, *Baptism: A Biblical Study* (Joplin: College Press, 1989) and F. LaGard Smith, *Baptism: The Believers Wedding Ceremony* (Cincinnati: Standard Publishing Company, 1989), although a more positive and extensive discussion about un-immersed believers would have been helpful.

156. Some dispute the English rendition of this passage, arguing that the preposition *eis* ("for the") somehow means that people are baptized "because of the" forgiveness of sins (making baptism simply a symbol of salvation previously received). Technically and linguistically, this is not correct. The English translations have it right; see Jack Cottrell, *Baptism: A Biblical Study* (Joplin: College Press, 1989), 55-61. For the syntactical and grammatical background, see Carroll D. Osburn, "The Third Person Imperative in Acts 2:38," *Restoration Quarterly* (1983): 81-84.

157. I. Howard Marshall, The *Acts of the Apostles*, in The Tyndale New Testament Commentaries (Grand Rapids: InterVarsity Press, 1980), 81.

158. We are not saying that every reference to baptism that uses this phrase means the same thing. In Matthew 28:19, it seems that "the name of the Father, Son, and Holy Spirit" has meaning as a reference to ownership. See the technical reference works listed above.

159. Walter Kaiser, Peter Davids, F.F. Bruce, and Manfred Brauch, *Hard Sayings of the Bible* (Downers Grove: InterVarsity Press, 1996), 718.

160. A child's inherent standing before God (Matthew 19:13-15) and the sanctifying influence of the parent's faith (1 Corinthians 7:14) influence children until they reach the necessary level of spiritual development where they can make the personal decision to turn away from sin (even as a future life path) to faith in Christ.

161. The explicit initiation of infant baptism dates to the latter part of the second century (one hundred years after the Bible was written). We know that the church father Tertullian opposed it on the grounds that it would be safer and more profitable to wait until faith was formed in the believing adult. Infant baptism did not become an established practice until the

fourth century. See F. LaGard Smith, *Baptism: The Believer's Wedding Ceremony* (Cincinnati: Standard Publishing, 1989), 115-16. See also Larry Stalley, *Baptism In The Early Post-Apostolic Church* (M. A. R. Guided Research, Harding University Graduate School, 1980); Jack P. Lewis, "Baptismal Practices of the Second and Third Century Church," *Restoration Quarterly*, vol. 26 (1983): 1-17; and Everett Ferguson, *The Early Christians Speak*, reprint (Abilene: ACU Press, 1994). Attempts to find infant baptism within the description of households coming to faith typically minimizes the fact that "households" in the ancient world typically included relatives, in-laws, and slaves. A careful examination of the conversions in Acts 10 demonstrates this truth.

162. For more information, see Walter Bauer, *A Greek-English Lexicon of the New Testament and Other Early Christian Literature.* 2nd ed., rev. by William Arndt and F. Wilbur Gingrich (Chicago: University of Chicago Press, 1979). Also, consult the comprehensive study of Thomas Conant, *The Meaning and Use of Baptizein* (Grand Rapids: Kregel Publications, 1977).

163. In Leviticus 14:15, in the Septuagint (the Greek translation of the Old Testament), each of these words is used to indicate the three distinct actions that they describe: pouring, sprinkling, and dipping.

164. The first instance of pouring is found in the Didache, written about 20 years after the last book of the New Testament. Pouring is referred to as the third and last method to resort to if one wants to be baptized. Widespread acceptance of something less than immersion did not occur until the fifth century. See F. LaGard Smith, *Baptism: The Believer's Wedding Ceremony* (Cincinnati: Standard Publishing, 1989), 96. See also Larry Stalley, *Baptism In The Early Post-Apostolic Church* (M. A. R. Guided Research, Harding University Graduate School, 1980); Jack P. Lewis, Baptismal Practices of the Second and Third Century Church, *Restoration Quarterly*, vol. 26 (1983): 1-17; and Everett Ferguson, *The Early Christians Speak*, reprint (Abilene: ACU Press, 1994).

165. In Colossians 2:11-12, the same point can be seen. Also, we may want to consider three further lines of related evidence. First, when a person wanted to be baptized in the New Testament, they went to the water. The Bible never recorded that water was brought to the person seeking baptism. People went to where there was an abundant supply of water ("much water"; see John 3:23 and Acts 8:36). This would be necessary only if baptism was an immersion in water. Second, the Bible teaches that when people arrived at a place where there was water, they went down into it. The Scriptures indicate that the person being baptized and the person doing the baptism both went down into the water (Acts 8:36; Matthew 3:5-6). Third, after baptism, both the person being baptized and the person performing the baptism

came up out of the water (Mark 1:10; Acts 8:39). For both people to go down into the water, then to perform the baptism in the water, followed by both people coming out of the water, only makes sense if baptism was by immersion. All of this would have been needless effort if baptism were by sprinkling or pouring.

166. *It is important to realize that God's saving power is not limited to proper baptism.* Instead of asking people to respond to Jesus' finished work on the cross by expressing faith and repentance in baptism, many Bible-believing churches encourage people to receive Jesus as Lord and Savior through saying a prayer. In this prayer, people invite Jesus to come into their hearts. In their understanding, this prayer is the full biblical method by which one is made a Christian. This specific method of becoming a Christian is a recent practice, not commonly followed until recent times (starting in the early 1800s). It is now standard teaching among most Bible-believing Protestants (Evangelicals). It has been made very prominent since Campus Crusade's Bill Bright popularized the Four Spiritual Laws in the middle of the twentieth century.

There is much to commend in this approach. Too often traditional churches miss the biblical emphasis on a personal relationship with God through trusting Jesus in our hearts. We do not hear enough of the central biblical teaching that we are saved by grace through personal faith. One can easily be drawn into accepting the sinner's prayer or simply asking Jesus into one's heart as being the full biblical way to become a Christian. After all, we know there is one Scripture which points to something similar to this. Romans 10:10 says: "For it is with your heart that you believe and are justified, and it is with your mouth that you confess and are saved." Such a confession is a good thing, in and of itself, even if it is done apart from baptism, as the Bible teaches.

But is it best to stop there? Is the sinner's prayer the full biblical response? For my part, I am glad to know that personal faith is the central issue and that God looks at the heart. However, there are no examples of anything like the sinner's prayer in all the conversions recorded in the book of Acts. The whole New Testament (including Acts) repeatedly teaches us that baptism is the full mode or method of expressing personal faith in Jesus Christ to become a Christian. This is the position which is more fully biblical.

But for me, it is another thing to say "a follower of Christ cannot be saved unless he or she has been properly baptized." To hold such a view, one must discount central elements of biblical teaching and the work of God's Spirit:

1. One must reject faith as the central and essential human response to God's grace (John 3:16; Romans 3:25; Romans 10:9-10; Ephesians 2:8-9). Although important, we believe that baptism is not on the same level, but is rather a secondary matter of God-given method-

ology for the purpose of expressing this faith. The Bible repeatedly teaches that salvation is by *grace through faith*.

2. One must minimize the biblical teaching that God looks at the heart to see what is most fundamental and essential in our motivations as we respond to his grace (1 Samuel 16:8; Acts 15:7-8). We believe God weighs the motives of the heart and central intentions as being more important than external religious ordinances, although both are important (Matthew 23:23; Mark 2:23-28; etc.).

3. One must discount the biblical teaching on the nature and work of the indwelling Holy Spirit of God. One must advocate that countless millions of devoted, but un-immersed followers of Christ throughout history have been deceived in their belief that the Spirit of God has in-dwelt and sealed them as his own. One must also hold that the majority of Christ's followers in the present have also been deceived about the Spirit's work in their lives and about their relationship with God through him. It would mean the majority of Christ's followers at present and in history are lost. This horrifying view not only denies God's promises, but it calls into question God's goodness and providence.

4. One must put undue emphasis and weight on the act of baptism. This would cause people to rely upon their baptism, something which they have done, as opposed to a complete reliance on Christ's blood.

God-ordained forms, methods, and rituals are important, but as even the Old Testament makes clear, God's gifts and acceptance of human faith are not strictly bound to proper modes. The substance of personal faith is far more important than the fullness of a proper external form given as the means to express this faith. We want to carefully practice what God has instituted about baptism, but the ultimate evidence or sign that God has made someone a Christian is the indwelling of the Holy Spirit. Biblical teaching and experience indicate that God's saving power is not limited to proper baptism (Ephesians 1:13-14; Romans 8:9).

Thus, there are three essential biblical qualities we should look for in assessing who are saved followers of Christ:

1. genuine repentant faith in Jesus Christ and focus upon him as the basis of one's salvation;

2. the indwelling Spirit's work, including the subjective testimony of God's Spirit within affirming that one is a child of God; and, most importantly,

3. the emerging objective fruit of the Holy Spirit transforming one's life into the likeness of Christ.

Such people have been saved and should be recognized as Christians by all followers of Christ, even when they have not experienced a biblical baptism.

Rejection of baptism as the method of becoming a Christian came about as a reaction to the baptismal regeneration stance of the Roman Catholic church and the *ex opere operato* view that was held and ratified by the Council of Trent in 1547. For a historical survey, see Donald Bridge and David Phypers, *The Water That Divides: The Baptism Debate* (Leicester: InterVarsity Press, 1977). The view that I advocate in this book is not that view. For an interesting consideration of these matters, see Geoffrey W. Bromily, "Baptismal Regeneration," in *The International Standard Bible Encyclopedia* (Grand Rapids: Wm. B. Eerdmans, 1979), 428, 429.

167. See Paul Chitwood, *The Sinner's Prayer: An Historic and Theological Analysis* (Doctoral Dissertation, The Southern Baptist Theological Seminary, 2001).

168. The material that follows is taken from John Mark Hicks and Greg Taylor, *Down in the River to Pray: Revisioning Baptism as God's Transforming Work* (Siloam Springs: Leafwood Publishers, 2004).

169. Ferguson, *The Early Christians Speak*, reprint (Abilene: ACU Press, 1994).

170. *Nicaeno-Constantinoplotan Creed* of A.D. 381 in Philip Shaff, ed., *The Creeds of Christendom*, 3 vols. (Grand Rapids: Baker Book House, 1996).

171. *Nicene Creed* of 381 CE states, "I acknowledge one Baptism for the remission of sins." See Philip Shaff, ed. *The Creeds of Christendom*, 3 vols. (Grand Rapids: Baker Book House, 1996).

172. Dallas Willard, "How To Be A Disciple," in *Christian Century* (April 22-29, 1998): 430-31. See also Dallas Willard, *The Divine Conspiracy* (San Francisco: Harper and Row, 1997).

173. Michael Wilkins, *Following the Master: A Biblical Theology of Discipleship* (Grand Rapids: Zondervan Publishing, 1992), 186.

174. See this point explained in the definitive biblical study on discipleship in Michael Wilkins, *Following the Master: A Biblical Theology of Discipleship* (Grand Rapids: Zondervan Publishing, 1992).

175. See Richard Longenecker, ed., *Patterns of Discipleship in the New Testament* (Grand Rapids: Eerdmans, 1996).

176. C.S. Lewis, *Mere Christianity* (New York: Simon & Schuster, 1996), 171.

177. Dietrich Bonhoeffer, *The Cost of Discipleship* (New York: Touchstone, 1995), 59.

178. For more on human freedom and personhood in biblical theology, see Leroy Forliness, *The Quest For Truth* (Nashville: Randall House Publishers, 2000).

179. Richard Foster, *Celebration of Discipline*, rev. ed. (New York: Harper and Row, 1988), 8.

180. Dallas Willard, *Renovation of the Heart* (Colorado Springs: NavPress, 2002), 22.

181. I am indebted to Bill Hull for his clear description of this mindset, see *The Disciple Making Pastor* (Grand Rapids: Baker Book House, 1998).

182. Mark Dever, *Nine Marks of a Healthy Church* (Wheaton: Crossway Books, 2000), 184.

183. For the biblical background on this point, see Robert Coleman, *The Master Plan of Evangelism* (Old Tappan: Fleming Revell Co., 1963) and *The Master Plan of Discipleship* (Grand Rapids: Baker Books, 1998).

184. The emphasis on "fellowship" as the focus of the church in the Bible is well documented by Robert Banks, *Paul's Idea of Community*, rev. ed. (Peabody: Hendrickson Publishers, 1994). This is the best book on the life of the local church, but we also must recommend Howard Snyder's *Radical Renewal: The Problem of Wineskins Today* (Houston: Touch Publications, 1996).

185. Dallas Willard, *The Spirit of the Disciplines: How God Changes Lives* (San Francisco: Harper and Row, 1988), 160.

186. The role of the apostles—meaning the 12, plus Paul—clearly does not exist today, because of the requirements laid down in Acts 1. It is also highly likely that prophets, in the sense described in Ephesians 2:20, do not exist. Many advocate that prophets exist today, but few seem to have the Ephesians 2:20 role in mind when they say this. See Wayne Grudem, *The Gift of Prophecy in the New Testament and Today* (Wheaton: Crossway Books, 1988) and David Aune, *Prophecy in Early Christianity and the Ancient Mediterranean World* (Grand Rapids: Wm. B. Eerdmans, 1983).

187. A careful reading of 1 Timothy 3:14-16 shows that 1 Timothy was written to help establish criteria and roles for a lasting structure in the local church. Within the canon of Scripture, there is a pattern of evangelists, elders, teachers, and deacons carrying on the ministry in the absence of the apostles. For more information, see Everett Ferguson, *The Church of Christ* (Grand Rapids: Wm. B. Eerdmans, 1996).

188. These terms are used interchangeably in Acts 20 and 1 Peter 5, referring to the same men and the same role. For more information, see Everett Ferguson, *The Church of Christ* (Grand Rapids: Wm. B. Eerdmans, 1996), 318-27. The most readily available book on elders is Alexander Strauch, *Biblical Eldership: An Urgent Call To Restore Biblical Church Leadership* (Colorado Springs: Lewis and Roth Publications, 1995). But see also the older work of J. W. McGarvey, *A Treatise on The Eldership*, reprint ed. (Murfreesboro: Dehoff Publications, 1956).

189. The best book on men and women by a single author is James B. Hurley, *Man and Woman in Biblical Perspective* (Grand Rapids: Zondervan Publishing House, 1983), and he does a decent job discussing male and female deacons. But see the discussion on female deacons in Carroll Osborn, *Women in the Church: Refocusing the Discussion* (Abilene: Restoration Perspectives, 1994) and Steven Sandifer, *Deacons: Male and Female* (Houston: Keystone Publishing, 1989). See also the website of the "Council of Biblical Manhood and Womanhood" for helpful material at www.cbmw.org.

190. C.S. Lewis, *The Screwtape Letters with Screwtape Proposes a Toast* (New York: HarperOne, 1996), 5.

191. See Dallas Willard's two books, *The Spirit of the Disciplines: How God Changes Lives* (San Francisco: Harper and Row, 1988) and *Renovation of the Heart* (Colorado Springs: NavPress, 2002).

192. Eric Metaxas, *Bonhoeffer: Pastor, Martyr, Prophet, Spy* (Nashville: Thomas Nelson, 2011), 268.

193. Cally Parkinson. Interview by Bobby Harrington. May 2010.

194. Robert Kolb, *Martin Luther: Confessor of the Faith* (Oxford: Oxford University Press, 2009), 58.

ABOUT THE AUTHOR

BOBBY HARRINGTON is the point-leader of Renew.org and Discipleship.org, both of which are collaborative, disciple-making organizations. He is the founding pastor of Harpeth Christian Church with graduate degrees from both Harding School of Theology and Southern Baptist Theological Seminary. He has authored or co-authored more than ten books on discipleship, including *DiscipleShift, The Disciple Maker's Handbook*, and *Becoming a Disciple Maker*. He lives in the Nashville area with his wife, children, and grandchildren.

9 781949 921342